The new jersey income-maintenance experiment

volume I

Operations, surveys, and administration

Institute for Research on Poverty
Monograph Series

The new jersey income-maintenance experiment

volume I

Operations, surveys, and administration

David Kershaw and Jerilyn Fair

Mathematica
Princeton, New Jersey

With a Foreword by Robert J. Lampman

ACADEMIC PRESS New York San Francisco London

A Subsidiary of Harcourt Brace Jovanovich, Publishers

This book is one of a series sponsored by the Institute for Research on Poverty of the University of Wisconsin pursuant to the provisions of the Economic Opportunity Act of 1964.

ACADEMIC PRESS, INC.
111 Fifth Avenue, New York, New York 10003

United Kingdom Edition published by
ACADEMIC PRESS, INC. (LONDON) LTD.
24/28 Oval Road, London NW1

Library of Congress Cataloging in Publication Data

Main entry under title:

The New Jersey income-maintenance experiment.

        (Institute for Research on Poverty monograph se-
ries)
        Bibliography: p.
        CONTENTS: v. 1.   Operations, surveys, and admin-
istration.
        1.   Negative income tax—New Jersey.   I.   Kershaw,
David.   II.   Fair, Jerilyn.   III.   Series: Wisconsin.   University—Madison.   Institute for Research
on Poverty.   Monograph series.
HC107.N73I53   1976   362.5   75-16882
ISBN 0—12—405001—8

Institute for Research on Poverty

The Institute for Research on Poverty is a national center for research established at the University of Wisconsin in 1966 by a grant from the Office of Economic Opportunity. Its primary objective is to foster basic, multidisciplinary research into the nature and causes of poverty and means to combat it.

In addition to increasing the basic knowledge from which policies aimed at the elimination of poverty can be shaped, the Institute strives to carry analysis beyond the formulation and testing of fundamental generalizations to the development and assessment of relevant policy alternatives.

The Institute endeavors to bring together scholars of the highest caliber whose primary research efforts are focused on the problem of poverty, the distribution of income, and the analysis and evaluation of social policy, offering staff members wide opportunity for interchange of ideas, maximum freedom for research into basic questions about poverty and social policy and dissemination of their findings.

Mathematica Policy Research (MPR), which was the Urban Opinion Surveys Division of Mathematica, Inc., during the New Jersey Experiment, was founded in 1968 to conduct the experiment. Since that time, MPR has expanded considerably and now conducts social policy research, social science experiments, and large-scale evaluation research in the areas of income security and welfare, health, housing, education and manpower policy, and simulation modeling. The company has a staff of over 500 members who specialize in economic, sociological, and survey research, policy analysis, systems design and implementation, and national sample and specialized survey operations.

MPR has attracted a professional research and operating staff with a strong commitment to social change through policy research. The activities of the company are thus intentionally limited to projects in the public sector.

Contents

part I   Operation of the experiment

part II   Research and technical issues

part III   Administrative issues

Appendices

The decision to undertake the new jersey experiment

Robert J. Lampman

The decision to mount a large-scale field experiment with negative income taxation may well turn out to be of historic moment in the development of social science. That decision resulted from three separate trends: (1) rapid spread of the belief, especially among economists, that negative taxation was an idea whose time had come; (2) ascendance within government of the methodology of measuring the cost-effectiveness of alternative means to attain a stated goal; and (3) rising interest among social scientists in attempting controlled experimentation with social-policy variables. These three trends contributed to the unprecedented "experimentation with legislation" and to the overriding of concern that such an experiment would be fraught with technical difficulties and might not contribute much to the illumination of the national debate on income-maintenance reform.

BELIEF THAT NEGATIVE INCOME TAXATION WAS AN IDEA WHOSE TIME HAD COME

President Johnson called for a "War on Poverty" in his State of the Union Message of January 1964. Congress adopted the Economic Opportunity Act later that year, by which time R. Sargent Shriver had been designated to direct the new agency—the Office of Economic Opportunity (OEO)—that was to spearhead and coordinate the efforts against poverty. Shriver emphasized that poor people would be counseled, retrained, rehabilitated, or otherwise "reformed" to take advantage of opportunities to be found in the American marketplace. The labor market was also to be reformed, by reducing discrimination, creating public jobs, and perhaps changing minimum wage rates. But the early statements from the OEO carried little hint of interest in the reform of income-maintenance institutions. Reform of the poor and reform of the job market were much preferred to welfare reform. As Shriver rather inelegantly put it, the "tax-eaters" were to be converted into taxpayers.

Within a year and a half, the OEO chief became a spokesman for negative income taxation. The goal of relieving poverty—if defined in terms of money income—dictated attention to a principal form of income for the poor (namely, transfer payments) and its obverse (tax payments). Economists were generally aware that the poor paid at least their proportionate share of taxes and were quick to point out that government could help the poor by relieving them of taxes. The 1964 legislation to promote recovery highlighted the prospect that tax relief was to be a recurring pattern for disposition of "economic growth tax dividends." However, ways to relieve taxes at the low-income end, and thereby to make the overall tax system more progressive, were seen by policymakers as rather limited. State and local sales and property taxes and payroll taxes for social insurance, although contributing to regressivity, were not easily modified. The light burden on the poor of the federal individual income tax could be removed by revising personal exemptions and by the notable social invention of the minimum standard deduction, enacted in 1965. In that year, Secretary of the Treasury Douglas Dillon hinted that "the next tax cut" would be for the poor but gave no clear indication of how this was to be accomplished. And, by definition, no tax cut could help those too poor to be paying any tax.

Many teachers of public finance have noted, when drawing a line on the blackboard to represent an income-tax-rates schedule, that the tax declines to zero at some income level for a family of a given size and that the tax effect on income level stops there. Thus, a family of four may pay the same tax (namely, zero) whether they have $3000 or $1000 of income. Instructors have also observed that the tax liability of the two families could be differentiated by negative taxation or income-conditioned transfer payments. Such an observation was generally offered merely as a curiosity, since no nation had legislated income taxation along these lines. (England was the first to do so with its Family Income Supplement of 1971.)

However, there was a fragmentary literature on ways to implement this idea. Lady Rhys-Williams, a Liberal party member in Britain, spelled out, in 1943 and again in 1953, what she called a "social dividend" that included a work test. A group in the Office of Tax Analysis of the U.S. Treasury discussed the general idea during World War II. Some members of that group, including Walter W. Heller and Milton Friedman, pointed out its possibilities in postwar papers, as did George J. Stigler. Two graduate students who explored variations of the approach in dissertations were Robert R. Schutz, at the University of California, in 1952, and Christopher Green, at the University of Wisconsin, in 1966.[1]

By 1965, the suggestion of extending cash help to the poor via a negative income tax was surfacing in many quarters and in many guises. Some called it a social dividend; others called it a guaranteed minimum income, an income-conditioned family allowance, a demogrant, or an income supplement. The key notion was to pay some amount (call this amount the guarantee) to families of a given size having no other income, and to pay nothing to a family of the same size but with income of a given level (call this the breakeven level of income). The way the benefit payment varies between the guarantee level and zero at breakeven is described by the implicit tax rate, which may be 100 percent (if the guarantee is, say, $3000 and the breakeven income is $3000), or 50 percent (if the guarantee is, say, $1500 and the breakeven is $3000).

This devastatingly simple notion was congruent with the proposition that poverty is merely lack of money. It competed with the notion that the poor needed sympathetic counseling, job training, and public-service employment or in-kind transfers, such as food stamps, medical care, and housing. It also competed with the notion that expansion of existing income-maintenance programs would do the job. Some of the more fanatical spokesmen for negative income taxation represented social insurance and public assistance as "parts of the problem" and recommended replacing them with one grand negative income tax.

In the mid-1960s, one commission or advisory group after another came up with recommendations for various negative-income-tax schemes, but Congress and the President gave these recommendations little attention. The Council of Economic Advisers and the Assistant Secretary for Research and Evaluation of the Department of Health, Education, and Welfare (HEW) showed interest in the idea. But the Research, Plans, Programs, and Evaluation group at OEO was perhaps the strongest in advocating the negative income tax to the President. In October 1965, OEO included a negative income tax, to cost $4.7 billion, as the centerpiece of a comprehensive national antipoverty plan that it forwarded to the Bureau of the Budget. The only response from the President was the announcement, in early 1967, of his intention to appoint a commission on income-maintenance programs.

---

[1] Christopher Green, *Negative Taxes and the Poverty Problem* (Washington D.C.: The Brookings Institution, 1967).

ASCENDANCE OF THE METHODOLOGY OF COST-EFFECTIVENESS

In spite of a lack of encouragement from inside the government, OEO continued to press for consideration of negative income taxation. Staff members had come to their conviction that it merited attention while carrying out OEO's mandate to review all the antipoverty efforts of the government and to assess their cost-effectiveness in reducing poverty. Emphasis on what "bang for a billion bucks" a program would yield against poverty was assured by the hiring of a key group of economists, many of them from the Pentagon or the Rand Corporation, who were informed by the ascending discipline of the Program Planning Budget System.[2] Following this method, they stated the goal (to eliminate poverty), arrayed all existing and alternative means to achieve the goal, and gave each a set of scores in terms of cost-effectiveness. It is significant that the staff members carrying out these studies were, in many cases, new to social-welfare study, and few of them had experience in or were loyal to old-line government agencies or philosophies wherein the antipoverty goal was not so sharply defined.

Negative income taxation, while only a dream, emerged with high scores from such a rating system. It could be targeted to the poor and could at the same time minimize disincentive to work. It could reach those members of the poor population not eligible for social insurance or public assistance. It could also establish a national floor under state assistance benefits and bring a department of the federal government (the Internal Revenue Service or the Social Security Administration) into a strong, if not exclusive, role in administering assistance. In policy analysis of the alternatives, OEO economists drew upon research findings wherever they could find them. But it was an uphill fight to persuade political decisionmakers that a negative income tax was a constructive alternative to existing antipoverty strategies. One recurring question was suggested both by common sense and by the economic theory of work–leisure choice: How great was the disincentive to work that would flow from even a moderate guarantee and a moderate tax rate? Little empirical work had been done by academics on this topic in general, and even less on what was taken to be a key issue, namely, the effect of transfer payments on work effort by non-aged, nondisabled men.

In retrospect, it appears that this was not the only, and perhaps not even the leading, question of policy interest. As debate in Congress developed over President Nixon's welfare-reform proposals in the years 1969–1972, there seemed to be equal interest in work effort by women heads of families, in the supplementing of federal cash benefits with state benefits, in work tests and

[2] Joseph A. Kershaw, *Government against Poverty* (Washington D.C.: The Brookings Institution, 1970); and Robert A. Levine, *The Poor Ye Need Not Have with You: Lessons from the War on Poverty* (Cambridge: Massachusetts Institute of Technology Press, 1970).

work opportunities, and in the articulation of cash benefits with such in-kind benefits as food stamps, Medicaid, public housing or rent supplements, and child day care. There also was concern over the numbers that would be added to "welfare rolls," the disruption of local labor markets, and the inducement to have children. But, in 1966, it seemed that the principal burden on those making cost-effectiveness statements about negative income taxation was to respond to fears that its costs would be high because of induced idleness. It is also worth mentioning that proponents labored under the handicap of alarming vagueness. Negative-income-tax proposals were being offered that would cost anywhere from $3 billion to $75 billion and that would extend benefits to anywhere from 5 percent of the total population to more than 50 percent.

Public discussion of the nature and purposes of negative-income-tax schemes was then, and has continued to be, relatively scattered and unfocused. Within OEO, however, the cost-effectiveness calculus led to a serious quest for ways to narrow disagreement on how much money "realistic" variants of negative income taxation would cost. Interestingly, the absence of a work test was seen as realistic, but differing tax rates (all well below 100 percent) and guarantees were entertained. The quest ultimately led to the idea of a controlled experiment.

RISING INTEREST IN SOCIAL EXPERIMENTATION

Heather Ross, then a candidate for a Ph.D. in economics at the Massachusetts Institute of Technology working with the United Planning Organization (funded by OEO) in Washington, D.C., came forward in December 1966 with a plan to experiment with negative income taxation.[3] Her proposal was turned down at HEW but was sympathetically received at OEO. Guy H. Orcutt, a leading econometrician, endorsed the Ross proposal as "exciting," and declared that research along the proposed lines could advance fundamental knowledge about the determinants of labor supply at the same time that it enhanced the decision-making process. The state of the art of empirical research was developed to the point—with small-sample theory, regression analysis, and computer processing of masses of data—where it could handle the shift to experimental methods.[4]

[3] Ross, "A Proposal for a Demonstration of New Techniques in Income Maintenance," Memorandum, December 1966, Data Center Archives, Institute for Research on Poverty, University of Wisconsin, Madison.

[4] Guy H. Orcutt, "Experimental Study of Negative Income Taxation," Memorandum, March 14, 1967, Data Center Archives; and Guy H. Orcutt and Alice G. Orcutt, "Incentive and Disincentive Experimentation for Income Maintenance Policy Purposes," *The American Economic Review* 58 (September 1968): 754–772.

Just as the idea of the negative income tax is breathtakingly simple, so is the idea to experiment with it. If you want to know how a social program will work, try it out on a sample of subjects! Perhaps one could legislate the program into existence in one community and observe how labor supply changed there compared to another community similar in all regards except that it lacked the experimental program. The problem with this approach is that since many factors can cause change in labor supply or demand, statistical methodology requires that numerous communities be subject to experimentation and control. The alternative chosen was to select a dispersed sample of families, subjecting some of them to one "law," some to each of several others for a period of three years, and watching carefully to see how the subject families behaved in response to separate provisions of a negative-income-tax formula.

Prior to 1967, students of the effect of legislation were forced to look for "natural experiments." One type of natural experiment or quasi experiment involves looking at several states with different welfare laws and observing variations in labor supply across the states. Another type is set up by the passage of a law in a single jurisdiction; this affords the researcher an opportunity to observe the labor supply of a group of individuals before and after the passage of the law. In neither of these cases does the social scientist have a degree of control comparable to that of the laboratory scientist or the agricultural field experimenter. Something like experimental evidence can be presented by information on the work efforts of a cross section of persons having varying amounts of nonlabor income; but the potential problem is that nonlabor income tends to be received by persons who are different in some systematic way from those who do not receive such income. In any event, one can move from such a study to predictions of how persons would respond to a negative income tax by only the roughest of analogies.

In the years since World War II, there had been a strong trend toward introducing new quantitative precision into the social sciences, with the hope of gaining predictive power over social events. Empirical scholars used data from natural experiments and from cross sections, as reviewed above. They developed new survey techniques to collect more useful data, including the use of continuing panels of individuals so as to trace changes through time. But the model for uncovering *causal* relationships was always that of the natural scientist, who has control not only of the stimulus to a subject but also of all other factors that might contribute to a response.

OEO was looking for new ways to establish the cost-effectiveness of alternative negative-income-taxation patterns, and academic econometricians were eager to take social science over the threshold into the realm of controlled experimentation. It was a rare combination of willing parties meeting at the right time, and it generated extraordinary enthusiasm to go ahead with an experiment. This enthusiasm was sufficient to prevail even in the face of serious questions about how well this experiment would serve the interests of policymakers or social scientists. These questions may be summarized, with the benefit of hindsight, as follows:

1. Were the guarantee and the tax rate the only critical variables for experimentation?[5] Early drafts of research plans asserted that there would be only two variables, guarantee and tax rate, in the "treatment" or "stimulus" to be applied to experimental subjects. However, subsequent inquiries led to the conclusion that there are numerous other variables in negative income taxation that might have relevance for policymakers, since they might alter transfer cost or work responses or both. These include definitions of the family unit (what about grandparents, what about young adults who marry during the three years of the experiment?), of income (what about in-kind income, what about an assets test, what about deductibility of work expenses, what about other benefits and taxes that are conditioned by earnings?), of the income-accounting period to be used in calculating benefits (should it be a month or a year?), and of methods of paying benefits (should the guarantee be paid in advance and reduced during the income period by a tax on earnings, or paid as a net of guarantee less implicit tax at the end of the period?), and, finally, of eligibility (should there be a work test, should self-employment or acceptance of welfare make one ineligible for negative tax benefits?).

2. Should the experiment be set up to yield the most generalizable result of how a negative income tax would add to the transfer cost of existing public programs (in which case the appropriate sample would be a nationwide cross section of the total population, including those on welfare as well as off)? Or should it be designed to give a relatively pure answer to the question of how a negative income tax would alter the work effort of a group experiencing a zero-guarantee–zero-tax-rate situation (in which case the effort should be to select a sample ineligible for welfare and to relieve them of all other guarantees and implicit and explicit tax rates prior to ministering unto them carefully controlled doses of the treatment)?[6] This dilemma was resolved in favor of the latter—that is, restricting the geographic location, sex, age, and health status of family heads—and seeking a site where there would be the least conflict with, or contamination by, welfare benefits. New Jersey was eventually selected. Even so, there was some doubt as to whether the pure work response to negative tax benefits could be discerned amidst the welter of other determinants of work

[5] Larry L. Orr, Robinson G. Hollister, and Myron J. Lefcowitz, *Income Maintenance: Interdisciplinary Approaches to Research,* Institute for Research on Poverty Monograph Series (Chicago: Markham, 1971).

[6] James N. Morgan, "Current Status of Income Maintenance Experiments–Discussion," *The American Economic Review* **62** (May 1971): 39–42.

effort, including wage rates, employment opportunities, family size, spouse's earnings, nonlabor income (including unemployment compensation), in-kind benefits (such as Medicaid), health status, occupation, and laws surrounding employment—all of which are subject to change over a three-year period.

3. Could researchers set up a "rule of law" that would be anything like that which would obtain if a nationwide scheme were enacted by Congress? Would experimental subjects cooperate? Would they fabricate information, knowing that sanctions were lacking and that many techniques of tax auditing were denied to the researchers? Would the base-line information on income and work effort, established by recall, be of different quality from information collected currently as the experiment proceeded? Could field workers be relied upon to remain detached from the subjects and to treat them in the manner administrators of a national program would? Would cooperators and nonattriters be a biased sample of the potential claimants under a national program? Would a scattered sample receiving benefits in secrecy behave about the same as people would under a national law, which would be given wide publicity? In particular, would the scattered sample be slower in learning how to maximize benefits? To the extent that experimental subjects are known to others, would they be subject to differential treatment by employers, by landlords, or by relatives?

4. Would the experiment suffer from a Heisenberg effect, that is, a response by the subjects to the fact of being watched? If so, would this effect differ among those (including the control group) receiving different treatments? Would the experiment suffer from a Hawthorne effect, that is, a response simply to being "treated" rather than to the specific treatment? (Researchers at the Hawthorne plant of the General Electric Company found that workers would respond favorably for a short time to virtually any experimental attention.) Would the experiment suffer from its short duration, that is, would workers consider the negative tax benefits transitory rather than permanent income and hence adjust to them in quite a different way from what they would to benefits under an ongoing program? On the other hand, would they realize in the third and final year of the experiment, that a vacation would cost very little that year compared to the following year? Did this mean the data from the second year would be the most reliable?

5. Would an experiment with human beings be morally objectionable and hence completely impracticable? Could it be considered damaging to human beings to offer them benefits for three years and then drop them? What obligations reside with researchers to protect research subjects against damage by employers or others that may flow from their being experimental subjects? Is it acceptable to watch an experimental family make what seems to be a mistake and not try to help them? Would such help amount to contamination of the experiment?

6. Would the experiment serve the needs of OEO?[7] To set up, administer, and analyze the results would take at least five years. Was that time lag compatible with antipoverty planning? (In 1965, it would not have seemed so, but in 1967 it apparently did.) Would results be suspect because the experiment was sponsored, designed, and even administered by "believers" in negative income taxation? Obviously, the answer to that question might depend upon what the results turned out to be. Would some kinds of results harm the prospects for political acceptance of a negative tax scheme? Suppose, for example, that little change in work effort were found to flow from a high tax rate? Would that undermine one of the leading arguments for negative taxation as opposed to public assistance? Would merely having an experiment running serve the needs of OEO, by keeping the issue of negative taxation alive and, perhaps, by serving as a useful "demonstration" (if nothing more) during the years 1967–1972?

It is at least possible that if OEO had had prior experience with controlled social experimentation and had been more aware of how likely a null hypothesis is to prevail in the face of multicausal social outcomes, they would have been less eager to support this experiment. They might also have been less eager had they known in advance that in the congressional discussion of Nixon's Family Assistance Plan and H.R. 1, numerous issues not covered by the experiment would be central to the debate and, perhaps, to the defeat of the proposed legislation. (Even in retrospect, it is not clear how any set of findings from the New Jersey experiment might have altered the course of the 1969–1972 deliberations.) Had OEO known all this in 1967, they might have concluded that some other use of the several millions of dollars, in lieu of devoting them to the experiment, would have done more to promote the cause OEO espoused. No easy answer is forthcoming to that question. On the other hand, another "cause" that OEO favored was more surely promoted by the sponsorship of the experiment, namely, that of the critical cost-effectiveness study of social programs.

In summary, the New Jersey experiment came about because of a favorable combination of three trends, none of which, by 1967, had gone "too far." One was the trend toward acceptance of the belief that negative taxation was an idea whose time had come. Yet initial efforts to get the idea accepted had failed, and there was no expectation in 1967 that it was going to be translated into legislation in the next few years. A second trend was that of bringing cost-effectiveness study to bear upon social programs. In OEO, at least, that trend had gone far enough to show that to learn more about the likely effect of an untried program would call for new methods of social research; but not far

[7] Walter Williams, *The Struggle for a Negative Income Tax* (Seattle: Institute for Governmental Research, University of Washington, 1972).

enough, perhaps, to show how unlikely such research was to have any predictable result in the political realm.

Finally, although no large-scale experiment with a piece of social legislation had ever been tried, empirical researchers had run out of "natural experiment" materials to test labor-supply determinants. They were ready to try a controlled experiment, even though there were some grounds for doubt that it could provide definitive answers to such questions as what causes people to work more or less, or what provisions of a negative income tax might make it more or less administrable and acceptable if and when its time has truly come.

Preface

The New Jersey Income-Maintenance Experiment is a three-volume series on the graduated work-incentive experiment undertaken in New Jersey and Pennsylvania by the Institute for Research on Poverty at the University of Wisconsin and Mathematica, Inc., on behalf of the Office of Economic Opportunity.[1] This volume provides a nontechnical description of the experiment and its operation. It is intended to serve both as a book about the experiment for the general reader and as an introduction to the other two volumes. Volumes 2 and 3 are entitled, respectively, *Labor-Supply Responses* and *The Impact on Expenditures, Health, and Social Behavior, and the Quality of the Evidence.* They provide technical analyses of the major experimental findings.

This first volume is organized into three main parts. Part I includes a summary of the history and results of the experiment and information about the essential operating elements—selection of sample families, methods by which data were collected from the families, and the administration of the transfer payments.

---

[1] The New Jersey Income-Maintenance Experiment is also known by several other names: The New Jersey Graduated Work Incentive Experiment, The New Jersey Negative Income Tax Experiment, The New Jersey–Pennsylvania Income Maintenance Experiment, The New Jersey–Pennsylvania Graduated Work Incentive Experiment, The New Jersey–Pennsylvania Negative Income Tax Experiment, and the Urban Experiment.

Part II addresses certain research and technical issues raised during the course of the experiment. Part III reviews some of the more interesting and complex administrative problems faced as the experiment progressed.

The data from the experiment are housed in the Data Center of the Institute for Research on Poverty, from which data tapes may be ordered. Also at the Data Center are the archives of the experiment—a collection of memoranda, forms, and other documents produced during the course of the experiment.

It is impossible to thank everybody who contributed to the administration of the experiment, since more than two hundred persons filled the various operational positions during the five years that the experiment ran. Specific acknowledgments to key staff members are contained within the chapters that they helped write or which represent operational systems they developed and/or supervised. We must, however, single out some individuals here for thanks. It is clear that the first eighteen months of activity—the beginning of the operational phase in Trenton in June of 1968 through enrollment in Scranton in the late fall of 1969—were crucial to the outcome of the experiment. The small group at Mathematica, which included Heather Ross, Michael Taussig, Albert Rees, William Baumol, Frank Mason, Cheri Marshall, and the two of us, received constant moral and technical support from James Lyday and Robert Levine at OEO and Harold Watts, director of the experiment, and Felicity Skidmore at Wisconsin. When things got hot with the welfare departments later, the strength of the support we could always count on from John Wilson and Tom Glennan at OEO was critical. The continued administrative interest in the experiment shown by Robert Lampman, Robinson Hollister, and Glen Cain at Wisconsin was of great assistance in improving the way the experiment was run. It is safe to say that the endeavor never could have gotten off the ground, and stayed airborne, without the close personal and professional relationship that developed among these people and the operating staff.

Our thanks also go to Laura Smail and Marjean Jondrow, who edited this volume, and to Wendy Haebig, who typed the final version.

A very special acknowledgment goes to the 1357 New Jersey and Pennsylvania families whose participation in the experiment provided the data that are reported in this and the other two volumes. It would be difficult to express too much gratitude to persons who allowed us to pry into their lives for three years. As a special gesture of thanks, we have assured them that we will never bother them again and have also ensured that others will not do so.

The two of us accept the blame for any errors of fact or judgment contained herein and absolve the other staff members, whose valuable thoughts we have massaged to produce this book. Nothing contained in the volume should be construed as representing the views of the Office of Economic Opportunity, the University of Wisconsin, or Mathematica.

part I
Operation
of the experiment

1   Overview of the operation and results of the new jersey experiment

The New Jersey Income-Maintenance Experiment was the first large-scale social experiment in the United States. It involved the systematic variation of certain economic influences (the "treatment") on a group of persons as they went about their everyday lives, and a comparison of their resulting behavior with the behavior of another group of persons (the controls) who were similar to the first group in every way except that they did not receive the treatment. Today, there are in operation several similar federally funded, controlled social experiments (described briefly in Chapter 5). But in 1966 and 1967, testing economic hypotheses in this manner was a new idea.

The central question the New Jersey experiment hoped to address was the cost of a nationwide guaranteed annual income as determined by the extent to which families would reduce their work effort in response to cash payments. It was also expected that the experiment would provide policymakers with estimates of the administrative costs of such a program.

The sections of this chapter on the history and results of the experiment were written by Felicity Skidmore. Evidence of her invaluable editorial assistance also appears throughout the volume.

HISTORY

The sequence of events leading up to the decision by the Office of Economic Opportunity (OEO) to fund an experiment in negative income taxation has been described by Robert J. Lampman in the foreword to this three-volume series, *The New Jersey Income-Maintenance Experiment*. Briefly, OEO had advocated a national negative-income-tax program in 1965, had been unable to persuade the President to introduce the legislation, and, therefore, had decided to fund a project designed to produce hard evidence as to its feasibility. This evidence, it was assumed, could then be used to persuade politicians and the American public that a negative income tax would be good social policy.

Mathematica, Inc., a for-profit research firm in Princeton, New Jersey, submitted a proposal for an experiment. It was written largely by Heather Ross (a Massachusetts Institute of Technology graduate student who had authored the first such proposal for the United Planning Organization in Washington, D.C., the previous year) and by Princeton University Professors William Baumol and Albert Rees. The OEO research staff were disposed to accept and fund this proposal, but Sargent Shriver was unwilling to award so large a contract to a private, profit-making firm. He recommended that the grant be given to the Institute for Research on Poverty at the University of Wisconsin, which could then subcontract with Mathematica.

On 30 June 1967, OEO approved a grant to the institute, which immediately signed a subcontract with Mathematica for the field operations and part of the research. The first fourteen months of the grant were spent in designing and planning the experiment. The next four years, from August 1968 through September 1972, constituted the payments phase.

In early 1968, Mathematica solicited bids from survey research organizations to select and enroll families for the experiment and to administer regular interviews to them. Opinion Research Corporation won the contract, but by the fall of 1968 Mathematica decided to do the rest of the enrolling and interviewing itself.

In August 1968, families were enrolled in the first site, Trenton, New Jersey. Enrollment took place in the other sites one by one over the next year, being completed in the fourth and last site in September 1969. On 1 January 1969—during this twelve-month enrollment period—the state of New Jersey instituted a new welfare program that overlapped the experiment in terms of both eligibility and generosity. This necessitated increasing the experiment's maximum benefit level. It also caused later legal problems with county welfare authorities, who alleged that certain experimental families had taken advantage of the overlap to receive payments simultaneously from welfare and from the experiment. These difficulties are described in detail in Chapter 12. They included a subpoena being served on the field director of the experiment in

October 1969 for family records we had pledged to keep confidential, and a payment to Mercer County officials from the experiment in January 1970 to compensate the local welfare authorities for overlapping payments to experimental families.

In September 1969, political reality caught up with the experiment on another front. This is described in detail in Chapter 12. The pilot site had been in operation just over a year and the last site had just been enrolled when President Nixon submitted legislation to the House of Representatives proposing a welfare-reform measure that included a negative income tax for families with children. In December 1969, Harold Watts, the director of the Institute for Research on Poverty and a principal investigator in the experiment, and David Kershaw, the field director of the experiment for Mathematica, were invited to testify before the House Ways and Means Committee on the proposed legislation. They were unable to be very specific in their testimony because no data were yet available from the experiment. After their testimony, Watts, Kershaw, and OEO staff members discussed the advisability and feasibility of compiling and providing preliminary data from the experiment for the committee. In February 1970, the decision was made to go ahead and issue a report on the experiment based on very preliminary and early data from the first two sites.

This preliminary report was received with enthusiasm by supporters of the legislation and stimulated intense criticism from opponents of the bill. The General Accounting Office (GAO) of the federal government visited Mathematica to check the data, issued a critical analysis of the OEO report in May 1970, and made plans to undertake their own analysis of the New Jersey data, over the strong protests of the experiment staff.

Meanwhile, the House passed the Family Assistance Act (HR 16311), often referred to as the Family Assistance Plan, or FAP, in April. The Senate Finance Committee began public hearings on it immediately. These and the critical GAO report stimulated Senator John J. Williams of the Finance Committee to request individual family records, which plunged the experiment back into the issue of protecting confidential family information. The summer of 1970 was taken up with negotiations between the experiment staff and OEO on the one hand and the Senate Finance Committee and the GAO on the other in an attempt to provide useful data without violating pledges of confidentiality to the families. By August, an agreement had been reached that the GAO could visit the Mathematica office on a regular basis to do a data audit but would not request individual family records. Senator Williams did not press further his request for family records. In December 1970, the Family Assistance Act, in any case, was killed in the Senate.

The year 1971 saw the Administration propose another welfare-reform bill to the Congress, H.R. 1, and local county welfare authorities in New Jersey begin another investigation into possible fraud by experimental families. The research staff of the experiment again provided information to the House Ways and Means Committee, the House again passed the bill, and the Senate again killed it, in February 1972.

The first experimental site ended its payments in September of 1971; the last site completed its field operations a year later. Chapter 13 describes how the payments were stopped and what the reactions of the families were. The data were analyzed during the following fourteen months, and the final report on the experiment was released in December 1973. (Appendix A provides a chronology of important dates in the history of the experiment.)

The rest of Chapter 1 provides a summary of the design, operation, and results of the experiment. Subsequent chapters provide detailed descriptions of the various facets of the experiment touched on in this summary.

DESIGN AND OPERATIONS

Specification of Experimental Treatments

A negative income tax is a cash-transfer system of income supplementation. The system can vary in generosity, but any negative income tax is defined by two variables: the guarantee level and the tax, or reduction, rate. The guarantee level is the amount paid to a family[1] or individual with no other income. The tax, or reduction, rate is the rate at which that amount is reduced as a family's other income rises. The higher the guarantee level and the lower the tax rate (other things equal), the more generous the resulting schedule of payments will be, and, according to economic theory, the more attractive it will be for people to decrease the amount of work they do.

Any combination of a guarantee level and a tax rate will produce a specific schedule of payments that decreases as income rises. As long as the tax rate is less than 100 percent, the recipient is always better off by having earnings than by relying solely on the negative-income-tax payments, because as income increases, the total of income plus transfer payment increases.

---

[1] Throughout the discussion in this and the other two volumes of *The New Jersey Income-Maintenance Experiment*, the words "household" and "family" are used interchangeably. This needs a word of explanation. In the specific rules of operation of certain other income-maintenance experiments (see Chapter 5), the two words have different meanings: "family" refers to those living under one roof in direct husband–wife–child relationship; "household" refers to all people in the living unit who pool income and expenses. In this sense, the unit of analysis for the New Jersey experiment was the household. Our rules of operation, however, called them families, our site-office communications referred to them as families, we thought of them as families. This perception is thus reflected in our writing.

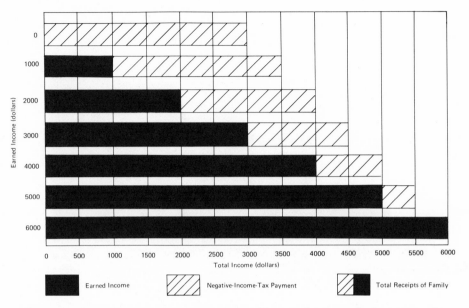

Figure 1.1 Relation between payment and earned income for a negative-income-tax plan with a $3000 guarantee and a 50 percent tax rate.

Figure 1.1 shows the relationship between a family's earned income and the payment it would receive under a negative-income-tax plan defined by a guarantee level of $3000 and a tax rate of 50 percent. Obviously, at zero earned income their payment would be $3000. The tax rate of 50 percent means that for every dollar earned the family is able to keep fifty cents. Thus, for earned income of $1000, the transfer payment is $2500 (the guarantee of $3000 minus 50 percent of the earned income, namely, $500).

The guarantee levels were specified as percentages of the poverty line adjusted for family size. The official poverty lines were refined somewhat for the experiment, because it was felt that there was no analytical justification for using nutritional requirements alone as the basis of need (as the Social Security poverty levels did), especially with respect to increases in the guarantee level with increases in family size.[2] The poverty lines used for the first year of the experiment are given in Table 1.1, along with those of the Social Security Administration (SSA) for 1967. (The experiment's poverty lines were increased every year by the percentage change in the consumer price index.)

[2] Albert Rees, "Variations in Support Levels with Family Size," Memorandum, February 1968, Data Center Archives, Institute for Research on Poverty, University of Wisconsin-Madison.

Table 1.1 Comparison of Poverty Lines Used in the Experiment
with Social Security Administration Poverty Lines, by
Family Size

Size of Family	Experiment (first year of operation)	SSA Poverty Line (1967)
2 persons	$2000	$2130
3 persons	2750	2610
4 persons	3300	3335
5 persons	3700	3930
6 persons	4050	4410
7 persons	4350	4925
8+ persons	4600	5440

Three guarantee levels were chosen as being the most relevant in terms of policy interest. The general rationale for the choice of guarantee levels was that levels higher than the poverty line were regarded as politically impossible to achieve in a national program. The most likely level, from a policy point of view, was considered to be 100 percent; 50 percent was chosen as the lowest feasible level; and 75 percent was a middle ground.

Three tax rates were also chosen: 30, 50, and 70 percent. The 50 percent rate had been used by many economists in their exposition of the negative income tax and, therefore, had come to be considered a central point; 70 percent was just slightly higher than the 1967 Social Security Amendments (and regarded by most social-policy experts as the highest feasible rate from the point of view of work disincentives); 30 percent was considered a reasonable lowest bound.

The actual combinations of tax rates and guarantee levels were chosen to keep the breakeven points (that is, the income level above which a family no longer receives benefits) within the range of political feasibility and reasonable cost. In March 1968, seven negative-income-tax plans were chosen for the experiment; they are shown in Table 1.2. Before the end of 1968, however, the low sample yield and new welfare regulations in New Jersey (described in Chapters 2 and 12) had combined to persuade us that a fourth guarantee level (125 percent) had to be added. The final set of eight experimental plans is shown in Table 1.3.

Composition of the Sample

There were two basic restrictions on the sample. First, sample eligibility required that a family have one male between eighteen and fifty-eight years old who was not disabled, and at least one other family member. Second, total family income could not exceed 150 percent of the poverty line.

Table 1.2 **Experimental Plans Originally Chosen**

Guarantee (percent of poverty line)	Tax Rate (percent)		
	30	50	70
50	X	X	
75	X	X	X
100		X	X

The decision to concentrate on healthy non-aged males with dependents was made by OEO before the grant was awarded, despite the fact that most of the welfare population consisted of female-headed families, because working-age men with no physical disabilities were the only people in American society who had never qualified for public assistance. The only benefits (except for the very low-level grants of local general assistance) they had traditionally been eligible for, such as Unemployment Insurance and Social Security, were dependent on their having had a history of regular employment.[3]

As Lampman has noted in his foreword, the fear was that offering able-bodied male heads of families transfer payments would cause widespread decreases in work effort, which would raise much higher than the country could afford the real cost of a universal negative income tax of the generosity and eligibility levels being talked about.

The need to find out more about the work behavior of female heads of household was also considered, but three arguments were seen as decisive in relegating it to a lower experimental priority. First, female heads were already eligible for public assistance; therefore, conversion of the program from a state to a national basis could be expected to have a relatively small effect on them. Second, their labor-force participation (comparatively speaking) was low and could be expected to remain so because they were typically heads of families with children and only one caretaking adult. Any new transfer program would not be expected to reduce their work effort further, thus adding significantly to the cost. On the contrary, since the nominal tax rates on public-assistance benefits for female-headed families, the Aid to Families with Dependent Children (AFDC) program, were running as high as or higher than 100 percent, a

---

[3] Although by 1966–1967 some twenty states had public-assistance programs for which two-parent families could qualify (AFDC-UP), these programs were small and relatively new, and nothing was known about their effects on work effort.

Table 1.3 The Negative-Income-Tax Plans
Used in the New Jersey Experiment

Guarantee (percent of poverty line)	Tax Rate (percent)		
	30	50	70
50	X	X	
75	X	X	X
100		X	X
125		X	

negative income tax with lower tax rates could be expected, if anything, to increase the attractiveness of work for them. Third, 1967 was the period when the Social Security Act was being amended to provide for a maximum tax rate on AFDC benefits of 67 percent. It was expected that empirical research projects would be built into the administration of this change (particularly in New York City), to produce new information on the labor-force behavior of female heads of families.

The decision to restrict eligibility to those families with incomes of not more than 150 percent of the poverty line evolved during the planning process. Our central interest was in measuring the response of low-income families. Two general considerations prevailed against raising the income[4] cutoff any higher than 150 percent of poverty. First, those close to the field operations wanted to be sure that most of the sample would qualify for significant payments to keep the goodwill of the experimental participants and to minimize the number who dropped out during the experiment. Second, OEO did not want to be in the position of funding a cash program that was primarily addressed to the nonpoor.

The decision as to the income cutoff had an unfortunate consequence that was not perceived as the decision was being made: It left working wives very

---

[4] The concept of income being discussed was not current income, but rather, some measure of normal, expected, or permanent income, to correct for the possible bias that might be introduced by having people with incomes that were unusually low (for them) overrepresented and people with incomes higher than usual (for them) excluded. For the final analysis, two statistically rather sophisticated measures of normal income were formulated. It was originally hoped that the same could be done for the normal income measure on which the sample was selected. However, the exigencies of the field-work schedule and data-processing facilities were such that the estimates for eligibility purposes were made by inspection of family data to see whether certain features of the family (education and training of the wife, for instance, if she was not working) would lead to the presumption that their normal income was significantly higher or lower than the average given for the previous year.

underrepresented in the sample. Only 15 percent of the wives who remained in intact families worked regularly throughout the experiment (although 40 percent worked at some time during the experiment)—an uncomfortably small sample for analysis.

Allocation of Families to Negative-Income-Tax Plans

The question of how sample units should be allocated to various experimental treatments or to the control group is always a complex statistical issue. Work on the sample allocation design for this experiment began at the end of 1967, continued throughout 1968, and finally ended in June 1969. Chapter 6 describes the process in more detail.

The objective was to estimate the cost of a national program (or at least the cost of covering urban wage earners in the Northeast). The central question was how to distribute eligible families among the various experimental plans according to their income level in order to maximize the information obtained for the money spent.[5]

As we have seen above, this initially involved seven and later involved eight experimental plans and a control group. It also involved a decision to stratify the sample according to the normal income of the families: The first stratum was to be those families below the poverty line (0–100 percent of the poverty line); the second stratum included those between the poverty line and 25 percent above it (101–125 percent); the third included those between 26 and 50 percent above it (126–150 percent).

The method by which a sample household was allocated to a particular negative-income-tax plan reflected a desire to make efficient use of funds. An intrinsic feature of negative-income-tax plans is that costs per observation unit vary systematically with guarantee, tax rate, and family income—with the poorest families costing most. Accounting for these cost differentials in the design led to an uneven allocation of household across experimental plans. It also led to the fact that the probability of assignment of a family to a particular plan was not independent of income—the higher the family income, the higher the probability of being assigned to a generous plan. This led to substantial numbers of families being assigned to plans with breakeven points below the families' incomes (and consequently receiving no payments). Basic principles of randomization were retained because all households within a given income stratum (that is, all

---

[5] A technical discussion of the design can be found in Charles Metcalf, "Implications of the Sample Design for Use of Experimental Data," in *The New Jersey Income-Maintenance Experiment,* vol. 3, *The Impact on Expenditures, Health, and Social Behavior; and the Quality of the Evidence,* ed. Harold W. Watts and Albert Rees, Institute for Research on Poverty Monograph Series (New York: Academic Press, forthcoming).

households identical in terms of stratification characteristics) faced the same set of assignment probabilities. Random number tables were used, and households in a specific income stratum were randomly assigned to the various cells relevant to that stratum, until all cells were filled. The final allocation of families to experimental cells (shown in Table 1.4) was, however, distinctly uneven.

Site Selection

The decision to concentrate on the urban Northeast was made by OEO in early 1967. Almost everyone concerned with administrative feasibility favored a focused experiment (that is, a sample consisting of a homogeneous group in a geographically limited area), rather than a national sample. In 1967, there was doubt as to whether it was possible to run a social experiment at all, and a limited sample was certainly considered more manageable than one spread across the country. At that time, there was no pool of administrative expertise or experience, such as has been developed in the intervening years by Mathematica and others. Nor was it clear that plans of differing generosity could be administered simultaneously without recipients making their own invidious comparisons and refusing to cooperate. The very concept of having a control group—families matching the experimental group in every respect except that they received no money—without community disruption was worrying. It was thought that, if trouble arose, geographical proximity of the administrators to the sites would be important in enabling the experiment to continue to function.

The planners also wished to have a sample in a relatively homogeneous labor market, another argument against an experiment with a national focus.[6] An OEO analysis of the labor markets of five northeastern states to determine which of them approximated most nearly the overall U.S. employment rate showed New Jersey to be a good potential site. Two further arguments favored New Jersey. First, cooperation by the state was promised. The concern over community disruption led the planners to put great weight on this factor. The New Jersey Department of Community Affairs and the New Jersey Economic Policy Council assured the planning group of support. Second, the planners of the experiment presumed that to select an unbiased sample and to produce usable data it was important to avoid sites where there were significant competing transfer-payment options that might allow overlapping welfare payments. That New Jersey had no AFDC program for unemployed parents (AFDC-UP) and was not projecting one in 1967 and early 1968 was an added advantage.

Early in the experiment, it was decided to enroll sites one after the other, rather than all simultaneously. In part, this was because of the difficulty of

---

[6] It was assumed that future experiments would concentrate on other populations, other geographical locations, and other kinds of labor market.

Table 1.4 **Number of Households Assigned to Each Plan, by Income Stratum**

Income Stratum	Guarantee/Tax Rate								Total Number		
	50/30	50/50	75/30	75/50	75/70	100/50	100/70	125/50	Experimental	Control	Sample
I: 100 percent of poverty line and below	5	32	31	5	18	23	11	50	175	229	404
II: 101 to 125 percent of poverty line	28	38	14	67	66	34	31	8	286	171	457
III: 126 to 150 percent of poverty line	13	6	55	45	1	20	44	80	264	232	496
Total	*46*	*76*	*100*	*117*	*85*	*77*	*86*	*138*	*725*	*632*	*1357*

getting field operations under way, but it was also due to the reasonable view that the first site could be treated as a pilot site from which lessons could be learned for the other site or sites. It eventually became clear that we could not find enough eligibles in the four New Jersey cities we chose; we would have to go outside New Jersey to complete the sample.

Trenton was chosen as the first site. As soon as the Trenton sample was complete, it was realized that the ethnic balance would be a problem. The 1960 Census showed blacks as only 22.4 percent of the Trenton population. When the tally of the Trenton eligibles was in, however, 66 percent of the sample was black, 16 percent was white, and 18 percent was Puerto Rican. The second and third sites were Paterson–Passaic and Jersey City. The tally when the Paterson–Passaic sample was complete was 40 percent black, 50 percent Puerto Rican, and only 10 percent white. In Jersey City, again we found a high proportion of Puerto Ricans. Even stratifying (that is, taking every second Puerto Rican family), the final sample distribution in Jersey City was 51 percent black, 13 percent white, and 36 percent Puerto Rican.[7]

In the face of these results, an explicit decision had to be made to go to a site where the population would be predominantly white. Since there were no other low-income areas in New Jersey where efficient sampling would produce the requisite number of whites, the decision was made to go to Scranton, Pennsylvania. With Scranton's overwhelmingly white sample, the experiment had an ethnically balanced sample (roughly one-third for each of the three major ethnic groups).

The field operations for the New Jersey experiment were spread over a four-year period, from August 1968 to September 1972. Originally enrolled in the experiment were 1216 families—725 in the various experimental groups and 491 in the control group. They were enrolled sequentially in four sites, as follows:

> August 1968–Trenton, New Jersey
> January 1969–Paterson–Passaic, New Jersey
> June 1969–Jersey City, New Jersey
> September 1969–Scranton, Pennsylvania

In October 1969, an additional 141 families were added to the control group in Trenton and Paterson–Passaic.

The sample selection process is fully described in Chapter 2. Suffice it to say here that the 1960 Census, our major source for identifying low-income areas, did not prove very helpful. Structural and socioeconomic changes since 1960 turned out to be frequent and usually impossible to identify from existing data

---

[7] The 1960 Census had shown Paterson as 15 percent black and Jersey City as low as 13 percent black.

sources; even within census poverty tracts, sample areas had to be redrawn by staff members of the experiment.

The Interviewing and Payments Processes

The interviewing process and the payments system were administered by two separate groups of personnel. To underline to the families the idea that the groups were independent of each other, two different names were used. The interviewing branch was entitled Urban Opinion Surveys, and the payments group was called Council for Grants to Families (a registered trade name). The processes of interview development and administration are described in Chapters 3, 9, and 10. The payments process is described in Chapter 4.

Twelve regular interviews, administered at three-monthly intervals, provided the main source of data from the experiment. Each was approximately one hour long and was in two parts: a twenty-minute section, repeated each time, on the labor-force status and participation of all family members sixteen years of age and older; and a forty-minute section that varied by quarter and covered at differing frequencies other kinds of economic-behavior items, such as expenditure and debt accumulation, plus information on health and social behavior. In addition to the quarterly interviews, there were eight special one-shot interviews, the most important of which was a short screening interview to assess eligibility for inclusion in the experiment; a "pre-enrollment" interview, to collect extensive base-line data on all the families selected before they were actually enrolled; and a follow-up interview administered three months after the last transfer payment, designed to explore labor-force behavior after payments had ended and to determine the families' understanding of the experiment and their reactions to the interviews and (for experimentals only) the transfer payments. The interviews were administered in the homes of the families by interviewers recruited from the area and trained for each interview by Mathematica staff members.

The payments were calculated by, and the checks were printed and mailed from, Mathematica's central office. Local field offices had to be established in each site, however, to deal with the inevitable problems connected with filling out the income report forms or losing track of a sample family that had failed to notify us of an address change. In addition, the local field offices were used as places to train the interviewers. Each of these field offices had an office manager—to help families, to provide "contextual" data to the researchers, and to deal with questions from the public.

Briefly, the payments process worked as follows. Every four weeks, each family in the experimental group filled out an income report form that provided the basis for calculating their payments—thus, every four weeks their payments were recalculated. The family then received the indicated amount in two biweekly checks. They were free to do whatever they wished with their payments, and could move anywhere within the United States without forfeiting participation in the experiment. The only condition for receiving the payments was that the family fill our their income report form. In addition to the negative-income-tax transfer payments, every family receiving payments was paid a biweekly amount of $10 (included in their regular check) in return for sending in the income report form. The controls were paid $8 a month for sending in a small card giving their current address. Both controls and experimentals were paid $5 for each interview.

The experiment staff requested from the Internal Revenue Service, and were granted, a ruling that excluded the transfer payments from taxable income. All other payments were considered taxable.

Experimental Staff and Costs

The size of the staff varied with the phases of the experiment. In the planning stage, the staff consisted of about twelve senior economists and sociologists at Wisconsin and Mathematica. At Wisconsin, staff requirements were fairly constant throughout the course of the experiment, but with the movement of the experiment into the field, additional administrative and interviewing personnel were required at the sites and in Princeton. Each field office had a roster of about fifteen to twenty interviewers, usually working twenty to thirty hours per week, four to six weeks out of every quarter. Administrative, data production, and research personnel in Princeton varied from about ten persons during start-up to thirty persons during full operation. The basic outline of the organization during full experimental operation can be seen in Table 1.5.

The cost of the experiment was just under $8 million, composed roughly of $5.4 million in research and administrative costs and $2.4 million in transfer payments (Table 1.6). Although the separation of research and administrative costs cannot be exact, partly because personnel performed both research and administrative tasks, an estimate of administrative costs is given in Table 1.7. Direct administrative costs, estimated at about $90 per family per year, were those costs involved in administering the payments system and performing a small amount of design and evaluation work. This figure, when combined with a relevant overhead factor, can provide a rough indication of what it would cost to administer a similar program on a national basis.

SUMMARY OF RESULTS

The two other volumes in *The New Jersey Income-Maintenance Experiment* are devoted to reporting the extensive and rigorous statistical analysis of the

Table 1.5 Operational Staff

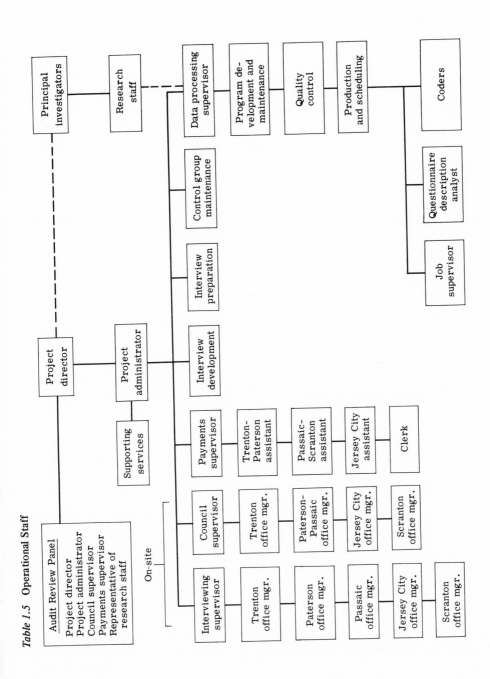

Table 1.6　Cost of the New Jersey Income-Maintenance Experiment

	Administration and Research			Transfer Payments	Total
	Mathematica	University of Wisconsin	Subtotal		
Prior to fiscal 1968	$　　1,608	$　　　0	$　　1,608	$　　　0	$　　1,608
Fiscal 1968	96,013	32,878	128,891	0	128,891
Fiscal 1969	638,194	89,672	727,866	188,258	916,124
Fiscal 1970	733,634	101,105	834,739	771,075	1,605,814
Fiscal 1971	1,010,619	113,954	1,124,573	719,662	1,844,235
Fiscal 1972	1,170,778	164,256	1,335,034	609,586	1,944,620
Fiscal 1973	776,012	310,783	1,086,795	86,608	1,173,403
Fiscal 1974	28,192	160,462	188,654	0	188,654
Total	*$4,455,050*	*$973,110*	*$5,428,160*	*$2,375,189*	*$7,803,349*

enormous quantities of data provided by the experiment. This volume would be incomplete, however, without a brief overview of the results of the experiment.

Perhaps the most important result was that there was no substantial withdrawal from work on the part of the experimental group. Tables 1.8, 1.9, and 1.10 show the average payment levels over the period of the experiment by site, by ethnic group, and (for the second year) by experimental plan.

Table 1.7　Estimated Annual Administrative Costs
per Family in 1970

Category	Annual Cost per Family
Administrative personnel	$ 9.76
Payments personnel	31.44
Field-office personnel	26.95
Audit (personnel and materials)	5.03
Appeals personnel	2.50
Computer time	2.55
Central-office supplies and services	7.07
Field-office supplies and services	4.49
Total annual administrative *cost per family*	*89.79*

NOTE: Costs vary with the administering agency, particularly on such items as employee benefits, fringes, and other overhead, which are thus *not* included in this table. For back-up data, see Fair, "Estimating the Administrative Costs of a National Income Maintenance Program," Internal Paper, May 1971, Data Center Archives, Institute for Research on Poverty, University of Wisconsin-Madison.

Table 1.8 Average Payments per Four-Week Period, Continuous Husband–Wife Families, by Site

	Total	Trenton	Paterson–Passaic	Jersey City	Scranton
First year	$91.03	$69.93	$79.43	$107.80	$91.46
Second year	93.25	71.91	80.67	109.86	94.72
Third year	96.84	58.67	84.92	120.35	98.26
Percentage change, first to third year	6.4	−16.1	6.9	11.6	5.2

Source: Albert Rees, "An Overview of the Labor-Supply Results," in *The New Jersey Income-Maintenance Experiment,* vol. 2, *Labor-Supply Responses,* ed. Harold W. Watts and Albert Rees, Institute for Research on Poverty Monograph Series (New York: Academic Press, forthcoming).

These payments show a mildly rising trend. In the first year of the experiment, for example, the average four-week payment was $91. In the third year this had increased to $97. When it is remembered, however, that a cost-of-living correction was made to the payment levels every year, amounting to increases in the guarantee levels of 5.5 percent in September 1969, 5.9 percent in October 1970, and 4.1 percent in September 1971, and that, further, the experimental period was a period of rising unemployment, the small extent of the increase in payments is evidence that there was no widespread decrease in work effort nor substantial falsification of income reports.

Table 1.9 Average Payments per Four-Week Period, Continuous Husband–Wife Families, by Ethnic Group

	Total	White	Black	Spanish-Speaking
First year	$91.03	$87.65	$97.65	$86.96
Second year	93.25	91.03	96.59	92.23
Third year	96.84	90.11	102.83	100.32
Percentage increase, first to third year	6.4	2.8	5.3	15.4

Source: Albert Rees, "An Overview of the Labor-Supply Results," in *The New Jersey Income-Maintenance Experiment,* vol. 2, *Labor-Supply Responses,* ed. Harold W. Watts and Albert Rees, Institute for Research on Poverty Monograph Series (New York: Academic Press, forthcoming).

Table 1.10 Average Payments per Four-Week Period, Continuous Husband–Wife Families, by Plan (Second Experimental Year)

Guarantee Level	Tax Rate (percent)		
	30	50	70
125	No plan	$187.28	No plan
100	No plan	123.72	$66.07
75	$103.54	44.17	34.91
50	46.23	21.66	No plan

Source: Albert Rees, "An Overview of the Labor-Supply Results," in *The New Jersey Income-Maintenance Experiment*, vol. 2, *Labor-Supply Responses*, ed. Harold W. Watts and Albert Rees, Institute for Research on Poverty Monograph Series (New York: Academic Press, forthcoming).

What did we find regarding the work effort of various members of the experimental families? To identify this we need to compare their experience with that of the controls.

The most important group for any national income-maintenance policy, and the group the experiment was specifically designed to examine, is that constituted by the non-aged, able-bodied males with family responsibilities. These are the people with the most solid attachment to the labor force. These are the people with the most labor to withdraw. These are the people about whom there is the most widespread fear that, given an income alternative, they will decide not to work. As it turned out, the effect for this group was almost undetectable. Over the central two years of the experiment (the period least contaminated by start-up and end effects), the employment rate for male family heads in the experimental group was only 1.5 percent less than that for the controls. For the number of hours worked per week, the difference amounted to just over 2 percent. For earnings per week, the experimentals actually were higher by 6.5 percent. This finding is at least partly spurious, due to a probable accelerated learning effect, whereby experimentals learned to report gross rather than net earnings faster than controls. It also appears to be partly due to the fact that the younger and better-educated experimentals were able to use the insurance provided by the payments to look for (and find) better, more stable, jobs.

The second group in terms of policy interest is the wives. The average family size in the sample was six, so the wives in the experiment were, on average, mothers of four children. For this group, the differential between experimentals and controls was substantial, with experimental wives working 23 percent fewer hours per week than the controls, their employment rate being 24 percent less, and their average earnings per week totaling 20.3 percent less. This can be regarded as a desirable outcome, given the fact that wives in six-person families work hard inside the home, and that this work could well be more beneficial (cost-effective) from a national point of view than low-wage market labor. It should be noted, in addition, that although this relative reduction is large, it in fact starts from an average figure of only 4.4 hours a week. So, from the point of view of family labor supply and national costs, it is not a large absolute change.

This brings us to total family labor supply—a composite of market work by the husband, the wife, and other adult family members. Predictably, these estimates lie between those for husbands and wives. Over the central two years, the number employed per family was 9.5 percent less for experimental families than for controls. The hours worked per week per family were 8.7 percent less for experimentals than for controls. The average earnings per week were almost the same. This disincentive was almost entirely made up of relative work withdrawal by secondary earners—wives who decided to work more inside the home, teenagers who may have been enabled by the payments to stay in school longer, and older workers who were able to take it a bit easier. As such, the disincentive effect may well be considered to be socially useful.

The analysis has shown a persistent difference in response according to ethnic groups—white, black, and Spanish-speaking. Such disincentive as was found for husbands was restricted mainly to whites. The substantial disincentive for wives was also largely due to white wives. For both males and females, the Spanish-speaking group showed more disincentive than the blacks, who showed none. No satisfactory explanation has yet been found for this difference. It is apparent that black controls had an unusually bad labor-market experience in the last year of the experiment, compared both with black experimentals and with the controls from the other two ethnic groups. Further research is under way to try to specify the causes for this ethnic difference.

Response in areas other than labor-force participation was generally slight. In the area of expenditures, the experimentals showed a tendency to move from public to private rental housing, and to buy relatively more homes. They also bought somewhat more furniture and other durables, and consequently incurred more debt.

In the area of psychological and sociological responses, the effects were negligible. Cash assistance at the levels involved in this study does not appear to have a systematic effect on the recipients' health, self-esteem, social integration, or perceived quality of life, among many other variables. Nor does it appear to have an adverse effect on family composition, marital stability, or fertility rates.

What we can say with certainty is that these benefits represented a net increase in family income, allowing these families greater command over material goods and services and enhancing their economic well-being. The antipoverty effectiveness of the payments was not seriously vitiated by offsetting reductions in earnings due to reduced work effort.

The following chapters examine in detail the issues touched on in this chapter. Chapters 2 through 4 describe the process of interviewing and making payments to the families. Chapters 5 through 10 address the research and technical issues of the experiment: the selection and implications of the operating rules, the issues in sample assignment, the problems of retaining a panel population for an extended period of time, the retrieval of information on families who dropped from the study, and the process and problems of interview development. Chapters 11 through 13 deal with the administrative issues of auditing the families, data processing, political problems encountered by the experiment, the difficulties of maintaining a confidential relationship with the families, and the ethical and practical problems of phasing out the families at the end of the experiment.

2   Sample selection

In accordance with the decision, described in Chapter 1, that the experiment should focus on the work effort of able-bodied, non-aged males with dependents, the following eligibility criteria were specified:

1. Each family had to have a male between the ages of eighteen and fifty-eight at the time of enrollment.
2. The family income the previous year had to be below 150 percent of the 1967–1968 poverty level[1] (below \$4950 for a family of four, for example).
3. The head of the household could not be a full-time student or a member of the military services or institutionalized.
4. At least one adult in the family had to be able to work (that is, to have been gainfully employed during the previous five years or to expect to be able to work in the next year).
5. The family had to have at least two members but did not have to include a child.

---

[1] The experimental poverty levels by family size differed slightly from the official figures, to make them more comparable across family sizes than the official ones (which were based on nutritional requirements alone).

As the experiment progressed, female-headed families came into existence through death, divorce, and desertion, and single individuals who left enrolled households remained eligible. The sample at the end of the experiment, therefore, was substantially more heterogeneous than at the beginning.

The selection of families was based on two preliminary interviews: a 44-question "screening" interview, administered to families in the four sites to determine eligibility, and a 340-question "pre-enrollment" interview, administered to families found eligible by the screening. Both interviews asked for income and family-composition data from which eligibility decisions could be made. In addition, the pre-enrollment interview obtained base-line measurements of selected sociological and economic variables.

The next task was to select the particular urban areas that would be sample sites. Trenton was selected as the first city because of its proximity to Princeton and Mathematica, because of the cooperative attitude of the local Office of Economic Opportunity (OEO) people there, and because it was the seat of the state government (whose cooperation at the time was considered important). It was decided to select a relatively small group from Trenton as a pilot. Other cities from which the next two sites were to be chosen were Camden, Newark, Jersey City, and the SMSA[2] containing Paterson, Clifton, and Passaic. Camden was eliminated because of its dependence on the labor market in Philadelphia and its sensitive political climate (there were a number of reports of impending riots). Newark was eliminating on the same basis: The devastating riot of 1967 had just taken place, and OEO could not risk putting the experiment in that highly sensitive city. Clifton was eliminated from the Paterson–Clifton–Passaic SMSA since it had no census poverty tracts.[3] This left Paterson, Passaic, and Jersey City for the sample sites. Paterson and Passaic were selected and sampled together, although they were regarded as two sites from an administrative point of view. Jersey City was the last New Jersey site selected.

As mentioned in Chapter 1, the three New Jersey cities yielded too few non-Puerto Rican whites for the experimental design, and the decision was made to expand into Pennsylvania. Two large areas relatively close to the existing experimental sites were considered for the Pennsylvania site: Scranton–Wilkes-Barre–Hazelton SMSA, and the Allentown–Easton–Bethlehem SMSA, both in Pennsylvania. The latter set was eliminated as being too prosperous for efficient sampling. Of the first set, Scranton was the largest and had a larger poor population than either Hazelton or Wilkes-Barre. After interviewing an explora-

---

[2] Standard Metropolitan Statistical Area: an integrated economic and social unit that includes a central city with a population of at least 50,000 and is usually contained within a single county.

[3] A census tract with a median income below the poverty level.

tory sampling of households, we decided to extend the experiment to Scranton.[4]

The procedure for locating the families within each city included the following steps. First, we examined existing data sources to determine the number of potentially eligible families and their geographical distribution within the city. This was particularly difficult in 1968 since the 1960 Census was so out-of-date, but there were other available data sources, such as special surveys done by city agencies and universities.

Next, members of the staff visited local officials to determine the political acceptability of the experiment. It was clear that there would be people having no official status who would be equally critical to the success of both the selection process and the operation of the experiment, and we made every effort to find out who these people were and to consult them as well. In Trenton, for example, the Puerto Rican community was split into two factions, and it was important to contact both factions to ensure that our interviewers would have access to members of the whole Puerto Rican community. In Passaic, a leader in a public-housing project spread the word that families should not open their doors to interviewers. This, of course, led to an exceptionally high refusal rate in the housing project. When the particular community spokesman was convinced that the project would not harm local residents, the refusal rate dropped. In Paterson, a black militant organization, in an effort to destroy the operation, encouraged its members to infiltrate the office by seeking interviewing and supervisory positions. They stopped when they became convinced that the experiment was not a threat and would, in fact, create additional jobs for the community. Jersey City had a notoriously oppressive political climate. Discussions with both the mayor and the chief of police were necessary before operations could begin there. As might be expected, clearances at city hall were all we needed. In Scranton, we did not have to go further than civic leaders (such as members of the Better Business Bureau and the head of the local real estate association).

Our next step was to locate target sampling areas within the cities. In Trenton, this was accomplished exclusively through the use of census data. We selected ten center-city tracts and five contiguous nonpoverty tracts. The latter were included to avoid possible biases from selecting only poor families in poor neighborhoods, since we thought that poor families outside of these areas might have different characteristics. However, sampling attempts outside the poverty tracts produced almost no eligible families, so we dropped the practice in the other cities.

[4] Kershaw to OEO and Wisconsin, Internal Memorandum, March 1969, Data Center Archives, Institute for Research on Poverty, University of Wisconsin-Madison.

It was clear from the Trenton experience that the 1960 Census data no longer identified current demographic distributions and that we would have to redraw sampling areas in the other experimental sites. In Jersey City and Scranton, staff members drove down every street, marking off on detailed maps commercial property, dangerous areas (those with unlighted streets, vacant lots, or warehouses, for example), and the ethnic characteristics of the various neighborhoods. By the time interviewers were sent into the field, the supervisors knew whether to send black, Puerto Rican, or white interviewers to an area, which blocks would not have dwellings, and which areas might be dangerous. Because structural and socioeconomic changes in urban areas are frequent and usually impossible to identify from existing data sources, this field inspection technique is necessary for a sound sampling procedure.[5]

After the target areas had been identified, the next step was to identify all dwelling units in the target area for subsequent sampling. The staff used listing sheets on which the boundaries of randomly selected blocks were marked. Each lister began at the northwest corner of his block (or segment, since some blocks had been combined for efficiency) and proceeded in a prescribed manner around and in the block until all households in the segment had been listed. A random group of 25 percent of the blocks was listed again in order to validate the listers' work.

The address of each dwelling unit marked on the listing sheet was then transcribed onto a separate card. The dwelling unit cards, when completed, constituted an accurate compilation of the households within the target area. These cards were then used to make assignments to interviewers for subsequent work. After a household was placed in final status (for example, the interview was completed or the household moved or refused to participate), its card was transferred to a new file, which constituted a continually updated report on what proportion of the listing task had been accomplished. This tight physical control over the process was particularly important, given the nearly 50,000 interviews that we attempted.

Following the listing and transcription of household addresses onto dwelling unit cards, a screening interview was administered to a sample of households. This brief interview was used to isolate those families potentially eligible for the experiment.

Families eligible on the basis of the screening interview received a longer, pre-enrollment interview. The pre-enrollment interview contained more detailed questions on income eligibility in addition to base-line attitudinal information.

---

[5] Other methods of sample selection—the use of rosters of community groups and churches, reverse telephone directories, tables at supermarkets, random telephoning—carry with them a substantial self-selection bias, and, although some are more efficient than household sampling, all were rejected because of obvious bias problems.

(See Chapter 10 for a more detailed discussion of the contents of the screening and pre-enrollment interviews.)

On the basis of income data collected, families were assigned to one of four income strata:

Stratum I: Income at or below the poverty line—for example, less than $3300 for a family of four.

Stratum II: Income between the poverty line and 125 percent of the poverty line—for example, between $3301 and $4125 for a family of four.

Stratum III: Income between 126 and 150 percent of the poverty line—for example, between $4126 and $4950 for a family of four.

Stratum IV: Income above 150 percent of the poverty line, ineligible—for example, more than $4951 for a family of four.

ENROLLMENT

After the assignment of families to plans, each family had to be convinced to enroll in the experiment. Given the resources already expended in locating, selecting, and interviewing these families, as well as the potential sample bias from refusals, the enrollment contact was a critical one. The major issues to be faced were the kind of persons to hire as enrollers, the approach to take with the families, the best method for training enrollers, and the materials to give each family. Decisions had to be made without any prior experience in large-scale social experimentation on which to draw.

Choosing and Training Enrollers

Initially, we assumed that enrollers needed a thorough background in the theory of the negative income tax. Accordingly, we used graduate students in the social sciences for almost all enrollments in Trenton and for most enrollments in Paterson and Passaic. Because of the resulting high attrition rate in these cities, it became clear that contact with the families would best be made by staff members who, while somewhat weaker in their command of the theory, thoroughly understood the attitudes and problems of recipients. For Jersey City and Scranton, rather than college students from outside of these cities, we used persons from the community being sampled.

The enrollers were trained at and operated from local field offices, which were centrally located in each site (including one in both Paterson and Passaic). The training sessions were held in the evening; and most of the enrollment attempts were also made in the evening, when the families were most likely to be at home. The people who trained the enrollers were professional staff from the

Princeton office of Mathematica. Enrolling was a more complicated procedure than the regular quarterly interviewing and usually was done by different people, although certain of the enrollers stayed on and became field-office staff and sometimes interviewer trainers.

The training procedure developed in an evolutionary way. The final (and most effective)[6] procedure was used in Jersey City and Scranton. It included the following elements:

1. Background material was provided to enrollers. Although the literature provided for enrollers varied, several items proved particularly useful, including a general article on the negative income tax[7] and the rules of operation of the experiment (see Appendix B).

2. The importance of the experiment was stressed. High morale on the part of the enrollers was very important in tracking down and convincing difficult families to enroll. Discussions of the importance of their work in the context of policy research helped keep up morale.

3. Enrollment procedures were reviewed. Enrollment techniques and policies were thoroughly discussed with enrollers, and a detailed explanation of all enrollment materials was given.

4. Members of the staff demonstrated an enrollment interview. The approach and a few typical problems encountered at enrollment were acted out for the enrollers.

5. The enrollers were put through stringent practice sessions before going into the field. To begin with, there was an assembly-line arrangement in which enrollers were confronted by staff members playing the role of persons eligible for enrollment. The enroller began by introducing himself and explaining the program to one of the staff who made the encounter appropriately difficult. The enroller then proceeded to another staff member experienced with the use of the income report form. Again, typical problems were posed for the enroller. Finally, each enroller was required to answer a list of questions that had been asked most often by families in the previous cities.

6. After the first few enrollment interviews, the staff met again with the enrollers and discussed any unusual problems. This session served as a review as well as being another method for maintaining enthusiasm.

Enrolling a Family

Enrollment of a family took anywhere from fifteen minutes to two hours, from one visit to several. Some families were more than willing to sign up,

---

[6] Comparisons among cities are difficult, but the refusal rate at enrollment and the subsequent attrition rate were considerably lower in Jersey City and Scranton than in the first cities. This is taken as an indication of a more effective enrollment procedure.

[7] James Tobin, Joseph Pechman, and Peter Miezscowski, "Is a Negative Income Tax Practical?" *Yale Law Journal* 77 (November 1967): 1–27.

especially since a check was a tangible part of the enrollment process. Other families were suspicious and insisted that the enroller go through the complete rules of operation with them, step-by-step. The following elements were basic to all enrollment contacts:

- General introduction to the experiment—who was sponsoring it, why, how long it would last.
- Explanation of the general benefits of the experiment for recipients.
- Description of the obligations of recipients, including accurate reporting of income on the monthly income report form, and change of address information.
- Explanation of further relevant information needed from the family on the quarterly interview, including accurate weekly earnings, welfare status, and other sources of income besides earnings.
- Cooperation with the family in making out the first income report form, to begin the process of filing. Administratively, this was the single most important part of enrollment. Adequately instructed families filed comprehensive and complete income report forms. Inadequately instructed families filed incomplete and incorrect forms for many months, necessitating several contacts by field personnel before these families learned correct filing procedures.
- Information concerning the local office as a place to obtain assistance with filing or with any other problems related to the experiment.
- Careful explanation of the rights of participants.

In addition to the verbal explanations given by the enrollers, an enrollment kit,[8] consisting of the following materials, was left with each family, to be examined at their leisure:

- A general brochure explaining the experiment.
- Rules of operation (short form).
- A list of community persons families could call to verify the legitimacy of the experiment.
- An income report form.
- Instructions on how to use the income report form.
- A payments calendar noting dates income report forms should be mailed and dates payments would be mailed.
- An identification card (to facilitate check-cashing).
- A tax table giving the amounts of experimental payments for specified weekly earnings according to the family's particular tax plan.
- A copy of the enrollment agreement signed by the family stating that they understood the basic rules of the program.

The families were told in detail about the experimental tax plan to which they

[8] See, for example, Scranton Enrollment Kit, September 1969, Data Center Archives.

had been assigned. They were not told about the other (more or less generous) plans that would face other families in the experiment, and they were not told about the control group. We reasoned that knowledge of the entire spectrum of plans would produce such serious self-selection bias as to make the data unusable and that the rights of the participants with respect to being able to make an informed decision were preserved by our detailed explanation of the specific options available to the family in question.

The enrollment contact was designed to equip the families with all the information they would need in order to participate. Except for the income report forms and occasional letters from the Princeton office, no future contacts with the families were planned from the payments branch of the experiment. Only problem filers were to be contacted, and those contacts were to be limited.

The primary reason for severely limiting direct contact between the staff and the families was to replicate insofar as possible the operation of a universal negative-income-tax program. One of the important elements of such a system, in contrast to existing public assistance programs, would be this lack of direct contact; it was important to learn the extent to which the families could function without casework contact. In addition, frequent contact could only increase whatever Hawthorne or other experimental effects there might be.[9]

RESULTS OF THE SAMPLING AND
ENROLLMENT PROCEDURES

Table 2.1 summarizes the sampling procedures that were used to select the sample. Since this was a multistep and complex procedure, each of the steps given in Table 2.1 is described in some detail.

Listing

As mentioned above, listing consisted of noting the address of each housing unit in the randomly selected blocks within the target areas of the sample cities. These target areas were widely drawn contiguous segments of the city parts of the SMSAs, located and defined by using 1960 Census income data modified by on-site inspection. As a practical matter, virtually all blocks within the target areas were selected for listing because as many eligible families as possible were wanted—given the difficulty in filling the sample. Once a block was selected, all dwelling units on that block were listed on a listing sheet and then transferred to

[9] The Hawthorne Effect is a response to the fact of being treated, not to a specific treatment.

Table 2.1   Results of the Sampling Procedure, by City

Interview Stage	Trenton	Paterson-Passaic	Jersey City	Scranton	All Cities
Listing					
Housing units listed	3530	14,781	18,002	12,334	48,647
Screening interview					
Interviews attempted	3497	14,781	18,002	12,334	48,614
Housing unit vacant	270	729	2668	1225	4892
Family never home	400	2954	3997	1063	8414
Refused interview	400	2449	3531	1578	7958
Completed interview	2427	8649	7806	8468	27,350
Eligibility from screening					
Ineligible for pre-enrollment	2200	7661	6567	7798	24,226
Eligible for pre-enrollment	227	988	1239	670	3124
Pre-enrollment interview					
Interviews attempted	227	913	1143	670	2953
Moved or could not be located	18	177	149	57	401
Refused interview	22	44	88	57	211
Completed interview	187	692	906	556	2341
Eligibility from pre-enrollment					
Ineligible for enrollment	50	246	358	174	828
Eligible for enrollment	137	446	548	382	1513
Enrollment					
Attempts	137	446	413	320	1316
Moved or could not be located	2	21	7	0	30
No longer eligible	0	3	5	0	8
Refused enrollment	9	40	11	2	62
Enrolled	126	382	390	318	1216

dwelling unit cards. Thus, each of the 48,865 housing units selected within the target areas of the four SMSAs was identified on a separate dwelling-unit card.

Screening Interview

The screening interview was designed to cut down the number of families who would receive the longer and more costly pre-enrollment interview. As the table indicates, a small number of dwelling unit cards were held in reserve and never used, and a total of 48,614 screening interviews were attempted; of these, 4892 housing units were found to be vacant. This seems a large number, but it should be remembered that throughout the period of the experiment there was general net migration *out* of the center-city areas. This left a potential of 43,722 households in which eligible families might dwell. Interviews were completed with 27,350 family-heads, or 62.6 percent of the households, leaving 8414 (19.2

percent) who were never found at home (after five tries) and 7958 (18.2 percent) who refused to speak with the interviewer. The latter called back four times, a standard procedure, varying the time of day and day of the week of each of the tries. In Jersey City, where a low initial yield caused concern about bias, eight callbacks were used.

Determination of Eligibility on the Basis of the Screening Interview

Among the completed screening instruments, 3124 (11.4 percent) turned up families considered eligible. As indicated above, eligibility requirements were that families have a male head able to work, that the head be between the ages of eighteen and fifty-eight, and that the total family income be below 1.5 times the 1967–1968 Social Security Administration poverty level (automatically adjusted for family size). As noted, the screening interview was brief and was not expected to determine eligibility with the precision of the longer instrument. A small number of families was held in reserve, even though eligible on the basis of the screening instrument, for use if needed subsequently. Most of these were Spanish-speaking families (in Paterson–Passaic and Jersey City, as shown) who were overrepresented in the sample.

Pre-Enrollment Interview

Of the pre-enrollment interviews attempted, 2341 (79.3 percent) were completed. The high pre-enrollment completion rate can be explained as a result of having weeded out the chronic refusers on the screening interview. Nevertheless, 6.9 percent of those contacted did not agree to submit to the longer pre-enrollment interview, and 13.6 percent could not be located even though they had taken a screening interview.

Determination of Eligibility on the Basis of the Pre-Enrollment Interview

Of the 2341 pre-enrollment interviews completed, 1513 (64.6 percent) contained data on families who were still considered eligible. Most of the reduction in eligible families came from the more detailed income information contained on the longer instrument. As a general rule, the more detailed and probing the income questions in an interview are, the more income is found.[10]

---

[10] For a more detailed discussion of this, see D. Lee Bawden and David N. Kershaw, "Problems in Income Reporting and Accounting," in *Income Maintenance: Interdiscipli-*

Enrollment

As before, a number of families, while eligible, were not enrolled, but kept in reserve. In Jersey City, the preponderance of Puerto Ricans in the sample was again the reason, and in Scranton, it was clear that the sample could be filled without using all eligibles from pre-enrollment. The reserve group in Scranton (62 families) were randomly eliminated from the potential enrollment group. We attempted a total of 1316 enrollments, resulting in a final sample of 1216, the enrollment completion rate (92.4 percent) again showing a tendency to climb over the previous pre-enrollment completion rate.

Thus, of the original target households, numbering 43,722, the number of families enrolled was 1216, or 2.8 percent of the households sampled. One hundred and forty-one extra control-group families were subsequently enrolled in Trenton and Paterson–Passaic, bringing the total final sample to 1357. The question then arises as to what kinds of bias may have been introduced by the elimination of so many families, not only for reasons of ineligibility but because of refusals and failure to be at home when an interviewer called.

REPRESENTATIVENESS OF SAMPLE

It is important to measure the extent to which the final experimental sample was a faithful representation of the families fitting the characteristics sought in the target cities. Fortunately, field work for the 1970 Census was conducted at about the same time that the field work for the experiment was conducted, so we can to some extent compare our figures with 1970 Census statistics (see Table 2.2).

The table is composed of the following entries:

Line 1: Percentage of non-aged, male-headed families, with income below 150 percent of the 1968 poverty line (1970 Census data). This entry includes all such families, regardless of whether or not they are in the labor force. Not included are disabled men (eliminated by the experiment) and others who simply do not want to work (not eliminated by the experiment). Because this number eliminates no heads on disability grounds, it overstates our eligibility rate.

Line 2: Percentage of non-aged, male-headed families, with heads in the labor force and incomes below 150 percent of the 1968 poverty line (1970 Census

nary Approaches to Research, ed. Larry Orr, Robinson Hollister, and Myron J. Lefcowitz, Institute for Research on Poverty Monograph Series (Chicago: Markham, 1971); and David N. Kershaw, "Administrative Issues in Establishing and Operating a National Cash Assistance Program," Joint Economic Committee, Congress of the United States, *Studies in Public Welfare,* Paper No. 5, Part 3, (Washington, D.C.: U.S. Government Printing Office, March 12, 1973).

Table 2.2 Comparison of the Final Sample with 1970 Census Statistics, by City

	Trenton	Paterson–Passaic	Jersey City	Scranton	All Cities
Census					
1. All non-aged, male-headed families, incomes below 150 percent of poverty line	7.0	9.7	9.0	8.2	8.6
2. All non-aged, male-headed families, in the labor force, incomes below 150 percent of poverty line	5.2	7.2	6.4	4.8	6.1
Experiment					
3. Eligibility rate based on screening interview	9.4 (8.2,10.6)	11.4 (10.6,12.1)	15.9 (15.1,16.7)	7.9 (7.3,8.5)	11.4 (11.0,11.8)
4. Eligibility rate based on pre-enrollment interview	6.8 (5.8,7.8)	7.4 (6.8,8.0)	9.6 (8.9,10.3)	5.5 (5.0,6.0)	7.4 (7.1,7.7)

NOTE: Figures are in percentages. Census estimates were derived by factoring up numbers on poverty families to include all those with incomes under 150 percent of the poverty line, eliminating single individuals and female-headed families, and adjusting the census age range for heads (14–64) to conform to that of the experiment (18–58). Numbers in parentheses are upper and lower 95 percent confidence limits for the above percentages.

data). Line 2 understates eligibility by eliminating all those families who, while otherwise eligible, did not have a male head in the labor force. Since it is impossible to apply the same disability measure to the census figures as to the experiment figures, we have to be satisfied that the true census eligibility rates, applying the experimental parameters, fall within the range represented by Lines 1 and 2.

Line 3: Percentage eligibility based on the experiment's screening interview. Line 3 is derived simply by dividing the families eligible for pre-enrollment by the total completions in screening. For the total,

$$\frac{3124}{27,350} = 11.4 \text{ percent.}$$

Line 4: Percentage eligibility based on the experiment's pre-enrollment interview. This is a more precise measure, using the detailed questions on income from the pre-enrollment interview. It is derived by factoring up the families eligible for enrollment (1513) by the ratio of the pre-enrollments attempted to the pre-enrollments completed (to correct for moves, refusals, and those eliminated). For the total,

$$\frac{1513 \times \frac{3124}{2341}}{27,350} = 7.4 \text{ percent.}$$

A priori, one would thus expect the number of those found eligible from the screening interview (Line 3) to fall within the bounds provided by the census (Lines 1 and 2), and the (more precise) number of those judged eligible from the pre-enrollment interview to fall near the bottom of or below that range.

As Table 2.2 shows, this is exactly what happened in Scranton and Trenton, and close to what occurred in Jersey City and Paterson–Passaic. As the Scranton column indicates, the number of those judged eligible from the screening interview falls in the top of the range (numbers in parentheses are upper and lower 95 percent confidence limits for the observed percentages), and the pre-enrollment eligibility falls at the very bottom of the range. Trenton, while slightly above in the screening eligibility, conforms quite well. A probable explanation for the differences in the comparisons for Jersey City and Paterson–Passaic is that the experiment, being very attentive to problems of bias introduced by traditional survey methods—which miss black families in cities (and for which the census has been criticized)—simply found more families on the screening in predominantly black areas (Paterson–Passaic and Jersey City). That this is not the case in heavily black Trenton may be accounted for by the fact that Trenton was a 1970 Census pretest site, and extra care may have been taken to avoid the black undercount problem.

In summary, Table 2.2 shows that the ultimate eligibility rate for the experiment falls just where it should, at least as compared to the only data source available for comparison. Thus, one may conclude that the sampling procedures provided a final experimental sample representative of other families in those cities with similar income and family composition characteristics.

CHARACTERISTICS OF THE SAMPLE
AT ENROLLMENT

Table 2.3 shows the ethnic composition of the sample.[11] After the enrollment in Trenton and Paterson–Passaic, 45 percent of the sample was black, 45 percent Spanish-speaking, and 10 percent white. OEO felt that extending the same proportions into Jersey City would overrepresent Spanish-speaking persons. Thus, a number of Spanish-speaking families otherwise eligible were eliminated from the sample in Jersey City. The underrepresentation of non-Spanish-speaking whites (125 families out of 1039 at the end of enrollment in Jersey City) was corrected by the enrollment of families in Scranton, where virtually all the sample was white. The final ethnic composition was roughly one-third for each of the three major ethnic groups.

Additional characteristics of the families at the time of the screening interview

---

[11] Characteristics given are based on the entire sample, that is, the original 1216 families plus the 141 families subsequently selected as additional control families.

Table 2.3 **Ethnic Composition of Sample, by City and by Treatment or Control**

Group	Trenton	Paterson-Passaic	Jersey City	Scranton	All Cities
Black					
Treatment	53	109	118	2	282
Control	52	84	81	1	218
Total	*105*	*193*	*199*	*3*	*500*
White					
Treatment	14	30	25	162	231
Control	11	18	27	153	209
Total	*25*	*48*	*52*	*315*	*440*
Spanish-speaking					
Treatment	20	137	55	0	212
Control	9	112	84	0	205
Total	*29*	*249*	*139*	*0*	*417*
All ethnic groups					
Treatment	87	276	198	164	725
Control	72	214	192	154	632
Total	*159*	*490*	*390*	*318*	*1357[a]*

[a]Includes the original 1216 families and 141 additional control families in Trenton, Paterson, and Passaic.

can be seen in Table 2.4. Average family size was 5.9 persons, and the mean age of the head of household was 35.8 years. These two characteristics did not vary substantially between control and experimental groups or among cities. Paterson–Passaic families had the lowest average education (7.7 years), and Scranton families had the highest (10.3 years).

At the time of the screening interview, 93 percent of the heads of household were employed. Employment of head of household was highest in Scranton, where 98.1 percent of the heads of household were employed, and was lowest in Trenton, where 83.5 percent of the family heads were employed.

About 65 percent of the family heads were skilled workers—professional, technical, managerial, and clerical workers; salesmen, craftsmen, foremen, and operatives; 35 percent were unskilled workers—persons employed in private households, in the service industries, and laborers. The relatively high number of people with skills is due to the fact that the sample was restricted to able-bodied males with dependents to support—a relatively stable family life.

An average of 10.6 percent of the families were receiving public assistance at the time they took the screening interview. Here, there is a marked contrast between cities. For instance, only 4.9 percent of the Jersey City sample was receiving public assistance, compared to 17.6 percent of the Trenton sample.

Table 2.4 **Characteristics of Families at Time of Screening, by City**

	Trenton	Paterson-Passaic	Jersey City	Scranton	All Cities
Sample size (families)[a]					
Experimental	87	276	198	164	725
Control	72	214	192	154	632
Full sample	159	490	390	318	1357
Mean family size (persons)					
Experimental	6.1	5.9	6.5	5.5	6.0
Control	5.8	5.6	6.0	5.5	5.7
Full sample	6.0	5.7	6.3	5.5	5.9
Mean age of head of household (years)					
Experimental	35.9	35.3	36.2	36.1	35.8
Control	34.7	34.5	35.3	38.3	35.7
Full sample	35.4	34.9	35.7	37.2	35.8
Mean education of head of household (years)					
Experimental	8.3	8.0	8.7	10.3	8.8
Control	8.7	7.3	8.7	10.3	8.6
Full sample	8.5	7.7	8.7	10.3	8.7
Mean family earnings, 1968 (dollars)					
Experimental	3860	4046	4332	4052	4283
Control	3634	4006	3875	4043	3933
Full sample	3758	4029	4107	4048	4024
Mean family income, 1968 (dollars)					
Experimental	4204	4153	4411	4389	4283
Control	3996	4304	4059	4398	4217
Full sample	4110	4219	4238	4393	4252
Families receiving public assistance (percent)					
Experimental	18.4	8.3	4.0	14.0	9.7
Control	16.7	12.6	5.7	15.6	11.7
Full sample	17.6	10.2	4.9	14.8	10.6
Occupational status of family heads (percent)[b]					
		Employed			
Experimental	82.6	91.6	95.4	98.2	93.1
Control	84.7	93.8	91.6	98.1	93.1
Full sample	83.5	92.6	93.5	98.1	93.1
		Skilled[c]			
Experimental	47.1	68.3	69.5	71.5	66.7
Control	56.1	66.8	58.4	64.1	62.4
Full sample	51.0	67.7	64.1	68.0	64.7
		Unskilled[d]			
Experimental	52.9	31.7	30.5	28.5	33.3
Control	43.9	33.2	41.6	35.9	37.6
Full Sample	49.0	32.3	35.9	32.0	35.3

(Continued)

37

Table 2.4 (continued)

Housing status of families (percent)

		Rental units			
Experimental	62.1	53.0	56.6	47.6	53.9
Control	48.6	70.3	59.4	40.1	57.5
Full sample	56.0	60.7	58.0	44.0	55.6
		Public housing			
Experimental	17.2	30.1	31.6	17.7	26.1
Control	34.7	19.3	23.4	30.3	25.2
Full sample	25.2	25.3	27.6	23.7	25.7
		Own home			
Experimental	20.7	3.4	7.7	31.7	13.2
Control	15.3	2.4	8.9	27.0	11.9
Full sample	18.2	2.9	8.3	29.4	12.6
		Other housing			
Experimental	0.0	13.5	4.1	3.1	6.9
Control	1.4	8.0	6.3	2.6	5.4
Full sample	.6	11.1	5.2	2.9	6.2

[a]Includes the original 1216 families and 141 additional control families in Trenton, Paterson, and Passaic.

[b]All heads were asked their occupational status, regardless of whether they were employed or not. Thus skilled plus unskilled equals 100 percent, not the percentage of employed.

[c]Skilled includes professional, technical, managerial, and clerical workers, salesmen, craftsmen, foremen, and operators.

[d]Unskilled includes persons employed in private households, in the service industries, and as laborers.

This reflects different administrative practices among the various public-assistance agencies, as well as differences in the sample population.

More than one-half of the families in the experiment lived in rented apartments or homes. Another one-fourth of the families were in public housing. Home ownership was low—12.6 percent. But this ranged from a high in Scranton, where 29.4 percent of the families owned their own homes, to a low in Paterson—Passaic, where only 2.9 percent of the families owned their own homes.

As a detailed inspection of the table will indicate, there did not exist the kind of differences between the experimental and control groups that would have caused differential behavioral responses based merely on the assignment strategy. In interpreting any comparison of characteristics between the experimental and control group, however, it is important to note that the assignment model did not allocate families uniformly across experimental cells. Differences in sample means must, therefore, be regarded with caution (see Chapter 6 for a discussion of the assignment model).

DISPOSITION OF FAMILIES
ELIGIBLE FOR ENROLLMENT

As discussed earlier, 1513 families were eligible for enrollment. In the search for additional control families for Trenton and Paterson–Passaic, we found another 141 families who were eligible. This brought the total eligible group to 1654. Of these, 1357 were enrolled. The status of the enrolled families and the 297 eligible families who were not enrolled is given in Table 2.5.

No attempt was made to enroll 197 eligible families located in Jersey City and Scranton. As mentioned earlier, we eliminated 135 randomly selected Spanish-speaking families in Jersey City, in order to maintain an ethnic balance of roughly one-third black, one-third white, and one-third Spanish-speaking families. Sixty-two families in Scranton were randomly eliminated because the cells to which they would have been assigned had been filled; thirty of the families we had selected to participate had moved or could not be located at the time of

Table 2.5 **Disposition of Families Eligible for Enrollment, by City**

	Trenton	Paterson–Passaic	Jersey City	Scranton	All Cities
Eligible for enrollment	170	554	548	382	1654
Enrolled					
Experimental	87	276	198	164	725
Control	72	214	192	154	632
Total	*159*	*490*	*390*	*318*	*1357*
Not enrolled					
Enrollment not attempted	0	0	135[a]	62[b]	197
Moved or could not be located	2	21	7	0	30
No longer eligible[c]	0	3	5	0	8
Refused enrollment	9	40	11	2	62
Total	*11*	*64*	*158*	*64*	*297*

[a]Spanish-speaking families randomly deleted from sample to maintain ethnic balance.

[b]Families deleted from sample because sample cells were filled.

[c]Families no longer eligible due to loss of male head.

enrollment; and eight families were no longer eligible because of the loss of a male head.

There remained a group of sixty-two families who, for one reason or another, chose not to participate in the experiment. This brought the overall refusal rate among families contacted for enrollment to 7.9 percent, with a high in Paterson–Passaic of 12.7 percent and a low in Scranton of 1.2 percent. The refusal rate by city is given in Table 2.6.

COMPARISON OF CHARACTERISTICS OF FAMILIES
WHO REFUSED ENROLLMENT OR WHO WERE ENROLLED

The small group of families who refused enrollment do not appear to differ significantly from the families who were enrolled. Table 2.7 shows that slightly more Spanish-speaking families refused enrollment than did white or black families. The higher refusal rates in Trenton and Paterson–Passaic (Table 2.6) are probably associated with the higher refusal rate of Spanish-speaking families, since it is in these two areas that the Spanish-speaking sample was concentrated.

Table 2.8 shows that the mean family size for refusals was comparable to that of the enrolled families—5.9 and 6.0 persons, respectively. The average age of the head of household was slightly higher for refusal families (37.7 years) than for enrolled families (35.8 years). Also, the working-age male in families that refused to enroll averaged one year less of education than the overall experimental average. Looking at occupational status, a larger portion of family heads who refused were unemployed (13.1 percent) than family heads who enrolled (6.9 percent); but a slightly greater proportion of the former were skilled workers (67.9 percent) than was the case among enrolled family heads (66.7 percent). At the time of the screening interview, 11.5 percent of refusals, compared to 9.7 percent of the enrolled families, were on welfare. This could have affected the refusal rate.

Table 2.6 **Number and Rate of Enrollment Refusals, by City**

	Experimental Families Enrolled	Families Who Refused Enrollment	Treatment and Refusals	Refusal Rate
Trenton	87	9	96	9.4%
Paterson–Passaic	276	40	316	12.7
Jersey City	198	11	209	5.3
Scranton	164	2	166	1.2
All cities	*725*	*62*	*787*	*7.9*

Table 2.7 **Number and Rate of Enrollment Refusals, by Ethnic Group**

	Experimental Families Enrolled	Families Who Refused Enrollment[a]	Treatment and Refusals	Refusal Rate
Black	282	24	306	7.8%
White	231	11	242	4.5
Spanish-speaking	212	26	238	10.9

[a]These numbers total only 61 (instead of the correct total of 62) because the records of one family are incomplete.

There were, thus, only minor inherent differences between families that refused enrollment and families that enrolled. There was one major difference, however, which was attributable to the experiment itself: the size of the enrollment check. The families had, or course, been assigned to a specific plan before they were visited by an enroller. When the enroller arrived to enroll a family, he or she was able to offer them a check based on the generosity of the plan to which they had been assigned in return for allowing themselves to be enrolled.[12] As can be seen from Table 2.9, the generosity of the plan, and therefore the size of the check, was very relevant to the enrollment decision. The average amount offered to those who chose to enroll was $36. The average amount offered to those who refused was only $8. In Paterson—Passaic, where the refusal rate was highest, the average amount offered to those who refused was only $6.

REASONS FAMILIES REFUSED ENROLLMENT

The reasons given by the families for not enrolling tended to fall into several broad and overlapping categories. It is difficult to classify these in any quantitative way, since the reasons could usually only be guessed at by enrollers. The following sampling of comments by enrollment personnel about families who chose not to participate is illustrative.

The work ethic:

He's a proud young man who finally insisted that he did not believe in taking

---

[12] The enrollment check was, in fact, the first in the series of regular checks the enrolled families would receive throughout the experimental period. It was calculated, therefore, on the basis of the experimental plan the family would face if they enrolled, plus family size and income (as measured in the pre-enrollment interview).

Table 2.8 Characteristics of Experimental Families and of
Families Who Refused Enrollment, as Shown from
Screening Interview

	Experimental Families	Refusal Families
Ethnic origin		
Black	38.9%	39.3%
	$N = 282$	$N = 24$
White	31.9%	18.0%
	$N = 231$	$N = 11$
Spanish-speaking	29.2%	42.6%
	$N = 212$	$N = 26$
Total	$N = 725$	$N = 61^a$
Mean family size	6.0	5.9
Mean age of head of household (years)	35.8	37.7
Mean education of head of household (years)	8.8	7.7
Mean family earnings, 1968 (dollars)	4103	3503
Mean family income, 1968 (dollars)	4283	3709
Public assistance recipients	9.7%	11.5%
	$N = 70$	$N = 7$
Occupational status^b		
Employed	93.1%	86.9%
	$N = 657$	$N = 53$
Skilled workers	66.7%	67.9%
	$N = 463$	$N = 36$
Unskilled workers	33.3%	32.1%
	$N = 231$	$N = 17$
Housing status of families (percent)		
Rentals	53.9	42.6
Public housing	26.1	31.1
Own home	13.2	13.1
Other housing	6.9	13.1

^{a}Total is 61, instead of 62, because the records of one family are incomplete.

^{b}All heads were asked their normal occupation, regardless of whether they were employed or not.

money for nothing. He lived on what he, himself alone, earned. He had a family, and it was his responsibility, not anyone else's, to take care of them.

No form of welfare would be acceptable to this man despite the guise of "basic income" and "experiment."

This man is sincerely obsessed with the Protestant ethic—he makes speeches about

Table 2.9 **Initial Payment Offered to Prospective Experimental Families, by Enrollment–Refusal Decision and by City**

	Sample Size	Average Amount of Check[a]
Trenton		
Enrollments	87	$38.73
Refusals	9	13.25
Paterson–Passaic		
Enrollments	276	27.04
Refusals	40	6.05
Jersey City		
Enrollments	198	47.80
Refusals	11	8.50
Scranton		
Enrollments	164	38.21
Refusals	2	22.75
All cities		
Enrollments	725	36.06
Refusals	62	8.07

[a]$2.50 minimum payments and $10.00 filing fees are not included in calculation of the average initial check.

the value of work in his neighborhood. Says it's a good program but not for him. Wishes us luck.

Suspicion about legitimacy of the experiment:

Respondent was incredulous, thought for sure program was a come-on.

He does not like America—may return to Puerto Rico—has gotten into too much trouble signing things and simply does not wish to get involved. The $2.50 check [minimum payment] simply was not enough to overcome his skepticism. His wife got him into this [by answering Urban Opinion Surveys] and he wants out.

Fear of loss of welfare payments, preference for welfare over experimental payments:

Miss_____ is receiving $175/month ADC. This is her sole income. She would not enroll because she was afraid of losing welfare, especially the hospitalization.

Not sure that he understood what his welfare status would be if he registered for the program.

Family was recently enrolled with welfare—sum they are receiving is more adequate to their needs than our program.

Program too much like welfare:

Respondent said, "What? Is this from welfare? No thanks!" and closed the door.

A feeling that the program was an invasion of privacy:

> Felt some of the pre-enrollment questions were too personal ("wouldn't even tell my wife").

> Doesn't want anybody prying into his family matters.

> Preferred privacy to insurance.

A feeling that participation was too much of a bother:

> Mr.____ thought filling out the monthly income report was too much work—even after I explained that it only takes five to ten minutes a month.

> Interviews took too much time.

> Husband is self-employed. Doesn't want to be bothered with the bookkeeping part.

Personal reasons:

> Cousin told them not to accept, that it will cost them in the future. Cousin has been living in this country for 15 years and no one ever gave him anything so why should they want to give it to respondent.

> Would have been willing to sign but will move to Puerto Rico with whole family in February.

> Wife has eye problem; husband can't read or write.

> Respondent, who was Italian, felt he didn't speak English well enough to participate.

> Too tired to sign.

3

Administration
of interviews

We made the decision in early 1968 to hire a professional survey research organization to conduct the survey part of the experiment. We were particularly interested in the National Opinion Research Corporation (NORC) because it was the most experienced social-policy interview firm in the country, but we also solicited proposals from Opinion Research Corporation (ORC), National Analysts, and the Market Research Corporation of America (MRCA).

To the disappointment of the staff, NORC indicated that it was not really interested in participating in the study, but would submit a bid, if pressed. When the bids came in, Charles Westoff, professor of demography at Princeton University, who helped the staff evaluate the proposals, said:

> The proposal that has come in from NORC is hardly a proposal and in the absence of any details cannot be evaluated comparatively with the other three bids. Unless they are willing to do more I would suggest not considering them any further at the moment.[1]

Special thanks are due to Diane Lewis and Sandra Carter, who supervised interviewers in the field in the early period of the experiment, and to Nancy Feldman and Andrea Schutz, who took over the supervision and provided much of the material for this chapter.
[1] Westoff to Mathematica, Internal Memorandum, February 1968, Data Center Archives, Institute for Research on Poverty, University of Wisconsin-Madison.

The MRCA and National Analysts proposals lacked evidence of what the staff thought to be the necessary experience with an urban poor population. Both showed a distinctly market research orientation.

The bid from ORC was accepted on the basis of their previous experience, their proximity to the Mathematica offices, and the existence of a trained interviewing staff in several New Jersey cities. One result of the proposal process was a feeling that the experiment presented some unique survey research problems. None of the bids had really shown an adequate understanding of this. As Frederick Stephan, a Princeton statistician and the other consultant brought in to evaluate the bids, stated:

> The purpose of a proposal for other-than-routine survey operations should include adequate evidence that the major problems involved in the work to be done are adequately comprehended and that the bidder stands ready to deliver what is required. In my opinion none of these proposals does this adequately to warrant awarding a contract without substantial further development of what work will be performed, how it will be controlled, and what quality can be assured. The approach seems to be influenced too much by the customary presentation of competitive bids and not enough by the unique requirements of this experiment.[2]

With this warning, the staff spent considerable time monitoring the operations of ORC. After ORC had conducted the screening and pre-enrollment in Trenton, the Mathematica staff decided that the experiment did, in fact, require rather extraordinary survey procedures that were not being provided by ORC. In particular, tighter controls, more substantial quality checks at the field level, more supervision by senior staff members, longer and more in-depth training, and a much greater use of staff and interviewing personnel who were familiar with poor areas of the city were needed. Since such attributes did not appear to exist in organizations willing to participate, a new organization was established within Mathematica itself (given the title of Urban Opinion Surveys) to conduct the interviews for the experiment.

In establishing this new operation, Mathematica staff members observed other organizations, went to training sessions given by the Bureau of the Census for its employees, invited a representative of NORC to conduct a seminar, and gathered training and other materials used by the Census Bureau and other organizations. With these experiences and materials to build on, and after a six-month trial-and-error period, we developed the procedures described in this chapter.

These procedures have been used by Mathematica in a large number of

---

[2] Stephen to Mathematica, Internal Memorandum, February 1968, Data Center Archives.

subsequent studies, and some of the new techniques, applicable to the rather special case of center-city interviewing, have been used by others.

STAFF FOR THE INTERVIEW PROCESS

Administration of the interviews took from four to six weeks every quarter in each of the four sites. During each interview wave, each site was staffed by an interviewing supervisor; an office assistant; quality-control readers; field checkers; and fifteen to twenty interviewers, depending on the size of the sample in the particular site. Overall supervision of interviewing in each city was done by an interviewing coordinator, whose base was in Princeton. Even though the two groups used the same office building, the interviewing staff should not be confused with the field-office staff, who dealt with the payment and address-reporting problems of the families on a regular basis. For a description of the site-office manager's responsibilities, see the section "The Field Offices" in Chapter 4.

Because there was a high turnover among interviewers, replacing them involved office personnel in repeated hiring and training processes. Some of the channels through which we located new interviewers were local colleges, newspaper ads, state employment offices, local poverty programs or civic organizations, and references from other interviewers.

Interviewing in urban areas is a difficult task and needs a substantial commitment on the part of the interviewer. Interviewers, who were paid by the hour and were required to have their own car, had a demanding job. Many of the subjects were suspicious of the questions asked, and some refused to open their doors. There were several instances of assaults and of interviewers being chased out of neighborhoods or having their wallets snatched.

Because the most important data being collected were on earnings, the best time to interview was evening, when the probability of finding the wage earner(s) at home was greatest. For this reason, even though there was more danger to the interviewers after dark, evening interviewing had to be scheduled.

Few efforts were made to match interviewers and respondents with respect to race, age, sex, or education. The qualitative finding was that empathy and confidence were more important than matching by characteristic. As in many aspects of the experiment, different procedures were required in different sites. The ability of the supervisors to adjust to these differences and to determine quickly such things as the necessity of sending older interviewers to Spanish-speaking homes, of race-matching whites in Jersey City, or of sending escorts to some areas with the interviewers, was important in completing the task. Table 3.1 indicates the characteristics of the interviewing staff in the winter of 1971, when all the sites were in operation.

Table 3.1 **Characteristics of Interviewers, 1971**

	Trenton (N=15)	Paterson–Passaic (N=35)	Jersey City (N=23)	Scranton (N=21)
Sex				
Male	67	57	35	29
Female	33	43	65	71
Race				
White	40	16	–	100
Black	53	42	78	–
Spanish-speaking	7	42	12	–
Average age				
(years)	27.1	27	26	22
Marital status				
Single	67	43	49	86
Married	27	37	39	14
Separated	6	2	4	
Divorced		10	8	
Widowed		8		
Education (years)	14	12	14	14
Average residence				
in area (years)	13.5	11.6	10.9	19.7
Persons with other				
employment	60	57	27	29
Persons with previous				
interviewing				
experience	33	51	52	39
Persons presently				
students	47	47	73	57

NOTE: Figures are in percentages except where stated to be otherwise.

INTERVIEWER TRAINING

The training of interviewers followed an evolutionary process, moving from the standard interviewing format used by many existing survey organizations to lengthy and repeated training sessions with heavy supervision. At the beginning of the project, training consisted of one three-hour session; by the end, interviewers were receiving four three-hour training sessions. In addition to being instructed on how to dress, how to probe for information, and the logic-flow of each instrument, interviewers were tested on the contents of the interview and were given details about the intent of the questions, practice interviews, retraining sessions, and extensive vocabulary reviews.

Halfway through the administration period of each quarter, a meeting of the field-interviewing staff, the central office personnel, and the research staff was held. Discussions at this midquarterly meeting addressed problems with particular questions on the interview, difficult field situations, and suggestions for revisions of the questionnaire. The purpose of the meeting was threefold: to serve as a retraining session for interviewers; to provide feedback to the researchers and interview development staff; and to enable the field staff to understand the connection between their efforts and those of the central office and the research staff.

QUALITY CONTROL

Approximately 75 percent of each interviewer's work was validated during the first two weeks of an interviewing period. If the interviewer did consistently high-quality work, the validation rate was then dropped to 25 percent. If the work was not of high quality, the validation rate remained at 75 percent and the interviewer underwent retraining.

To validate, a staff member contacted the respondent, either in person or by telephone. Three to six questions, from various sections of the interview, were asked; the respondent was then asked how long the interview had taken and whether or not he had any comments to make. This process enabled the supervisory staff to check the information on the questionnaire and to make sure that the interviewer had not merely put in an appearance, asked a few questions, and then falsified the rest of the information—which, in fact, happened very infrequently.

Each field office had, also, at least two field checkers and two quality-control readers. The field checkers were primarily responsible for catching those mistakes that could be corrected by discussion with the interviewer after the questionnaire was returned to the office (for example, inadequate explanations in open-ended questions, questions skipped that should have been answered, clarification of abbreviations, and missing signatures). The field checkers tried to have the questionnaires read by late afternoon of the working day following the interview, in order that any missing information might be retrieved during a daily reporting session. Sometimes interviewers had probed sufficiently but had forgotten to record all the information obtained. If it was a matter of misspellings or bad handwriting, this could easily be corrected. In most other cases of error, the interviewer had to go back and get the information from the family.

Quality-control readers were assigned the task of checking those items in the interview that required particular sensitivity on the part of the interviewer to the issues of clarity, codability, and conceptual consistency.

SCHEDULING AND GENERAL FIELD-OFFICE PROCEDURES

Most interviewers were in the field office for six weeks: one week for preparation and interviewer training, four weeks for actual interviewer-respondent contact, and one week for cleanup. Each interview was roughly one hour long, with twenty minutes for the regularly repeated labor-force questions and the other forty minutes taken up with questions that varied from interview to interview.

In order to keep on schedule, a daily production chart was maintained in each field office. Interviewers were expected to report to the field office in the late afternoon to pick up their interview forms and answer any questions from the quality-control staff on their previous night's work. They were then assigned specific families to interview and were expected to report back to the office after the evening's work. In no case was an interviewer allowed to take questionnaires home.

INTERVIEWING FAMILIES OUTSIDE THE ORIGINAL SITES

Families could move anywhere within the continental United States and still remain in the experiment. If the families were in the experimental group, they had to continue to file the income report forms in order to receive payments. All the families who could be found, whether experimental or control, were administered the quarterly interviews.

There were various ways of interviewing out-of-town families. If a family moved only a few miles from an experimental site, they were contacted by one of the regular interviewers. If a family moved somewhere close to one of the other negative-income-tax experiments, in Gary, Seattle, Denver, Iowa, or North Carolina, the family was interviewed by the staff of that experiment (a reciprocal arrangement). As might be expected, families who moved fanned out over a large area. During the course of the three years, families moved to Florida, Georgia, North Carolina, South Carolina, Virginia, Maine, Massachusetts, New York, Ohio, Illinois, and California. Where necessary, interviewers for families who had moved were recruited through local universities and through organizations such as the League of Women Voters, which had selected welfare reform as a national issue in 1971 and was happy to contribute to the experiment.

PREPARATION OF INTERVIEWS FOR ADMINISTRATION

All interviews required precoding of certain information onto the questionnaire in Princeton, before being sent into the field. In the case of the screening interview, only the location of the household was indicated but all other interviews required (in addition to the address) the name, age, sex, and relationship to head of household of all family members. This precoding ensured that the interviewer had a factual basis on which to assess changes since the previous interview.

In addition to precoding, there were often materials to be included in the interview packet, such as various supplemental questionnaire sections and special interviewer instructions. The $5 checks received by the families for answering each questionnaire were prepared and included with the interviews before they were released by the Princeton office.

During the administration of an interview, the interviewing coordinator in Princeton was in daily contact with the field supervisor. The field supervisor reported the number of interviews completed and discussed with the central office any problems that may have arisen that day. If a family could not be located or refused an interview, the interviewer reported to the field supervisor, who checked the central office records to find out whether the family had filed a recent address change, had indicated some kind of personal problem, or had a history of interview problems. Based on available information, a recommendation to try once more or give up was made.

When the interviews were completed, the questionnaires were returned to the Princeton office and tallied against those from earlier interviews. This process indicated completed and uncompleted interviews, the reasons for noncompletion, the number of attempts made to interview the family, and the field supervisor's recommendations for future interviewing. In addition, the field offices compiled, for the Princeton office, a list of the families who had caused problems during administration of the questionnaires—by breaking appointments, refusing to answer particular sections, or refusing to answer the entire instrument.

Before being turned over to the research staff, the data on the questionnaires were checked for information relating to changes in the family's name, status, address, or the number of its members, and this was entered into the records. Any discrepancies were checked with the field supervisor prior to administration of the next interview.

4

Administration

of transfer payments

The payments system was administered by a group consisting of the payments department in Princeton and a site manager and staff in each of the experimental sites. The payments department consisted of a payments supervisor, a clerk, and three payments assistants, each responsible for calculating and disbursing payments to approximately 240 families. The calculation of payments also required the services of a computer programmer for about fifteen hours per week.

This chapter will discuss the payments process and the functions of the field office, as well as the modifications that were made during the course of the experiment.

THE INCOME REPORT FORM

In order to receive a biweekly payment, each family was required to file an income report form (IRF) every four weeks. In addition to filling out the form

The payments system was developed under the supervision of Gwendolyn Cavanaugh and Marsha Shore. Field-office management was under the supervision of Kathleen Roche for much of the experiment and then of Michaelyn Olsen and Anne Freeman, who saw field operations to a conclusion and contributed to the writing of the sections on field operations. Marsha Shore wrote much of the section on the payments system.

completely, accurately, and on time, the family was required either to send in all the paystubs received by all working members of the family or to give an explanation if stubs were not provided. The $10 biweekly payment (called the filing fee) received by the families in return for filling out their income report form also provided a filing incentive for families who received small payments or who were not eligible for payments because their income was above the break-even point.

The filing fee was introduced in June of 1969, about ten months after the start of the experiment, as part of the solution to the experimental design dispute described in Chapter 6. Prior to this, a minimum payment of $2.50 was made to families whose income was above the breakeven point, but families receiving a regular grant received no additional compensation.

The families had four weeks within which to return the IRF to the payments department. The first two weeks of the filing period were known as the "regular filing period." The second two weeks were the "late filing period" (see Figure 4.1). If the IRF was not returned in four weeks, both payments (checks 1 and 2) were forfeited as well as the $10 filing fee that accompanied each payment. All IRFs on which payments had been forfeited had to be filed before any subsequent payments could be made.

Data collected on filing showed that about 50 percent of the families filed during the first week of the filing period, even though they had two weeks to do so without causing payment to be delayed. In the second week, a further 39 percent filed, resulting in an 89 percent return in the regular two-week period.

Fifty percent of the IRFs returned in the first week and 56 percent of those returned in the second week were from families who were receiving just the filing fee, suggesting that the size of the payment was not necessarily a great influence on a family's promptness in filing. A summary of the data on IRF returns in the first and second weeks is given in Table 4.1.

THE BIWEEKLY PAYMENT SCHEDULE

The first biweekly payment (check 1) was made on the last day of the four-week filing period. The second payment (check 2) was made two weeks later, or two weeks following the end of the filing period (see Figure 4.1). If the IRF was filed late, that is, during the second two weeks of the filing period, check 1 was delayed two weeks. The first and second biweekly payments were then paid together on the date regularly scheduled for payment of check 2. If the IRF was filed after the four-week filing period, both check 1 and check 2 (as well as the filing fee) were forfeited. Given the small size of the experimental group it would have been possible to decrease the turn-around time consider-

Table 4.1 **Numbers and Percentage of Income Report Forms Returned in Regular Filing Period, by City**

	IRFs Returned	IRFs That Could Be Processed	IRFs with Problems	Families Receiving Filing Fee Only[a]
Week 1				
Trenton (*N*=78)	37	33	4	24
Paterson (*N*=131)	64	57	7	36
Passaic (*N*=89)	49	47	2	28
Jersey City (*N*=189)	93	85	8	36
Scranton (*N*=163)	82	78	4	37
Total (*N*=650)	*325* (50%)	*300* (92%)	*25* (8%)	*161* (50%)
Week 2				
Trenton	28	27	1	21
Paterson	46	41	5	28
Passaic	32	27	5	24
Jersey City	74	69	5	32
Scranton	71	66	5	35
Total	*251* (39%)	*230* (92%)	*21* (8%)	*140* (56%)
Week 1 and Week 2 Combined				
Trenton	65	60	5	45
Paterson	110	98	12	64
Passaic	81	74	7	52
Jersey City	167	154	13	68
Scranton	153	144	9	72
Total	*576* (89%)	*530* (92%)	*46* (8%)	*301* (52%)

NOTE: The IRF periods shown here are 10 April 1971–7 May 1971 for Trenton, Jersey City, and Scranton and 17 April 1971–14 May 1971 for Paterson and Passaic.

[a]That is, families receiving no transfer payments because their income was above the breakeven point.

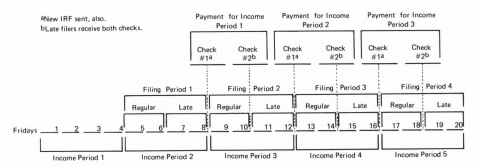

Figure 4.1 Income report period, filing period, payment cycle.

ably. However, in order to replicate the responsiveness of a national program, a "realistic" time period deliberately was used.

INCOME PATTERNS FOR EXPERIMENTAL FAMILIES

As Figures 4.2 through 4.6 indicate, there was considerable month-to-month fluctuation in both the earnings and the total income of experimental families. In retrospect, this is not surprising considering that the income, particularly of low-income families, is influenced by such factors as odd jobs, sporadic overtime, and layoffs. The degree of fluctuation came as a surprise to the research staff, however, because previous earnings-and-income studies had rarely collected data in such a form that it could be disaggregated to show detailed within-year patterns. Nor had those studies been restricted to low-income families.

The clear upward trend in earnings shown in the tables should not be seen as reflecting a lack of effect of the transfer payments on family earnings. The

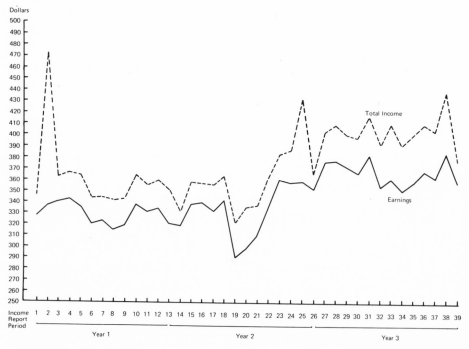

Figure 4.2 Earnings and total income by income report period, experimental families: Trenton.

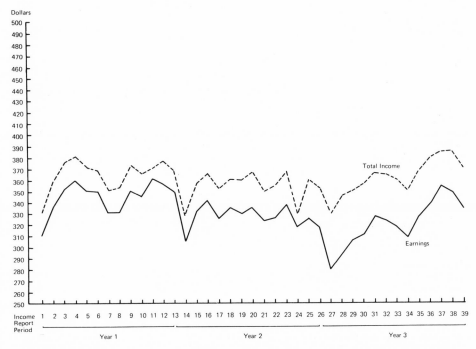

Figure 4.3 Earnings and total income by income report period, experimental families: Paterson–Passaic.

earnings of both experimentals and controls did, in fact, follow a generally increasing trend during the period of the experiment, both because of general country-wide wage increases and because the level of economic activity over the period was relatively high.

COMPUTING THE PAYMENT

The negative tax payment was based on the formula

$$P = \frac{G}{52} - (r \times y),$$

where
    P = weekly negative tax grant,
    G = yearly dollar guarantee based on plan assignment and family size,
    r = tax rate,
    y = average weekly income.

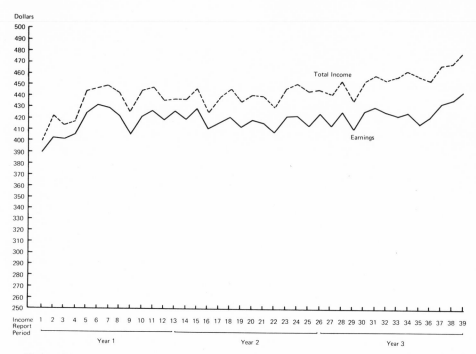

Figure 4.4 Earnings and total income by income report period, experimental families: Jersey City.

The average weekly income (y) was calculated using the three-month accounting period and carry-over system described in Chapter 5.

The basic process of analyzing the IRFs involved checking the paystubs against the amounts entered in the earnings section of the IRF, determining if all four weeks had been accounted for, and looking for any change in family composition or address. As the payments assistant read the IRF, he or she checked the payments record book, which contained the complete record of every type of income and expense reported on all preceding IRFs, every payment made, and the plan to which the family had been assigned. Checking the payments record familiarized the payments assistant with the family's filing habits and served as a preliminary audit.

If there were any questions or problems concerning an IRF, the payments assistant checked the family's file. This file contained all correspondence, field-office memos, and other information related to the family, as well as all IRFs filed by the family. Where the same problem had arisen before, an answer from the field manager was on file. Particular filing idiosyncrasies could also be identified by consulting previously filed IRFs and the record that contained each family's entire income history. If the problem could not be resolved by checking

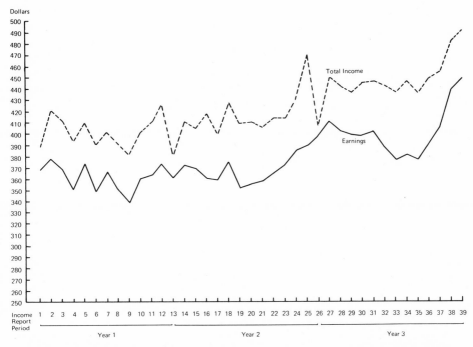

Figure 4.5 Earnings and total income by income report period, experimental families: Scranton.

the records in the payments office, the payments assistant sent a question card to the family and a memo to the field manager. On the average, about 8 percent of the IRFs in each filing period required field attention.

Most of the IRFs were usable as they came in or could be clarified from records in the payments department. The complete IRF information was then entered into the record book, the IRF filed in the family's individual folder, and the paystubs placed in an envelope to be returned to the family with the next payment.

As the payments assistant read the IRFs and recorded the data, he or she also coded the data onto coding sheets. The data were then keypunched and entered into the computer system. The computer calculated the payments, stored the check information until it was ready to print the checks, and stored the IRF and payment data in a permanent disc file. This file of data was essentially a duplicate of the record book but contained, in addition, the components of the payment calculation. Printouts of the computer file were produced on a regular basis for the payments assistant to check, update, and use for reference.

Originally, a "wage-payment transaction" printout was checked against the record book to verify that the data were correct before the check was printed.

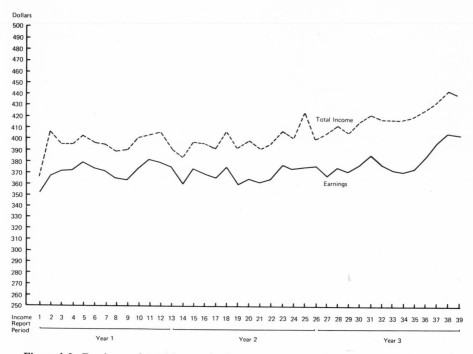

Figure 4.6 Earnings and total income by income report period, experimental families: all cities.

This resulted in the discovery of so few errors, however, that subsequently the checks were printed at the same time as the wage-payment transaction printout. Any incorrect checks were simply voided and rewritten by hand.

THE TAX REBATE SYSTEM[1]

In order to maintain control over the tax parameter, it was necessary to counteract the effects of other taxes. Although there were several such taxes, the experiment in fact controlled only for the major one, the federal income tax. If no adjustment had been made between the negative tax rates and those of the positive tax, families rising over the breakeven point would have experienced a sudden drop in disposable income.

Figure 4.7 illustrates how the current positive income tax works. The vertical axis, DY, is disposable income after taxes; Y is total income of the family before

[1] For more details, see Fair and Freeman, "The New Jersey . . . Experiment Tax Rebate System," Internal Paper, September 1971, Data Center Archives, Institute for Research on Poverty, University of Wisconsin-Madison.

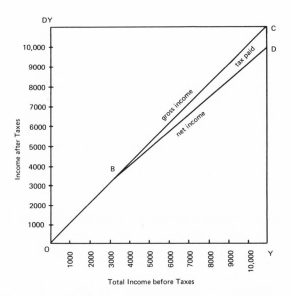

Figure 4.7 Positive income tax, family of four: (B) start of positive taxes; (OBC) gross income; (OBD) disposable income.

exemptions and deductions. The line *OBC* on the graph indicates gross income before taxes, and *OBD* represents net income after taxes. Using a family of four as an example, gross income equals net income up to about $3600 (point *B*); that is, no taxes are paid. After $3600, *OBD* takes on successively lower slopes as income increases and progressively higher tax rates apply. Total tax is the vertical distance between *OBD* and *OBC*.

A negative income tax is illustrated in Figure 4.8 for a family of four with a $3848 guarantee and a 50 percent tax rate. Point *E* represents the guarantee level. Point *F* is the breakeven point where negative tax payments are no longer received. The total negative tax payments for varying amounts of income are represented by the vertical distance between *OF* and *EF*.

Because the maximum income level at which no tax was paid was lower than the income levels (experimental breakeven points) at which experimental payments were reduced to zero, superimposing one system on the other with no adjustment would produce a range in which some experimental families faced their experimental tax (benefit reduction) rate plus the positive tax rate. If taxes were reimbursed up to a family's experimental breakeven point and not any higher, the family would face a tax "notch," meaning that the earning of one additional dollar above their breakeven level would lead to a *fall* in their disposable income (Figure 4.9).

A decision was therefore made that families would be reimbursed in full or in part for positive taxes paid, so as to maintain a constant tax rate (dictated by the

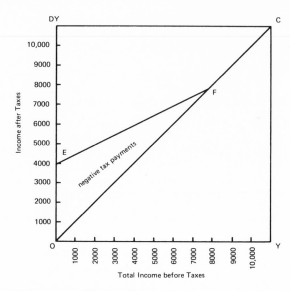

Figure 4.8 Negative income tax, family of four: (E) guarantee level; (F) breakeven point; (OFC) earned income; (EFC) disposable income.

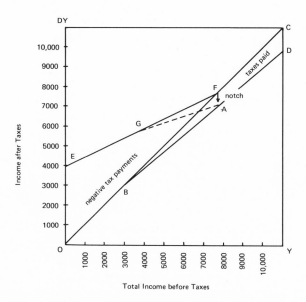

Figure 4.9 Combined positive and negative income taxes, unadjusted, family of four: (E) guarantee level; (F) breakeven point; (B) start of positive taxes; (EFGC) gross income; (EGFAD) disposal income, 1; (EGAD) disposable income 2.

62

experimental plan they were assigned to) up to the "tax breakeven point," defined as the income level at which positive taxes would begin to be paid if the Internal Revenue Service were using the same tax rate as the experimental plan to which the family was assigned (Figure 4.10). Families paying no positive tax were thus unaffected; families with incomes below the breakeven point of their experimental plan and paying positive taxes had all taxes reimbursed; families with incomes over the breakeven point of their experimental plan but not so high as their "tax breakeven point" were partially reimbursed.

Reimbursements, or rebates, were made at the end of each year. Each January, a letter requesting copies of all W-2 income-tax withholding forms was mailed to the families. Late in the month, a second letter was mailed requesting a copy of the 1040 income-tax payment forms. Families were told that they might be eligible for a tax rebate and that they would receive $6 upon our receipt of the 1040 form.

Administratively and experimentally, the procedure for rebating taxes did not prove effective, primarily because of the large lag between the date taxes were paid and the date the rebates were made. Taxes paid in January, for instance, could not be rebated until a year from the following April, when the 1040 forms were due. In practice, the time was even longer, since two months were allowed after collection of the 1040 forms to process the data and calculate the rebates.

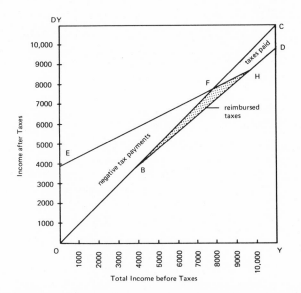

Figure 4.10 Combined positive and negative income taxes adjusted by tax rebate, family of four: (B) start of positive taxes; (E) guarantee level; (F) breakeven point; (H) tax breakeven point; (EFC) gross income; (EFHD) disposable income.

A refinement of this procedure was used in the Seattle–Denver Income-Maintenance Experiment, where tax rebates were made along with the payments on the basis of a "tax estimation" technique. Federal taxes owed were calculated for taxable income on a current basis. A reconciliation was then employed that later adjusted for the difference between the actual amount of taxes paid as documented by 1040 forms and the estimated taxes paid. Lag time for the reconciliation process was approximately one year, although the amount was usually small.

THE REVISED INCOME REPORT FORM

The function of the IRF was to provide sufficient data for the calculation of payments on a form families could fill out themselves. During the course of the experiment, we used two IRFs, the second version replacing the first version in the fall of 1970 (see Figures 4.11 and 4.12). (The IRFs, along with all other forms, were printed in both English and Spanish.)

The original IRF did not call for sufficiently detailed information and lacked space to report support payments. In addition, the earnings section failed to pick up precise information. Unless the family sent in all paystubs, for example, it was not clear whether the amount entered was for one week, two weeks, three weeks, or four weeks. There was no way for the family to indicate the number of jobs held, making it impossible for the payments assistant to know whether all sources of earnings had been accounted for.

The note at the bottom of the form requested the family to send in paycheck stubs. Not all jobs, however, provide paystubs. The form contained no space for the family to explain these circumstances, and when stubs were not sent, the payments assistant had to ask the field office to contact the family for clarification. Families who, because of illness, slack work, or lost paystubs, sent in less than four stubs also had to be contacted if no explanation was provided.

It became apparent that many requests for information or clarification resulted not so much from the families' inability to file as from the inadequacies of the form itself. In an attempt to distinguish "filing problems" from "IRF problems," a study was made in March 1970 of the IRF and the types of filing errors. In a 25 percent random sample of families over twenty periods in Trenton, fourteen in Paterson–Passaic, nine in Jersey City, and six in Scranton, the IRFs were analyzed to determine if a payment could be calculated on the basis of the IRF as filed without having to contact a family for further information or clarification.

Of the 1862 old IRFs analyzed, 74 percent were immediately usable and 26 percent were not. The results of the study were very useful in the development of a new IRF. The major changes were made in the earnings section. The family

COUNCIL FOR GRANTS TO FAMILIES

120 Alexander Street   Princeton, New Jersey 08540

FAMILY INCOME REPORT

Covering the period_____to_____

_____   _____
(name)   (telephone number)

_____
(street number)   (city)   (state)

_____Check here if there has been any change in your address in the last
four weeks.

Have there been any changes in your household during the last four weeks?

_____NO, no new people have been added and no people have left our
household during the last four weeks.

_____YES, there have been changes.
Please explain:_____

_____

I.   EARNINGS BEFORE TAXES (Wages, Salaries, Tips, and Commissions)

(1)   Husband . . . . $_____
(2)   Wife . . . . $_____
(3)   All Others. . . . . $_____

II. OTHER INCOME

(4)   Business Income (after all expenses) . . . . $_____
(5)   Rent (including room & board payments from roomers). . . . $_____
(6)   Interest or Dividends (on savings and investments) . . . . . $_____
(7)   Social Security Benefits (including disability & retirement). . $_____
(8)   Unemployment Insurance. $_____
(9)   Welfare Benefits . . . . $_____
(10) Veteran's Benefits (including veteran's disability) . . . . . $_____

All Other Income (please explain)

(11)   _____ . . . . $_____
(12)   _____ . . . . $_____
(13)   _____ . . . . $_____

Income from the value of owner-occupied housing will be computed
by the Council.

TOTAL FAMILY INCOME. . . . . $_____

X_____   _____
(signature of head of family)   (date)

NOTE: YOU MUST INCLUDE ALL PAYCHECK STUBS OR PAY
ENVELOPES WITH THIS REPORT. THEY WILL BE RETURNED
WITH YOUR NEXT FAMILY INCOME REPORT.

Figure 4.11 Income report form.

was required to report earnings on a weekly basis, filling in an amount for each
of the four weeks before entering a total. The question about paystubs at the
bottom of the earnings section provided space for the family to explain missing
paystubs and acted as a reminder to include the paystubs when returning the

65

Do not detach. Mail both copies to the Council.

COUNCIL FOR GRANTS TO FAMILIES
120 Alexander Street   Princeton, New Jersey 08540
FAMILY INCOME REPORT ☐

Name_____ Telephone Number_____

Address_____ City_____ State_____

PART 1: EARNINGS BEFORE TAXES (Gross wages, Salaries, Commissions)
You must send in ALL PAYCHECK STUBS or PAY ENVELOPES received by ALL members
of your family from ALL JOBS for the 4 weeks starting and ending on the following dates:

	to	

	Husband	Wife	All Others	
How many jobs did you work at during the 4 week period?	____ Jobs	____ Jobs	____ Jobs	
How many of the 4 weeks did you work?	____ Weeks	____ Weeks	____ Weeks	TOTAL 4-WEEK FAMILY EARNINGS
Week #1..............	$_____	$_____	$_____	
Week #2..............	$_____	$_____	$_____	
Week #3..............	$_____	$_____	$_____	
Week #4..............	$_____	$_____	$_____	
4-WEEK TOTAL	$_____	$_____	$_____	$_____

Did all working family members send in all paystubs?
☐ YES   ☐ NO ——▶If NO, please explain why:_____

PART 2:   OTHER INCOME RECEIVED DURING THE 4-WEEK PERIOD

(1) WELFARE	$	(6) Rent collected from roomers or rental property	$
(2) Social Security (including disability and retirement)	$	(7) Business income (after all expenses)	$
(3) Unemployment Insurance	$	(8) Interest or Dividends	$
(4) Veteran's Benefits (including Veteran's Disability)	$	(9) Other:	$
(5) Child support or alimony received	$	(10) Other:	$

PART 3:   TOTAL FAMILY INCOME

MY TOTAL FAMILY INCOME IS (add amounts in PART 1 and PART 2):	$

PART 4: EXPENSES

(1) Did you pay someone to care for your children or dependents in order to go to a job?	☐ NO ☐ YES	$
(2) Did you pay alimony or child support payments?	☐ NO ☐ YES	$

PART 5: CHANGES

(1) Have you moved in the last 4 weeks? ☐ NO ☐ YES	New address:
	New telephone number:
(2) Has anyone been added to your household in the last 4 weeks? ☐ NO ☐ YES Name of person added	Age
(3) Has anyone left your household in the last 4 weeks? ☐ NO ☐ YES Name of person who left	Age

X_____   _____
SIGNATURE OF HEAD OF HOUSEHOLD   DATE

COMMENTS_____

Figure 4.12 Revised income report form.

66

IRF. As before, a total income figure was requested, as a double check. Part 4 of the new IRF asked the questions about child care and alimony and support payments that the original form had omitted. The "changes" section was expanded to two questions instead of one, in order to distinguish members added to the household from members who left it, and to include the name and age of each.

The new form resulted in a decrease in the number of IRFs that the payments department had to refer to the field. It was simply mailed to the families as usual, with no announcement or special instructions, and it presented no new problems to the families. One year after the second IRF had been brought into use, the filing problems to be handled by the field office per IRF period had gone down from 25 percent to 8 percent.

LATE FILING AND FORFEITURES

Late filing was concentrated in a small group of families who were aware of the rules and procedures but simply chose to file late and receive payments late. Notices, calls, personal visits, and even forfeiture of payment had little effect on their filing interest or ability. Because of the administrative difficulty in getting cooperation from such families, they were dropped after they had refused to continue to participate or had failed to file three successive IRFs. The field-office manager periodically contacted these families to see if they would like to rejoin the program; if they wished to rejoin, they were reeducated in the rules and procedures of proper filing.

In general, late filing and forfeitures fluctuated considerably between periods and among cities but maintained a rather constant level over time (see Figure 4.13). Variables such as change in season, point in time over the three-year program, and treatment of late filers seem to have had virtually no effect on the extent of late filing.

THE FIELD OFFICES

The negative-income-tax experiment, in contrast to the welfare system, was explicitly designed to minimize personal and face-to-face contact between participants and staff members. Although such contacts did not have to be made with many families very often, there was a need for a local field office in each site. These offices were responsible for any problems or questions from families, community contacts, and special research projects. They were also ideally located to serve as early warning systems for problems and trends in the

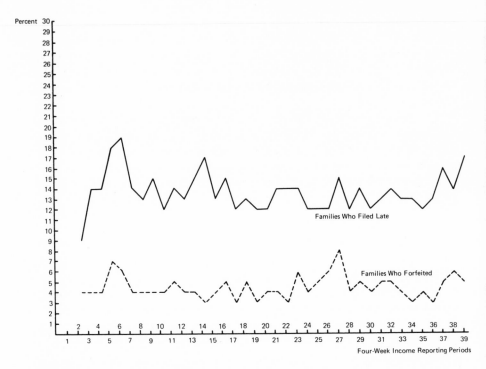

Figure 4.13 Percentage of families who filed late or forfeited for income reporting periods 1–39, covering three years: all cities.

experiment. Field-office staff members were often the first to became aware of problems or misunderstandings on the part of families. They also read the local newspapers and informed the central office of community events and issues that might affect the experiment. The offices also came to be used for training interviewers, although the personnel involved in interviewer training and the interviewers themselves were different from the field-office and payments staff.

The offices were originally set up with a full-time office manager and one or more assistants, usually people hired from the surrounding community. After the first year, the staff was reduced to one office manager for each city. By the second year the staff was reduced again. In Jersey City, the original two field offices were combined. In Scranton, the field operations were handled by one part-time person working two days a week. Responsibility for both the Paterson and Passaic field offices was assigned to one office manager who spent three days a week in one city and two days in the other. By the third year of the program, only the Trenton office remained open full time, due to its pivotal status as the pilot city. Overall supervision was provided by a coordinator based in Princeton.

CONTACTS WITH FAMILIES

As we have said, we tried to avoid unnecessary contacts with families to minimize behavioral responses induced by the contact itself. (It must be remembered that we are referring here to contacts with respect to experimental payments. The regular interviews every three months were a separate operation.) When contacts about IRFs or payments difficulties were required, an attempt was made to keep them as impersonal as possible. A form letter was always tried first as the least personal and most easily administered method. If within a few days the family did not respond to such a letter, the telephone was the next method used. Since many families did not have telephones, this means of contact was not always available. The third method was a handwritten note asking the family to call the office. This sometimes brought results where a form letter had failed. Home visits were a last resort since they were the most personal type of contact and encouraged the family to think of the office manager as a caseworker.

Most contacts related to filing the income report form. Since late filing was a frequent reason for contacting the families, a strict schedule was developed outlining the types and number of contacts that could be made to prompt families to file. This was done so that standardization could be maintained across sites and so that the experiment might reasonably be replicable in a national program.

Whenever the information on an IRF was insufficient for a payment to be computed, the family was contacted by the office manager and asked to explain or supply the missing information. Routine questioning of all unclear or incomplete income report forms solved many reporting problems and often prevented payment errors. Other problems such as changes in family composition, changes in welfare status, and change of address, also resulted in contact with the families. Families who indicated that they no longer wished to participate were also contacted by the office manager. Sometimes they merely wanted a chance to voice a complaint and were willing to continue in the program once they had been heard. Although the office managers made every effort to make participation in the program as convenient as possible, no family was pressured to remain in the study.

Families who moved were a major problem for some office managers. In Paterson, where extensive urban renewal projects made low-income housing quite scarce and families were especially mobile, an average of eight families moved each month. Some families moved to Puerto Rico or to the South and then moved back. Some moved from one block to the next. Some moved from one apartment to another and then back. Several moved twice in a single month. Some reported address changes either on their income report form or by calling the field office. Others simply disappeared and had to be traced.

Table 4.2 Field-Office Contacts with Participants per Month, by Subject and Type of Contact

Reason for Contact	Note or Letter			Telephone			Office Visit		
	Average No. of Contacts	Average Time per Contact (in minutes)	Total Time (in minutes)	Average No. of Contacts	Average Time per Contact (in minutes)	Total Time (in minutes)	Average No. of Contacts	Average Time per Contact (in minutes)	Total Time (in minutes)
Initiated by field office									
Insufficient information on income report form	5.9	9	53	56.0	10	560	5.2	18	94
Late filing and forfeits	47.2	11	519	31.2	8	250	1.6	25	300
Change in family size	1.8	6	11	7.7	5	39	1.1	10	11
Change of address	6.4	9	58	5.2	5	26	1.8	8	14
Initiated by family									
Request for information on payment	—	—	—	16.1	20	322	6.0	20	120
Request for help with income report forms	1.4	15	21	2.0	9	18	1.0	13	13
Other requests, such as for information on jobs, housing	4.6	10	46	14.7	9	132	5.2	22	114
Full sample	67.3		708	132.9		1347	21.9		666

Reason for Contact	Home Visit			All Types of Contact		
	Average No. of Contacts	Average Time per Contact (in minutes)	Total Time (in minutes)	Total No. of Contacts	Total Time (in hours)	Average Time (in minutes) per Month per Family (Based on 668 Families)
Initiated by field office						
Insufficient information on income report form	17.8	60	1068	84.9	29.6	2.7
Late filing and forfeits	5.6	45	252	85.6	22.0	2.0
Change in family size	2.5	45	113	13.1	2.9	.3
Change of address	2.5	35	88	15.9	3.1	.3
Initiated by family						
Request for information on payment	1.1	50	55	23.2	8.3	.7
Request for help with income report forms	1.4	45	63	5.8	1.9	.2
Other requests, e.g., for information on jobs, housing, etc.	1.7	40	68	26.2	6.0	.5
Full sample	*132.6*		*1707*	*254.7*	*73.8*	*6.6*

71

Over the course of the experiment the office managers kept records of all contacts they had with the families. Table 4.2 gives the average number of such contacts and the time spent on each per month, by subject and type of contact. The figures are averages taken midway in the experiment. There was approximately one contact per month for every two and one-half families in the program.

part II
Research and
technical issues

5   The rules of operation

In an operating program, regulations define the rights and obligations of participants so that the program can be operated in an equitable, standardized, and efficient way. Without such regulations, administrators have no clear guidelines for policy and participants have no protections. An experiment needs a detailed set of rules for the same reasons, and for an additional reason. Rules affect behavior, and a nonexhaustive set introduces uncontrolled, and therefore unknown, variation in behavior.

RULES OF OPERATION FOR THE NEW JERSEY EXPERIMENT

The most important regulations concerned the definition of the family (that is, the collection of persons eligible to fill out a joint income report form as a filing unit and receive the payment as a group), the definition income, and the accounting period. (A complete set of the rules of operation of the experiment is to be found in Appendix B.)

Definition of the Family

The filing unit chosen as the family for purposes of the calculation and receipt of payments was defined as the head of the family plus his or her dependents. A dependent was defined as any blood, or adopted, relative living with the head, or a person not so related but living with the head and receiving no more than $30 per month from income sources outside the family income.

The general intent of the family-unit regulations was to replicate insofar as possible the conditions of a national program. However on two specifics—when a member leaves a family unit and when a new member joins—it did not seem possible to replicate a national program.

The decision was made that children leaving the family unit because they became of age could take their marginal payment with them but *not* start a new filing unit of their own. This was to prevent the creation of a "dowry effect" (whereby children in experimental families would be more than usually marriageable for the three-year experimental period).

An analogous decision was made that families could admit no new members for payments purposes except natural-born children or other children after a six-month continuous period of residence within the new family. This was to prevent experimental families from becoming artificially attractive as lodging places for relatives or friends.

When a spouse left the original household, the regulations allowed that spouse to take that portion of the family guarantee allotted to him or her, but not to form any new family units eligible for experimental payments. The guarantees for both spouses were always equal. The children's guarantees went to the spouse who took custody.

Definition of Income

The purpose of the income definition was to devise a measure of overall economic well-being that would enable the payments calculation to reflect adequately and uniformly differences from family to family.

The earnings of all family members were counted as income, as were rent; net business income; interests and dividends; annuities and pensions; Unemployment Insurance, Workmen's Compensation, and Social Security benefits; veteran's benefits; strike benefits; training stipends; and alimony and court-ordered support payments.

Families who lived in owner-occupied or subsidized housing were imputed the difference between the monthly rental for subsidized housing (or monthly taxes and insurance in the case of homeowners) and the average rental value of nonsubsidized housing of the same number of rooms. Homeowners were allowed a fixed percentage of taxes and insurance for maintenance and improvements. The standard rental values and the housing status of the families were reviewed on a yearly basis. The housing imputation was adjusted for individual families each time they moved. Although rental income was counted at 100 percent, room-and-board receipts up to $12 per week were deducted to cover expenses.

Certain other deductions were allowed, including full support of children and other dependents outside the home and partial dependent-care expenses (such as child care) incurred in order to enable a member of the household to enter the labor force. The dependent-care deduction from the earnings of the released worker was allowed up to a maximum of $80 per four-week period for one member receiving care, $120 for two or more members.

In the original set of rules, welfare payments were treated in the same way as such other cash transfers as Social Security benefits; that is, they were counted as income. This was because New Jersey had no public-assistance program for which families with an able-bodied male were eligible.

As described earlier, on 1 January 1969, New Jersey introduced a generous AFDC-UP program for which most of the experimental sample was eligible. Only Trenton had been enrolled for any length of time, so it was decided that for all the other sites the rules of operation would be changed so that every payment period experimental families would have to decide whether or not to accept welfare (with welfare accounting rules) or experimental payments (with experimental accounting rules). They were to remain in the sample for the purposes of sending in income report forms and answering the quarterly interviews, and they could change back and forth as many times as they liked between welfare and experimental payments. The Trenton sample was to be allowed to continue as it had started, reporting any welfare payments to the experiment as income.

In November 1969, however, the Mercer County prosecutor's office began investigating overlapping payments, as described in Chapter 12. It was eventually established that several Trenton families had had welfare overpayments. The Trenton rules were changed, therefore, to conform to the rest of the cities.

The Accounting Period

The time period during which income received by a family is included in the calculation of its payment is the accounting period. (For the current welfare system, the accounting period is, generally, one month. That for the positive tax system is one year.) The accounting period affects the degree to which equity is maintained among families, that is, the extent to which families with the same income over a given period of time are treated equally, regardless of the pattern in which the income is received. The objective of the experiment (and presumably of any national program) was to treat families equally, however much the pattern of their earnings varied. The range of earning patterns included families with unemployed members whose incomes were zero all year; families with constant, but low, incomes; families whose incomes fluctuated substantially over a year; farm and other families who received all their income in a lump sum once or twice a year; and families with incomes that steadily rose or steadily fell over a period.

The concept of equity was assumed to mean annual equity; therefore, the goal of the accounting system was to pay the same amount each year to families who were in the same plan and had the same income, regardless of the pattern of their earnings. As is explained later, achieving this annual equity without completely sacrificing responsiveness to changes in need was both conceptually and administratively complicated.

It is instructive to compare two ways of achieving annual equity. The first is to make payments based on the family's income for the most recent month, and then reconcile any difference between total payments during the year and the total that would be appropriate for the family's annual income at the end of the year.[1] The second is to use a twelve-month moving-average system, in which the current month's income is averaged with the income of the preceding eleven months to reach an average income figure upon which each month's payment is based. This system requires no year-end reconciliation.

Table 5.1 illustrates why, under the former, monthly accounting, system, an end-of-year reconciliation is necessary to achieve annual equity. It shows how four families, all with the same annual income, would be treated under the monthly accounting system. Each family in the table has a guarantee of $3000, a tax rate of 50 percent, and an annual income of $4000; the total annual payment for each should be $1000.[2] All four of these families have equal annual incomes, yet the only one receiving the correct annual payment is the steady earner. The three with irregular earnings receive substantially larger total payments over the year (a family with steadily increasing earnings would also be mispaid).

Under the monthly accounting system, families substantially above a given *annual* eligibility level could still be eligible in some months. Consider a family with an annual income of $15,000, in which the wage earner loses his job for three months. Under the monthly accounting plan, the family would be eligible for payments for three months. Given that many families in the United States have incomes that fluctuate, a national program with a monthly accounting system could have a caseload at any one time of double or triple the number of families eligible on an annual basis, with consequent major increases in disburse-

---

[1] The time period used was actually a four-week period, since it was felt that wage earners were more likely to be paid on a weekly than monthly basis. A monthly accounting system is, however, a less cumbersome concept than a four-week accounting system and is used here for purposes of discussion.

[2] Yearly payment = guarantee − (tax rate × income) or, in this case, $3000 − (.5 × $4000).

Table 5.1 Payments to Families with Various Types of Earnings under a Monthly Accounting System

	Steady Earnings		Declining Earnings		Irregular Earnings		Farm Income	
	Income	Payment	Income	Payment	Income	Payment	Income	Payment
January	$333	$84	$600	$ 0	$600	$ 0	$ 0	$250
February	333	84	550	0	800	0	0	250
March	333	84	500	0	200	150	0	250
April	333	84	450	25	0	250	0	250
May	333	84	400	50	0	250	0	250
June	333	84	350	75	300	100	0	250
July	333	84	325	87	500	0	0	250
August	333	84	275	113	600	0	0	250
September	334	83	225	138	600	0	0	250
October	334	83	175	163	0	250	4000	0
November	334	83	150	175	200	150	0	250
December	334	83	0	250	200	150	0	250
Total	*4000*	*1004*	*4000*	*1076*	*4000*	*1300*	*4000*	*2750*

ment cost,[3] and (in the absence of annual reconciliation) also in transfer cost. A monthly accounting system without annual reconciliation rewards the "bunching" of income during the year, thus creating an incentive to move away from regular jobs and toward other forms of earning.

Recapturing payments in an ex post factor attempt at equity is, however, administratively cumbersome and often, in fact, impossible. In the example given, annual equity would require the recovery at the end of the year of $300 from the irregular earner and $1270 from the farm family. This could, of course, create severe hardship for these families; in most cases it would also be both difficult and self-defeating for the experiment to try to recapture large amounts from a family with earnings totaling only $4000 per year.

The alternative twelve-month moving-average system ensures automatic annual equity. It is, however, very unresponsive to changes in family income. For example, a family of four with a guarantee level of $3000, a tax rate of 50 percent, and a steady income of $500 per month would receive zero dollars in

[3] See "Estimates of Caseload Size, Family Benefits Administration Staff Requirements and Transfer Payment Costs for HR-1 (Title XXI–'Family Programs')," prepared for the Office of Family Benefits Planning, Department of Health, Education, and Welfare, by Mathematica, Inc. (Princeton, N.J., 1972): 22–23.

payments. If, however, the family's income dropped to zero in one month, the *average* monthly income would drop to $458 [(11 X $500 + 0)/12]. This would yield a payment for that month of only $21, instead of the maximum monthly payment of $250 allowable for an income of zero dollars. For a family with an earner who had just been permanently laid off, it would be twelve months before they received the maximum payment.

In addition to this type of problem, differential labor-force responses can be expected to result from different accounting schemes. In the twelve-month moving-average system, neither a rapid rise in income nor a drastic drop in income is reflected very substantially in the level of payments. Therefore, it could be argued that work effort would be affected very little by experimental payments. In the monthly accounting system, however, families receive an immediate response in payments to a change in income; this could well act as an inducement for people to work less.

The experiment was interested in testing possible work-incentive differences induced by various accounting systems. Therefore, it was decided to test two different systems. The annual, retrospective (twelve-month moving-average) system was put into effect for a small subsample of 65 families. The most highly responsive system—with a monthly accounting period—was not used, because OEO was unwilling to risk the major bunching in earnings they feared would occur. A compromise was struck with the decision to institute a three-month moving average for the rest of the sample. Earnings of the most recent month were averaged with those of the previous two months, slightly lessening the response of the payments to changes in income. In the case of the family with steady earnings of $500, a sudden drop to zero income would result in an average monthly income of $333 [(2 X $500 + 0]/3]. Under the three-month moving average, this would yield a apyment of $84, compared with $250 for the monthly system and $21 for the twelve-month moving average.

When the three-month moving-average system was instituted, it was assumed that the payment flows would be smoothed sufficiently to make the annual reconciliation problem a minor one. Family incomes fluctuated so much, however, that it was still necessary to recover large sums of money from certain families. For example, in Trenton, at the end of the first calendar year of operations (five months of payments), substantial readjustments had to be made for 40 percent of the families, and amounts to be recaptured (through lower future payments) ranged as high as $463 for one family.

The recapture problem was finally solved through the use of an old inventory concept. Professor of Law William Klein and Professor of Economics D. Lee Bawden, both of the University of Wisconsin, devised a "carry-over" method of accounting, under which payments made to a family were based not only on the average income of the last three months but also on any income in excess of the

Table 5.2 Payments to a Family with Irregular Earnings under a Monthly Accounting System with Carry-over Provision

	Earnings	Accumulated Carry-Over Sum	Net Income (earnings plus carry-over sum)	Newly Added into Carry-Over	Payment[a]	Total Income Received
January	$600	$ 0	$600	$100	$ 0	$600
February	800	100	900	300	0	800
March	200	400	600	0	0	200
April	0	100	100	0	200	200
May	0	0	0	0	250	250
June	300	0	300	0	100	400
July	500	0	500	0	0	500
August	600	0	600	100	0	600
September	600	100	700	100	0	600
October	0	200	200	0	150	150
November	200	0	200	0	150	350
December	200	0	200	0	150	350
Total	*4000*				*1000*	

[a]Annual breakeven is $6000, and monthly breakeven is, therefore, $500.

breakeven amount earned in any of the preceding twelve months.[4] This "excess income" was carried over until the excess had been worked off or for a maximum of eleven subsequent months. As long as a carry-over sum existed, the payment was zero. When all the carry-over was used up and the moving average was below the breakeven point, payments resumed. The carry-over was used up in a "first in, first out" fashion. That is, carry-over generated in month 1 was used up before that generated in month 2, and so forth. If the carry-over was not used up within twelve months, it was dropped off. In this way, families were not accountable for income more than one year old nor were they ever in the position of having to repay a sum at the end of the year. If a family's income went over the breakeven point, a continuously changing amount was added to their income in each future month until the excess was either used up or dropped because a year had passed since it had been accumulated.

Even under a monthly accounting system, a carry-over provision solves the problem of annual equity, no matter how irregular the earnings. Returning to the same example with which we began, Table 5.2 shows how the irregular earner depicted in Table 5.1 would fare under a monthly accounting system that included a carry-over provision. As the table shows, total income (earnings plus

[4] Klein, Internal Memorandum, July 1969, Data Center Archives, Institute for Research on Poverty, University of Wisconsin-Madison.

payments) has been substantially smoothed, and total payments for the year add up to the correct annual amount.

DIFFERENCES IN RULES OF OPERATION
ACROSS EXPERIMENTS

During the planning for the New Jersey experiment, it was recognized that rules had to be standardized to permit the effects of the negative-income-tax treatment to be isolated. It was not realized, however, that regulations could, if varied systematically, constitute actual treatments. This has become much clearer in the years since the New Jersey experiment was begun. It is best illustrated by looking at three other income-maintenance experiments whose rules differ from the New Jersey ones in important respects.

An income-maintenance experiment focusing on rural families was financed by OEO and administered by the Institute for Research on Poverty. Families were all enrolled simultaneously in December 1969, and payments lasted for three years, that is, until December 1972. Another such experiment, funded by the Department of Health, Education, and Welfare (HEW) and conducted by an independent group, was run in Gary, Indiana. This was the only experiment with a saturation component, and its area of special interest was the interaction of income-maintenance schemes with the provision of subsidized day care. A saturation experiment is one in which every eligible family in a given geographical area is enrolled. In the Gary case, part of the experiment was situated in a Model Cities area, and in this section of Gary all eligibles were enrolled. The payment period was three years (with the exception of a small two-and-one-half-year high-income subsample). Enrollment was spread over an eight-month period, with the first payment being made in January 1971 and the last payment in August 1974. The most recent income-maintenance experiment, funded by HEW and run by the Stanford Research Institute and Mathematica, is being undertaken in Seattle, Washington, and Denver, Colorado. Its area of special interest is the interaction of income-maintenance schemes with manpower training. Most families are being paid for three years or five years, with a small subsample being paid for twenty years. The first payments were made in November 1971, and the last payment (with the exception of the twenty-year subsample) will be made in August 1977.

Looking at two important regulations across the various experiments will illustrate their potential as treatment variables: (1) the definition of the family unit and (2) the definition of income.

Comparisons of Definitions of Family Unit

The rules defining the family unit for the New Jersey experiment were designed in an effort to minimize any influence that the rules themselves might have on behavior. If the rules as well as the negative-income-tax payments influenced behavior, any resulting differences between experimental and control behavior could not be attributed simply to the treatment. However, the concept of "neutral" rules is itself ambiguous. As Table 5.3 indicates, the effort to develop such a set has produced family-unit rules that vary substantially across income-maintenance experiments.

As the table indicates, there are important differences among the experiments in the regulations governing both initial eligibility and conditions for subsequent entry. The experimental effect of varying these rules is clear. For example, most of the experiments were concerned with measuring changes in family composition over time as a function of the payments. Presumably, the results of these measurements will form the basis for decisions at the national level regarding family-unit rules in national income-maintenance systems. Consider the differences in the rules, as illustrated in Table 5.3. In the Gary experiment, a dependent must be 21 years of age before being able to leave the original household and take his payment with him; in the others the age is 18. One could easily hypothesize that under these conditions, new units would be readily formed by dependents from ages 18 to 21 in all the experiments except Gary, where the incentive is for the dependent to remain in the unit until age 21 in order to continue to receive payments. This alone could force at least marginal differences in the pattern of new-family formation among experiments and provide substantially different research results.

This potential difference is further increased by the regulations governing the addition of new adult members. In most of the experiments new adults cannot be added to an existing eligible unit under any circumstances—a rule designed to protect the experiment from expansion through outside adults moving into eligible households; but in Gary such an adult becomes eligible for full experimental status after a three-month waiting period. Whether or not new families are formed or old ones are expanded has critical implications for the cost and impact of a national program, and it is at least possible that the various experiments will come out quite differently on cost estimates because of differences in their operating rules.

Another significant difference in the family-unit rules of the various experiments concerns the payment to a spouse who leaves the household. In all the experiments, the annual guarantee is a composite figure constructed of payments attributable to each family member. See Table 5.4 for the figures pertaining to the New Jersey experiment. The New Jersey regulations provided that when a

Table 5.3 Comparison of Rules Defining the Family Unit in Four Income-Maintenance Experiments

	New Jersey	Seattle–Denver	Rural	Gary
1. Family members to be related for initial eligibility	No	No	No	No
2. Family or household as the basic unit	Household	Family	Family (may be several families)	Household
3. Initial family size: maximum	None, but no increase in payments if over eight persons	Seven	None	None
4. Initial family size: minimum	Two	Two	None	Two
5. Initial age limitation of head	18–58 years	18–58 years	18–58 years if married; otherwise, 21–58 years	No limitation
6. Initial requirement regarding sex of head	Male[a]	Male or female	Male or female	Male or female
7. Child required for initial eligibility	No	No	No	No, but there must be a dependent of whom the head is the parent or legal guardian
8. Age of majority; dependent, if leaving unit, retains portion of payment	18 years	18 years	18 years	21 years
9. Requirements for new spouse to qualify for eligibility in a newly formed unit	Cannot become eligible	One-month wait for spouse of any enrolled person over 18; otherwise, when enrolled person reaches 18	Immediately for spouse of any enrolled person over 18; otherwise, when enrolled person reaches 18	Immediate

10. Requirements for adding a new adult other than spouse in original or new unit	Cannot be added	Cannot be added	Cannot be added	Anyone over 18 not paying rent after residing with family for 3 months; relatives become eligible immediately
11. Requirements for adding a new child in any unit other than by birth	Persons under 18 after six-months residence, on formal adoption	Six months residence unless: 1. natural or legal child (immediate); 2. child of new spouse (when spouse becomes eligible)	Six months if under 18 or immediately if formal application for adoption has been made.	Immediately if a natural child or stepchild or a child for whom formal application for adoption has been made
12. Size of guarantee for leaving spouse	One-half guarantee for a two-spouse family	$1000 (1971 dollars)	One-half guarantee for family of two	Zero for the spouse who does not have custody of the dependent children
13. Size of guarantee for a leaving dependent 18 years or older	Marginal payment	$1000 (1971 dollars)	Marginal payment for persons 18–20; if 21 or older, receives same guarantee as does spouse (see #12)	None
14. Size of guarantee for a leaving dependent under 18	Marginal payment	None	None	None
15. Treatment of income from nonrelated individuals in household	Same as family member	Income counted if individual is eligible; if not, only explicit transfers to eligible family members are counted	Same as family member	Same as family member; must renounce AFDC benefits

NOTE: "Family" refers to those under one roof in direct husband–wife–child relationship. "Household" refers to all people in the living unit who pool income and expenses.

[a] Strictly speaking, the family head could be either male or female, as long as a male, able-bodied, non-aged potential wage earner was present. In fact this meant that the vast majority of New Jersey families were male-headed.

85

Table 5.4 **Payments Attributable to Each Household Member by Guarantee Level, New Jersey Experiment, 1968–1969**

Household Member	Guarantee Level			
	50%	75%	100%	125%
Spouse	$500	$750	$1000	$1250
Spouse	500	750	1000	1250
Dependent 1	375	562	750	937
Dependent 2	275	413	550	688
Dependent 3	200	300	400	500
Dependent 4	175	262	350	437
Dependent 5	150	225	300	375
Dependent 6	125	188	250	313
Dependent 7 and more	0	0	0	0

spouse left the original household, he or she was given an annual guarantee equal to his or her portion of the family guarantee, ranging from $500 to $1250 in 1968–1969, depending on the plan. The portion of the guarantee that the spouse took was deducted from the original unit's guarantee. Seattle–Denver gives a flat payment ($1000 in 1971, adjusted by the cost-of-living increase every year) to a spouse who leaves the unit, and Gary does not make a payment unless the spouse has custody of a child. There appears to have been a neutral to slightly positive incentive for spouses to stay in the unit in New Jersey and Seattle–Denver (Although there may have been a slight negative incentive for spouses in high-payment plans in New Jersey and low-payment plans in Seattle–Denver) and a substantial positive incentive to stay in the family in Gary.

A close examination of these tables (Tables 5.3 and 5.4) reveals a number of important differences in the incentive structure for family-composition changes that indicate how important regulations are both for analysis and for generalization to national policy. If recommendations are made for national policy, the extent to which the rules of operation of an experiment resemble the intended regulations of a national program will determine the extent to which research results will serve as accurate predictors of program results.

Comparisons of Definitions of Income

Table 5.5 compares the experiments in terms of the items countable as income for payments purposes. As the table indicates, there are significant enough differences in the regulations to have an impact on the behavioral responses of families. Some of the differences in the regulations can be accounted for by the different populations in the experiments. For example, the rural experiment was

Table 5.5 Comparison of Rules Regarding Income Inclusions in Four Income-Maintenance Programs

Items Included as Income for Payment Calculation	New Jersey	Seattle–Denver	Rural	Gary
1. All income defined in federal (positive) income tax	Yes	Yes, except for interest	Yes	Yes
2. Prizes and awards	Yes	Yes, but $100 disregard of each prize	Yes, but $100 disregard of each prize	Yes
3. Gifts	Yes, but first $100 of total of #3 + #6 + #11 + #16 is deductible	Yes, but $100 disregard per family per year	Yes, all gifts in excess of $200 per family member	Yes, but first $100 of total of #3 + #11 is deductible
4. Scholarships	Yes, in excess of tuition, books, and fees. Includes room and board, whether supplied in cash or in kind	Yes, in excess of tuition, books, and fees	Yes, in excess of tuition, books, and fees. Includes room and board, whether supplied in cash or in kind	No rule
5. Alimony and court-ordered payments	Yes	Yes, including payments in kind, but taxed at 50 percent, no matter what the experimental tax rate is	Yes, but first $100 received from a person living with the family excluded	Yes, whether periodic, lump sum, or installment
6. Support	Yes, but first $100 of total of #3 + #6 + #11 + #16 is deductible	Yes, but taxed at 50 percent, no matter what the experimental tax rate is	Yes	Yes, but first $100 of total of #3 + #6 + #11 is deductible
7. Pensions and annuties	Yes	Yes	Yes	Yes

(Continued)

Table 5.5 (continued)

Items Included as Income for Payment Calculation	New Jersey	Seattle–Denver	Rural	Gary
8. Other transfers	Unemployment, strike benefits, Social Security, V.A. benefits, training allowances taxed as regular earnings	V.A. pensions and disability and income continuation benefits that come from a fund to which family has voluntarily contributed counted as income. Unemployment, Social Security, training, other transfers taxed at 100 percent	Unemployment, strike benefits, V.A. benefits, training allowances, surplus commodities, food stamps	Unemployment, strike benefits, Social Security, V.A. disability benefits, training stipends
9. Dividends	Yes	No, treated under asset imputation (see #17)	Yes, including returns on capital. Does not include insurance dividends that serve only to reduce premiums	Yes, including payments that are wholly or in part a return on capital
10. Interest on government obligations	Yes	No, treated as an asset (see #17)	Yes	Yes
11. Inheritance	Yes, but first $100 of total of # 3 + #6 + #11 + #16 is deductible	Yes	Yes	Yes, but first $100 of total of # 3 + #6 + #11 is deductibe
12. Life insurance	Yes, less first $1000	Yes, less first $1000 Reimbursement for medical expenses not counted. Any settlement or "damages" counted as regular income	Yes, less first $1000	Yes, net of premiums
13. Insurance as compensation for a loss	Yes		Yes, but not value of medical care or payment for related medical care	Yes, all damages, insurance payments, workmen's compensation for physical or mental injury or sickness

88

14. Rent in public housing	Yes, market value of housing, in excess of actual rent paid	Not counted; but changes in rent due to changes in income all offset at 100 percent	Difference between market value and the actual rent paid	Ignored
15. Realized capital gains	100 percent	100 percent of short-run. Long-run gains excluded	100 percent	Short-run same as non-wage income. Long-run, excluded if proceeds entirely reinvested within 6 months of sale; otherwise gain taxed as income
16. Accumulated income in trusts	Yes, but first $100 of total of #3 + #6 + #11 + #16 is deductible	No, only counted when distributed	Not specified	Yes
17. Imputed value to capital assets	No, except for the rental value of owner-occupied housing	Imputation for stocks, savings accounts, owner-occupied housing, etc., based on current rate for 1-year savings certificates	10 percent of net "usable wealth," i.e., (1) equity in business property above $20,000 (if includes owner-occupied house above $30,000); (2) equity in home above $10,000; (3) cash in excess of $1000; (4) cash value of life insurance above $5000; (5) all other property except clothing, furniture, auto, and personal effects, less secured debts	No

(Continued)

Table 5.5 (continued)

Items Included as Income for Payment	New Jersey	Seattle–Denver	Rural	Gary
18. Rental income from properties	100 percent of net	If rental property is owner-occupied or if income is less than $150 per month gross, income treated as in #17 above. If rental property is not owner-occupied and grosses more than $150 per month, income treated as business income	100 percent of net	100 percent of net
19. Earnings of children	Counted in full	Counted in full	Counted in full for 16 years and older. Earnings of children under 16 not counted	Counted in full for 16 years and older. Earnings of children under 16 not counted
20. Small and infrequently received income.	Counted in full	Counted in full	Counted in full	Counted in full
21. Need-conditioned payments by a state, political subdivision, or private agency exempt from tax under IRS Code of 54-501 (2), (3), or (4) or federal agency (such as public assistance)	Receipt of any such payments a complete bar to receipt of payments above filing fee	Receipt of any such payments a complete bar to receipt of payments above filing fee	Receipt of any such payments a complete bar to receipt of payments above filing fee	If family on AFDC, payments made to family and reimbursed to the experiment by AFDC. All other kinds of welfare counted as taxable income
22. Foster-child care	No	No	Income received for care counted in full	Foster children not counted as members of unit, and assistance

90

Table 5.6 Comparison of Rules Regarding Deductions from Income in Four Income-Maintenance Programs

Items Deducted From Income for Tax Calculation	New Jersey	Seattle–Denver	Rural	Gary
1. Cost of earning	Yes, for business income; no deductions for nonbusiness, such as uniforms, transportation to work	Yes, except on capital items costing more than $200, which must be depreciated on a straight-line basis. But no exclusion for nonbusiness cost, such as uniforms, transportation to work	Yes, including property taxes and any asset valued at less than $200 or with a useful life of less than one year. All other items must be depreciated on a straight-line basis	Yes, for business income; no deductions for non-business costs, such as uniforms, transportation to work
2. Day care	Up to $80 per 4 weeks for one or $120 per 4 weeks for two or more children if it enables a family member to be gainfully employed. But limited to the replaced earner and for current earnings, that is, not to release parent for school or training	Reimbursement of actual cost to family if it releases the last able-bodied adult for employment. May not exceed gross earnings of lowest-paid worker. Maximum $5 per day per child. All single-parent families eligible for full reimbursement of child-care expenses up to the $5 per day per child maximum.	Up to $80 per 4 weeks for one or $120 per 4 weeks for two or more children. But limited to the income of the replaced earner per family	Not deductible

(Continued)

Table 5.6 *(continued)*

Items Deducted From Income for Tax Calculation	New Jersey	Seattle–Denver	Rural	Gary
3. Care of incapacitated	Treatment same as for day care, including re-quirement that it must release an earner, limited to $80 per 4 weeks for one or $120 per 4 weeks for two or more people in care	Same as day care.	Up to $80 per 4 weeks for one or $120 per 4 weeks for two or more. But limited to the income of the released earner per family	Care treated as medical expense (see #4 below)
4. Medical insurance	No	Yes, full amount in excess of $60 times the number of the family members per year	Full amount of premium on doctor and hospital insurance; amount in excess of $60 per person per accounting period	Yes, medical expenses over $30 per person per 6-month period. Medical insurance not deductible
5. Capital losses	Up to amount of capital gains	100 percent of short-run capital losses. Long-run losses not deducti-ble. (Note that long-run gains do not count as income.) Limited to total income, with a 12-month carry-forward	100 percent of realized capital losses	Losses in excess of gains deducted from gross income for 12 months

6. Costs of owner-occupied housing	Yes	No	Yes	No
7. Rental income from a roomer	$12 per week if meals are included	If the rent paid is less than $150 per month, ignored. If more than $150 per month, treated as business income	Not covered by rules	Not covered by rules
8. Alimony paid out	Yes	50 percent of the payments reimbursed	Yes, up to $150 per person, unless a higher amount is court-ordered	Yes
9. Support for persons living outside	Yes, $30 per person supported per month if court-ordered, and when payment equals or exceeds $30 per person per month	50 percent of the payments are reimbursed	Yes, up to $150 per person, unless a higher amount court-ordered	Yes, actual costs for alimony, child support, and court-ordered payments. Children away at school treated for tax calculations as members of household
10. Federal and state taxes paid	No	No	Total times reciprocal of tax rate of family's assigned plan	No

93

concerned with income from self-employed individuals, particularly farmers. This required substantially different rules on self-employment from those in the New Jersey experiment, mainly in terms of greater detail. Note, for example, the special arrangement in the rural experiment's rules for treating the value of capital assets.

A marked difference among experiments is in the taxing of income (see Table 5.6). The New Jersey, Gary, and rural experiments tax income at a constant rate. The Seattle–Denver experiment uses different tax rates for different income items. For example, alimony and court-ordered support payments are taxed at 50 percent, and other items such as Unemployment Insurance, Social Security payments, and short-term capital gains are taxed at 100 percent, that is, totally taken away. The fact that Seattle–Denver taxes certain types of income at 100 percent can be expected to introduce greater incentives to underreport those items than in the other experiments.

Finally, the treatment of certain other items of income—reimbursement for medical expenses incurred, the value of public housing in excess of the market value, the value of owner-occupied housing, income from trusts—differ across the experiments, with a correspondingly different impact on families, both with regard to the collection of these items and with regard to earnings behavior.

In a short-term experiment, such rules may also induce families to defer until after the experiment the collection of payments due to them, if these are taxable by the experiment. (In New Jersey, it was discovered that one family had a large insurance settlement for an industrial accident deferred until a week after the last payment.) As the table indicates, Seattle–Denver has a tax rate associated with deductions that differs from that of the other experiments and which could stimulate differential behavior patterns as compared to them. Note the comparative treatment of day-care expenses, alimony payments, and support for persons living outside the home.

In the New Jersey experiment, few serious problems arose with respect to definition of income, except for the problem of welfare benefits. Careful work on all the other major issues at the beginning of the experiment meant that only minor modifications were required as the experiment progressed.

In summary, the regulations were a critical part of the experiment. Families strained the family-unit rules in many ways, with new units formed and re-formed and units reunited in different forms. Having to allow for all the family composition changes that occurred helped us to reformulate the rules of operation into a more effective and comprehensive tool. It has become clear that the regulations themselves constitute an important part of the experimental environment, a part that may well interact with the tax rate and guarantee treatments, producing differences in subject response that are caused by experimentally induced stimuli other than the primary treatments.

6 The sample assignment

The purpose of this chapter is to provide a nontechnical description of the process by which families were assigned to the experimental plans in the New Jersey experiment. As mentioned in Chapter 1, the experimental families were stratified into three groups according to income level (or stratum). Stratum I (low) contained those families with incomes below the poverty level, Stratum II (medium) included those families with incomes between 100 and 124 percent of the poverty level, and Stratum III (high) included those with incomes between 125 and 150 percent of the poverty level. The eight experimental plans, the control group, and the three income strata produced 27 experimental cells. The sample-assignment problem was to distribute eligible families among the 27 cells in such a way that maximum information could be obtained subject to the constraint placed on the experiment by the Office of Economic Opportunity (OEO) that no more than $1.2 million should be paid out annually in transfers.

One way of allocating families would have been simply to put the same number of families in each cell. Assuming that families would exhibit equal variance in earnings behavior regardless of cell, this would permit independent estimates for each cell. The costs to the experiment, however, are very different for the various cells.

ELEMENTS IN THE ASSIGNMENT PROBLEM

The cost for each cell is computed by adding two factors: (1) the fixed cost of finding and then maintaining a family in the experiment (roughly equal for all cells, although families receiving lower payments are slightly harder to maintain in the sample) and (2) the transfer costs for each family in each cell. By definition, control-group families have a zero cost in terms of transfers. Also by definition, the higher the income stratum of a family, the lower their transfer payments for any given negative-income-tax plan, and the more likely they are to be above the breakeven point of that plan and therefore receiving no payments. Table 6.1 indicates the breakeven income levels of the various experimental plans in terms of percentage of the poverty level, to facilitate comparison between them and the minimum-income levels for the three income strata of the experiment. As is readily apparent, the 50–50 and 75–70 plans have such low breakeven levels that virtually no family assigned to either plan whose income placed them in either Stratum II or Stratum III would be in a position to receive positive payments unless their income dropped during the program.[1] Assuming no work disincentive, families in these two strata on these two plans could therefore be maintained at zero cost each. At the other extreme, a Stratum I family assigned to the 125–50 plan would cost an average of $3300 a year in transfer payments. An average family of four in Stratum III (assuming an income of $4538) in the 125–50 plan would cost $1856 annually—much less than a Stratum I family in that plan, but a great deal more than a Stratum III family on, say, the 75–70 plan. Thus, for every Stratum I family assigned to the 125–50 plan, the experiment could assign thirty-three Stratum III families to the 50–50 and 75–50 plans. If the information to be gathered from each of these families is the same, then it would be clearly inefficient and wasteful to allocate the same number of families to the costly cells as to the low-cost cells. Thus, cost per observation was an important assignment issue.

The following additional considerations were also important:

Policy weight. Each plan was assigned a weight based on an estimate of how important it was in terms of national policy. Thus, the 75–50 plan was assigned a high policy weight, as was the 100–50 plan. Plans at the extremes received low policy weights. See Table 6.2.

The "M" point. The "M" point was the point at which a family's income, relative to the plan to which it was assigned, was so high that the plan could be expected to have no effect on the labor-force behavior of the family. For example, a family assigned to the B plan with an annual income of $10,000

---

[1] As can be seen from Table 6.3, the final experimental design called for 108 families to be so assigned.

Table 6.1 Breakeven Levels in Comparison to Income
Eligibility Levels of Experimental Cells

Plan (guarantee–tax rate)	Breakeven Income Level (percentage of poverty line)
A. 50–30	167
B. 50–50[a]	100
C. 75–30	250
D. 75–50	150
E. 75–70[a]	107
F. 100–50	200
G. 100–70	143
H. 125–50	250

	Income Eligibility Levels
Income Stratum I (low)	0 percent of poverty line
Income Stratum II (medium)	100 percent of poverty line
Income Stratum III (high)	125 percent of poverty line

[a]Plans on which virtually no one family in Stratum II and no one family in Stratum III could receive positive payments.

might not respond to the existence of the plan. The M point, according to principal investigator Harold Watts, professor of economics at the University of Wisconsin,

... should be at least as high as the breakeven point, since families below the breakeven point are directly affected by both a net transfer and a change in the substitution rate between leisure and income. Reasoning from the conventional indifference curve representation of the income/leisure choice problem, one would expect deflection even for those currently at equilibrium above the breakeven point. For a given breakeven point, indeed, one would expect the range of possible responses to be greater the greater the marginal tax rate.[2]

The M point was thus set above the breakeven point, by an amount that increased with the tax rate. The assignment would thus be ineffective for those families allocated to plans where they were above their M point.

Attrition rate. It was assumed that attrition would be a function of the generosity of the plan, with families receiving high payments having a greater incentive to remain in the experiment than those receiving low payments. Therefore, an attrition-rate expectation was associated with each cell, including the control group, where attrition was expected to be as high as 50 percent.

[2] Watts, Internal Memorandum, November 1968, Data Center Archives, Institute for Research on Poverty, University of Wisconsin-Madison.

Table 6.2 Policy Weights Attached to the
Experimental Plans

Guarantee	Tax Rate (percent)			
(percentage of poverty line)	0	30	50	70
125			5	
100			10	3
75		6	10	3
50		3	4	
0	0			

To allow for attrition, the lower the expected payment in a cell the more families (below their M points) were assigned to that cell.

Variance. In the absence of empirical evidence with respect to the probable differences in variance among plans—or even between the control and treatment groups—assumptions had to be made with regard to the variance in response to different plans. It was assumed that variance in earnings behavior would be lower in the treatment cells than in the control cells. As James Tobin eventually argued:

> A priori, should treatment households be expected to show wider variance than control households? It is not clear. On the affirmative side is the fact that treatment households receive on the average a larger income gain than control households, and variety in indifference curve means variety of response to this income gain. Both kinds of households respond, in a variety of ways, to a variety of changes in wage rates. These responses are superimposed on the response to the income effect. But for the same happenings in the labor market the effective wage change is smaller for treatment than for control observations. . . . This is a reason for variance to be smaller in treatment cells, not larger.[3]

The expectation of larger variance in the control group meant that relatively more families should be allocated to the control group, in order to get equally precise behavioral response estimates.

Continuity assumption. One of the most important assumptions was that the experimental data could be used to estimate a response function that would be continuous across cells. This did not mean that it had to be linear. On the contrary, as Watts pointed out:

> It should be explicitly noted that the variables tax rate (r), guarantee level (G), and normal earnings (E) can be squared, cubed, logged (or what have you); but

[3] Tobin, Internal Memorandum, June 1969, Data Center Archives.

however they are transformed or combined, each such term should appear as the coefficient of one of the parameters to be estimated.[4]

The theory that the labor-supply function was continuous across cells meant, essentially, that it was analytically unnecessary to have equal numbers of observations in each cell. Indeed, it was theoretically defensible to leave some of the cells completely empty, since response in those cells could be estimated by responses in other cells. Thus, the continuity assumption alone was enough to produce a quite uneven allocation of families to the various cells.

THE ASSIGNMENT MODEL DISAGREEMENT

Taking all these considerations into account, the University of Wisconsin economists produced an assignment model that was presented to members of the research staff of both Mathematica and Wisconsin at a meeting in Princeton in December of 1968. It assumed differential costs among cells, differential policy weights among cells, an M point above which response would cease (and observations would have no value), differential attrition rates among cells, differential amounts of variance among cells, and a continuous-response surface across cells.[5] Relating the variables and the constraints, the model then provided, as Watts said,

> optimal allocations of experimental households relative to an explicit experimental objective and subject to overall budget constraints, as well as a variety of further constraints. It allowed for explicit introduction of regularity restrictions and for a differential weighting of interest among possible inferences obtainable from the experiment.[6]

The Mathematica group was upset at the unevenness of the allocations, particularly the fact that so many families were allocated to low-payment plans. In response to the Wisconsin model, they proposed an analysis of variance (ANOVA) approach, which would have gone some distance toward balancing the allocation, although it, too, would not have been even across cells. Several arguments were made for a more even allocation, as follows.

1. If the Wisconsin group proved to be wrong about the assumption regarding the form and continuity of the response function, it would be impossible to estimate anything from the experiment, having thrown away the possibility of

---

[4] Watts, Internal Memorandum, November 1968, Data Center Archives.

[5] John Conlisk and Harold W. Watts, "A Model for Optimizing Experimental Designs for Estimating Response Surfaces," *Proceedings of the American Statistical Association* (1969): 150–156.

[6] Watts, Internal Memorandum, 1968, Data Center Archives.

reverting to ANOVA. This risk was regarded by Mathematica as worse than the risk of overspending (or undersampling) if Wisconsin proved to be correct.

2. Mathematica was unwilling to risk excessive attrition by low-paid families, fearing it would jeopardize the opportunity to study the feasibility of running a self-administrable transfer program.

3. The sociologists on the project were concerned that even if the economists could estimate labor-supply functions with uneven allocations, the sociological analysis would suffer if only a relatively small number of people got substantial payments. For example, it would be difficult to estimate the effects of high payments on changes in family composition, organizational participation, health status, and attitudes. They were less concerned with guarantee levels and tax rates as such and more concerned with making a substantial financial impact on poor families.

4. The Mathematica group suspected that the Wisconsin model would be too difficult to explain to the public on completion of the experiment. As one of the principal investigators, William Baumol, and Heather Ross, a staff economist of Mathematica, put it:

> Public understanding and acceptance of the outcome is critical to the success of the program. Asking the public to make a judgment on the basis of an intricate design model is risky in any circumstance. In the present case, where there is no professional agreement on the optimal design, and where the proposed models yield highly unbalanced outcomes (40 percent of our experimental families are presently above their breakeven lines) it is much more than risky.[7]

5. Finally, the field staff at Mathematica was concerned that low payment levels, particularly in the highly volatile political climate in Paterson and Passaic, would cause community groups to turn against the experiment. The field people had barely held off militant groups in both cities by explaining to them that the experiment would bring financial assistance to the community, and they were afraid that the new allocation would lend credence to the accusation of community exploitation.

There ensued a period of intense debaté between Wisconsin and Mathematica over the design model. The Wisconsin group took the position that the model was only as good as the assumptions behind it and that the Mathematica group was free to suggest different assumptions that Wisconsin would run through the model. During this period, the Mathematica group suggested changes in those assumptions that were thought to have the greatest bearing on the uneven allocation, namely, those relating to continuity, functional form, and the M point. Mathematica did not contest the assumption of continuity but did stress the high risk of not being able to perform adequate analysis if continuity did not hold. While some suggestions for changes in functional form were briefly

[7] Ross and Baumol, Internal Memorandum, April 1969, Data Center Archives.

pursued, realistic ones did not, in fact, have a great impact on outcomes, and the argument on these specifications was eventually dropped.

The matter was finally taken to OEO for settlement. The OEO people recognized that the level of complexity of the argument was such that an outside expert should be consulted; by mutual consent, Mathematica and the University of Wisconsin (with OEO's agreement) selected James Tobin, professor of economics at Yale University, to arbitrate the dispute.

Both groups supplied Tobin with memoranda, Wisconsin adhering to the original model with modifications introduced earlier and Mathematica submitting a compromise plan. The Mathematica plan suggested that the cells be divided into *regions* in terms of the generosity of plans:

1. The control region
2. The zero-payment region
3. The low-payment region
4. The moderate-payment region
5. The high-payment region

Each of these regions would be composed of a number of cells, without regard to precise guarantee levels and tax rates but with regard to the absolute level of payments that would be made to families in those cells. The authors wrote:

> By specifying minimum sample size in terms of broader regions, rather than individual cells, considerably greater latitude is left for the allocation design. Within each income stratum, these regions define themselves naturally in terms of combinations of cells that differ from those in other income strata. Thus . . . [see Figure 6.1] we see that for the low income group the .75G/.5r tax plan falls into the moderate payment region, while for other income groups it constitutes part of the low income areas.[8]

They went on to argue that, for the purposes of sociological and administrative analysis, it would be important that at the end of the experiment each stratum have a certain minimum number of families (arbitrarily set at 50 in the memorandum) in each of the key regions. Assuming some attrition, they then proposed that 65 families, as a minimum, be allocated to most of the key regions, 50 to the high-payment region in the lower stratum (assuming no attrition), and 100 to each of the control regions. They concluded:

> The cost to the Watts model of this proposal is how much the "region" constraints affect the value of the objective function. By allowing the model considerable flexibility across cells (as opposed to regions) the percentage increase in the value of the objective function should be quite small if not negligible. . . . In short, the loss in efficiency for the model should be considerably smaller than the gain in information content for the sociological and administrative analysis.[9]

[8] Mathematica to Tobin, Internal Memorandum, May 1969, Data Center Archives.
[9] Ibid.

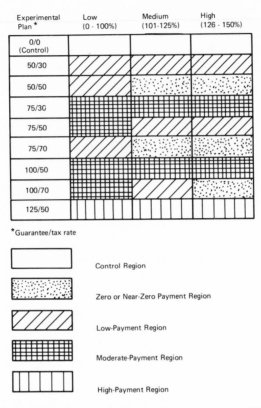

Figure 6.1 Level of payment for low-income, medium-income, and high-income groups, by guarantee–tax plan.

In June 1969, the Mathematica and Wisconsin staffs received the Tobin recommendation. Tobin's recommended allocation of families was based on computations made under the following assumptions:

1. Average cost in each cell takes account of the flat payments recommended [$100 per year for control households, $260 per year for treatment households] and the original Wisconsin assumptions about attrition are revised to assume [an] 80 percent retention of observations not receiving NIT [negative income tax] payments.
2. The cost of induced response is computed on the assumption . . . that a fraction $1/2\,r$ makes a zero income-response, while a fraction $1-1/2\,r$ makes a zero work response.
3. The conditional variance of response . . . is twice as large in certain cells as in others. . . . The effect of assuming differential variance is, generally, to place more observations in the more variable cells. . . .
4. Watts' basic specification [that experimental effects decline as income approaches "M"] is assumed. The constant term in the relationship [is] assumed

to differ from city to city, in accordance with the argument . . . that exogenous nonexperimental effects on earnings are city-specific. . . . [However, it is assumed that differences in] responses to different treatments are *not* city-specific. Thus earnings differentials from the appropriate city-specific base can be pooled across cities to measure the effects of variation in G and r.

5. The usual realistic constraints on available sample sizes by income strata were assumed, including the limits on new control observations in old cities. The actual cell assignments in old cities were, of course, taken as irreversible.

6. The usual total budgetary constraints were assumed, both on total outlay and on the fraction (1/3) to be spent on the 1.25/.5 [125–50] program. However, the total budget was reduced 5 percent to allow for an anticipated annual cost-of-living escalation in guarantee levels.

7. An improved version of the Watts–Conlisk "h function," which I regard as a rough way of allowing for the fact that the probability of no response rises as average income rises relative to the breakeven, was used.

8. The agreed standard policy-interest weights, population frequencies, etc., needed to translate variances of observed behavior into weighted variances of aggregate costs of various programs were used.[10]

In addition, Tobin made a number of minor changes in the cell sizes that resulted from these calculations, as follows:

1. I paid some attention to an analysis of variance model calculation of the proper *de novo* allocations of the 650 observations available in the new cities. In particular, I wanted to be sure that there were enough observations of programs of high policy-interest value so that estimates of their responses and costs would not depend too exclusively on interpolation. The operational effect of this consideration was to shift observations into the 1.00/.5 plan [100–50]. For the rest, I observed that the initial allocations in old cities have insured a fairly complete coverage of plans and strata. . . .

2. I wished to provide a sufficient spread of observations to meet the informational requirements of studies other than the central estimate of work response and associated costs, i.e., sociological variables and administrative experience. This led, in particular, to a large allocation of high-payment observations in [the low income stratum] –9 more than the basic calculation suggested. On the administrative side, it appears important to gain experience with the problems of arranging and regulating the making of substantial payments to poor people. . . .

3. I arbitrarily determined that no cell in the new cities should have a size between 0 and 5.[11]

Other provisions of the Tobin plan were (1) control-group members should be paid $100 per year to counter attrition; (2) treatment families should receive a $10 biweekly filing fee in addition to any transfer payments they received; and (3) 150 new control-group families should be added in Trenton, Paterson, and Passaic, in each city distributed 45, 45, and 60 among the three income strata.

[10] Tobin, Internal Memorandum, June 1969, Data Center Archives.
[11] Ibid.

The Tobin proposal was accepted in full, and families were enrolled in the plans to fill out the allocation model as specified (Table 6.3).

Table 6.3 **Tobin Allocation Model**

	Income Stratum			
	Low	Medium	High	Total
Experimental plan (guarantee– tax rate)				
A. 50–30	5	31	12	48
B. 50–50	29	37	5	71
C. 75–30	30(5)	14	50(5)	94(10)
D. 75–50	5	57(10)	36(10)	98(20)
E. 75–70	13(5)	51(15)	0	64(20)
F. 100–50	22	34(5)	20	76(5)
G. 100–70	11	26	33(10)	70(10)
H. 125–50	50	8	80	138
Total	*165(10)*	*258(30)*	*236(25)*	*659(65)*
Control	*238*	*165*	*247*	*650*
Total sample	*403(10)*	*423(30)*	*483(25)*	*1309(65)[a]*

NOTE: Additional "lagged" accounting group families given in parentheses.

[a]This differs from the 1357 total of families actually enrolled, because of a sampling shortfull.

7   Sample maintenance and attrition

The dropping out of families from the experiment (attrition) was a continuing problem. Although we had built allowances into the sample design to accommodate some attrition, an excessive and nonrandom loss of families could have constituted a serious threat to the validity of the results. When it became apparent early in the experiment that attrition was growing rapidly, extensive efforts were made to develop profiles of the families who were dropping out, to analyze the reasons why families were leaving the program, and to devise means for retaining such families.

The primary focus of this discussion will be the extent of and reasons for attrition of entire family units. Although the loss of data on individuals within the household was of importance, the more important consideration was the loss of data on whole family units.

As Tables 7.1 and 7.2 show, 273 whole family units were lost over the course of the three years—an attrition rate of 20 percent. As could be expected, the attrition rate for control families was higher, 25.3 percent, than that for experimental families, 15.6 percent. The highest rate of attrition was in Paterson and Passaic, where approximately 30 percent of the families were lost, the lowest rate was in Scranton where only 1.8 percent of the experimental and 7.8 percent of the control families were lost.

Table 7.1 Cumulative Attrition of Entire Family Units, by Quarterly Period, in Numbers

Group	Cell Count	Quarterly Period											
		1	2	3	4	5	6	7	8	9	10	11	12
Trenton													
Treatment	87	4	5	10	7	11	15	13	15	15	16	18	19
Control	39	10	10	10	10	12	11	13	13	13	14	14	13
Total	*126*	*14*	*15*	*20*	*17*	*23*	*26*	*26*	*28*	*28*	*30*	*32*	*32*
Paterson													
Treatment	163	7	13	22	23	28	27	33	38	36	39	42	45
Control	68	3	12	18	14	14	11	14	16	16	19	23	24
Total	*231*	*10*	*25*	*40*	*37*	*42*	*38*	*47*	*54*	*52*	*58*	*65*	*69*
Passaic													
Treatment	113	1	5	12	17	19	23	24	24	25	22	27	28
Control	58	1	6	9	9	10	13	11	14	13	15	15	17
Total	*151*	*2*	*11*	*21*	*26*	*29*	*36*	*35*	*38*	*38*	*37*	*42*	*45*
Jersey City													
Treatment	198	5	8	7	9	16	14	13	13	16	16	18	18
Control	192	20	21	16	21	29	31	40	43	46	52	52	54
Total	*390*	*25*	*29*	*23*	*30*	*45*	*45*	*53*	*56*	*62*	*68*	*70*	*72*
Scranton													
Treatment	164	1	2	1	1	2	4	4	4	3	3	3	3
Control	154	5	4	5	6	6	9	10	11	12	12	12	12
Total	*318*	*6*	*6*	*6*	*7*	*8*	*13*	*14*	*15*	*15*	*15*	*15*	*15*
All cities													
Treatment	725	18	33	52	57	76	83	87	94	95	96	108	113
Original controls	491	39	53	58	60	71	75	88	97	100	112	116	120
Total	*1216*	*57*	*86*	*110*	*117*	*147*	*158*	*175*	*191*	*195*	*208*	*224*	*233*
New controls													
Trenton	33	–	–	–	–	2	3	2	3	3	3	6	5
Paterson	64	–	–	3	6	4	5	11	13	15	17	15	21
Pasaic	44	–	–	1	2	3	7	7	9	10	11	12	14
Total	*141*	*–*	*–*	*4*	*8*	*9*	*15*	*20*	*25*	*28*	*31*	*33*	*40*
All controls	*632*	*39*	*53*	*62*	*68*	*80*	*90*	*108*	*122*	*128*	*143*	*149*	*160*
Total sample	*1357*	*57*	*86*	*114*	*125*	*156*	*173*	*195*	*216*	*223*	*239*	*257*	*273*

Table 7.3 shows attrition by guarantee level. Under the most generous guarantee (125 percent of the poverty line), only 6.5 percent of the families attrited, but under the lowest guarantee (50 percent of the poverty line), 22.1 percent attrited. The 75 percent guarantee and the 100 percent guarantee showed almost no difference in attrition rates, which were 16.6 percent and 16.5 percent, respectively.

The rate of attrition also appeared to be related to the tax rate. As seen in Table 7.4, attrition rose as the tax increased, both for the total sample and for most of the individual cities; the higher the tax rate, the higher the rate of

Table 7.2 Cumulative Attrition of Entire Family Units, by Quarterly Period, in Percentages

Group	Cell Count	Quarterly Periods											
		1	2	3	4	5	6	7	8	9	10	11	12
Trenton													
Treatment	87	4.6	5.7	11.5	8.0	12.6	17.2	14.9	17.2	17.2	18.4	20.7	21.8
Control	39	25.6	25.6	25.6	25.6	30.8	28.2	33.3	33.3	33.3	35.9	35.9	33.3
Total	*126*	11.1	11.9	15.9	13.5	18.3	20.6	20.6	22.2	22.2	23.8	25.4	25.4
Paterson													
Treatment	163	4.3	8.0	13.5	14.1	17.2	16.6	20.2	23.3	22.1	23.9	25.8	27.6
Control	68	4.4	17.6	26.5	20.6	20.6	16.2	20.6	23.5	23.5	27.9	33.8	35.3
Total	*231*	4.3	10.8	17.3	16.0	18.2	16.5	20.3	23.4	22.5	25.1	28.1	29.9
Passaic													
Treatment	113	.9	4.4	10.6	15.0	16.8	20.4	21.2	21.2	22.1	19.5	23.9	24.8
Control	38	2.6	15.8	23.7	23.7	26.3	34.2	28.9	36.8	34.2	39.5	39.5	44.7
Total	*151*	1.3	7.3	13.9	17.2	19.2	23.8	23.2	25.2	25.2	24.5	27.8	29.8
Jersey City													
Treatment	198	2.5	4.0	3.5	4.5	8.1	7.1	6.6	6.6	8.1	8.1	9.1	9.1
Control	192	10.4	10.9	8.3	10.9	15.1	16.1	20.8	22.4	24.0	27.1	27.1	28.1
Total	*390*	6.4	7.4	5.9	7.7	11.5	11.5	13.6	14.4	15.9	17.4	17.9	18.5
Scranton													
Treatment	164	.6	1.2	.6	.6	1.2	2.4	2.4	2.4	1.8	1.8	1.8	1.8
Control	154	3.2	2.6	3.2	3.9	3.9	5.8	6.5	7.1	7.8	7.8	7.8	7.8
Total	*318*	1.9	1.9	1.9	2.2	2.5	4.1	4.4	4.7	4.7	4.7	4.7	4.7
All cities													
Treatment	725	2.5	4.6	7.2	7.9	10.5	11.4	12.0	13.0	13.1	13.2	14.9	15.6
Original controls	491	7.9	10.8	11.8	12.2	14.5	15.3	17.9	19.8	20.4	22.8	23.6	24.4
Total	*1216*	4.7	7.1	9.0	9.6	12.1	13.0	14.4	15.7	16.0	17.1	18.4	19.2

(*Continued*)

Table 7.2 (continued)

	Cell Count	Quarterly Periods											
		1	2	3	4	5	6	7	8	9	10	11	12
New controls													
Trenton	33	–	–	–	–	6.1	9.1	6.1	9.1	9.1	9.1	18.2	15.2
Paterson	64	–	–	4.7	9.4	6.3	7.8	17.2	20.3	23.4	26.6	23.4	32.8
Passaic	44	–	–	2.3	4.5	6.8	15.9	15.9	20.5	22.7	25.0	27.3	31.8
Total	141	–	–	3.7[a]	7.4[a]	6.4	10.6	14.2	17.7	19.9	22.0	23.4	28.4
All controls	632	7.9[b]	10.8[b]	10.4[c]	11.4[c]	12.7	14.2	17.1	19.3	20.3	22.6	23.6	25.3
Total sample	1357	4.7[d]	7.1[d]	6.5[e]	9.4[e]	11.5	12.7	14.4	15.9	16.4	17.6	18.9	20.1

NOTE: Calculated on a base reflecting entry of new controls into sample, i.e., Paterson and Passaic at third quarterly, Trenton at fifth quarterly.

[a]Base = 108 (Paterson and Passaic new control families only).

[b]Base = 491 (original control families only).

[c]Base = 599 (original controls plus Paterson and Passaic new controls).

[d]Base = 1216 (original sample only).

[e]Base = 1324 (treatment families plus Paterson and Passaic new controls).

108

Table 7.3 Attrition of Entire Family Units, by Guarantee Level

			Guarantee			
	Control	50%	75%	100%	125%	Total
Trenton						
Number in group	72	27	35	25	NA	159
Number attrited	18 (25%)	6 (22%)	8 (23%)	5 (20%)	NA	37 (23%)
Paterson						
Number in group	132	31	67	45	20	295
Number attrited	45 (34%)	13 (42%)	18 (27%)	11 (24%)	3 (15%)	90 (30%)
Passaic						
Number in group	82	17	53	32	11	195
Number attrited	31 (38%)	4 (24%)	14 (26%)	8 (25%)	2 (18%)	59 (30%)
Jersey City						
Number in group	192	26	81	32	59	390
Number attrited	54 (28%)	4 (15%)	9 (11%)	2 (6%)	2 (3%)	72 (19%)
Scranton						
Number in group	154	21	66	29	48	318
Number in attrited	12 (8%)	0 (0%)	1 (2%)	0 (0%)	2 (4%)	15 (5%)
All cities						
Number in group	632	122	302	158	138	1357
Number attrited	160 (25%)	27 (22%)	50 (17%)	26 (17%)	9 (7%)	273 (20%)

NOTE: NA = not applicable.

attrition. For the same guarantee, in all but two cases, a 50 percent tax rate shows a higher rate of attrition than does a 30 percent tax rate, and a 70 percent tax rate shows a higher rate of attrition than does a 50 percent tax rate.

The effect of the generosity of the payment on attrition is also reflected in a comparison between the average last payment received by those families who dropped out before the end of the experiment and the average final payment received by those who remained in the experiment for the full three years (78 payments). This is shown, by site, in Table 7.5.

Several types of attrition can be distinguished (see Table 7.6). A large group of families (4.7 percent), for instance, moved to Puerto Rico, thereby becoming ineligible. An even larger group of families moved and could not be located; seventy-six families (5.6 percent of the sample) fell into this category.

The largest group of attriters, however, was composed of those families who simply refused to continue; there were 123 families in this category. Most of the reasons given for dropping out closely paralleled the reasons given by families who decided not to enroll in the first place, that is, (1) preference for or fear of repercussions from welfare or other public agency, (2) dislike of infringement on privacy, (3) dislike of the filing procedure or payments calculations, (4) distrust

Table 7.4 Attrition of Entire Family Units, by Tax Rate within Guarantee Level

| | Guarantee–Tax Rate | | | | | | | | | | |
| | G = 50% | | G = 75% | | | G = 100% | | G = 125% | Treatment Groups | Control Group | Total Sample |
	r=30%	r=50%	r=30%	r=50%	r=70%	r=50%	r=70%	r70%			
Trenton											
Number in group	13	14	13	13	9	14	11	NA	87	72	159
Number attrited	1 (8%)	5 (36%)	2 (15%)	3 (23%)	3 (33%)	1 (7%)	4 (36%)	NA	19 (22%)	18 (25%)	37 (23%)
Paterson											
Number in group	6	25	21	26	20	21	24	20	163	132	195
Number attrited	2 (33%)	11 (44%)	3 (14%)	6 (23%)	9 (45%)	5 (24%)	6 (25%)	3 (15%)	45 (28%)	45 (34%)	90 (31%)
Passaic											
Number in group	4	13	14	28	11	12	20	11	113	82	195
Number attrited	1 (25%)	3 (23%)	2 (14%)	7 (25%)	5 (45%)	4 (33%)	4 (20%)	2 (18%)	28 (25%)	31 (38%)	59 (30%)
Jersey City											
Number in group	14	12	30	27	24	17	15	59	198	192	390
Number attrited	3 (21%)	1 (8%)	2 (7%)	3 (11%)	4 (17%)	2 (12%)	1 (7%)	2 (3%)	18 (9%)	54 (28%)	72 (19%)
Scranton											
Number in group	9	12	22	23	21	13	16	48	164	154	318
Number attrited	0 (0%)	0 (0%)	0 (0%)	0 (0%)	1 (5%)	0 (0%)	0 (0%)	2 (4%)	3 (2%)	12 (8%)	15 (5%)
All cities											
Number in group	46	76	100	117	85	72	86	138	725	632	1357
Number attrited	7 (15%)	20 (26%)	9 (9%)	19 (16%)	22 (23%)	12 (17%)	15 (17%)	9 (7%)	113 (16%)	160 (25%)	273 (20%)

NOTE: G = guarantee; r = tax rate; NA = not applicable.

Table 7.5 Average Final Biweekly Payment for Active and
Attrited Units

	Active Families		Attrited Families	
	Amount of last (78th) payment	N^a	Amount of last payment	N^a
Trenton	$20.54	74	$14.15	19
Paterson	31.77	117	4.02	45
Passaic	23.00	81	14.88	36
Jersey City	51.46	171	23.76	25
Scranton	35.35	167	21.00	3
All cities	42.75	*610*	12.89	*128*

[a]Figures includes split units; do not correspond to entire-unit figures.

of the experiment, and (5) various personal reasons. Interestingly, the reason
most frequently cited for not signing in the first place, the "work ethic" (dislike
of receiving income they had not earned), was not the most commonly given
reason for wanting to drop out. Examples of the reasons given by families for
dropping from the program are given below (as reported by the field offices):

Fear of loss of welfare payments (or other public benefits):

> Family fears welfare. Filing [income report forms] isn't too much trouble but the
> family needs money from welfare and fears other payments will upset welfare.

> Decided to quit because they were on welfare and didn't want any trouble from
> welfare.

> Mr. _____ complains that welfare is dropping their payments by $22.66 now that
> they know he is getting $20.00 every four weeks from us in filing fees. He doesn't
> have to save stubs and file forms for welfare, and it was just so much trouble that
> he wanted to get off.

> The family's mother is on welfare, and no matter what we tell them, they are
> afraid it will affect their welfare payments. They were not impressed with the new
> filing fee [from $2.50 to $10.00 every two weeks]. According to Mrs. _____ any
> money that we give her will be deducted from her welfare payment.

> On November 13 Mr. _____ called Princeton office to notify us that he did not
> want to receive any more checks from us if he had to report them to the Public
> Housing Authority. He said that it he reports a $5.00 raise they increase his rent
> $3.00 above what it is, so he would rather not have a check from us if his rent is
> going to be raised.

Felt program was an infringement on privacy:

> Not married, don't want to be bothered by interviewers. . . . Invasion of privacy.
> Mr. _____ doesn't want people to know he is living there.

Table 7.6 Number of Attritions, by Category

	Original Cell Count	Refused to Continue		Could Not Be Located		Moved to Puerto Rico		Other		Total	
		Number	Percent	Number	Percent	Number	Percent	Number	Percent	Number	Percent
Trenton											
Treatment	87	9	10.3	4	4.6	4	4.6	2	2.3	19	21.8
Control	72	8	11.1	9	12.5	1	1.3	0	0	18	25.0
Total	*159*	*17*	*10.7*	*13*	*8.2*	*5*	*3.1*	*2*	*1.3*	*37*	*23.3*
Paterson											
Treatment	163	25	15.3	13	8.0	7	4.3	0	0	45	27.6
Control	132	22	16.7	11	8.3	11	8.3	1	.8	45	34.1
Total	*295*	*47*	*15.9*	*24*	*8.1*	*18*	*6.1*	*1*	*.3*	*90*	*30.5*
Passaic											
Treatment	113	14	12.4	5	4.4	9	8.0	0	0	28	24.8
Control	82	10	12.2	9	11.0	11	13.4	1	1.2	31	37.8
Total	*195*	*24*	*12.3*	*14*	*7.2*	*20*	*10.3*	*1*	*.5*	*59*	*30.3*
Jersey City											
Treatment	198	9	4.5	5	2.5	3	1.5	1	.5	18	9.1
Control	192	15	7.8	19	9.9	18	9.4	2	1.0	54	28.1
Total	*390*	*24*	*6.2*	*24*	*6.2*	*21*	*5.4*	*3*	*.8*	*72*	*18.5*
Scranton											
Treatment	164	2	1.2	0	0	0	0	1	.6	3	1.8
Control	154	9	5.8	1	.6	0	0	2	1.3	12	7.8
Total	*318*	*11*	*3.5*	*1*	*.3*	*0*	*0*	*3*	*.9*	*15*	*4.7*
All cities											
Treatment	725	59	8.1	27	3.7	23	3.2	4	.6	113	15.6
Control	632	64	10.1	49	7.8	41	6.5	6	.9	160	25.3
Total	*1357*	*123*	*9.1*	*76*	*5.6*	*64*	*4.7*	*10*	*.7*	*273*	*20.1*

> Felt program was an invasion of privacy. . . . "If you want to help me, that's fine, but I don't want to give you any more information than what I make."

Dislike of filing or payments procedure:

> Does not want to be on program because he runs his own business and does not get paystubs.

> Mrs. _____ and her two sons are embarrassed about collecting the paystubs—the sons feel funny about their mother seeing their paystubs and Mrs. _____ is embarrassed about seeing them. Mr. _____ too tired to keep accurate income records of what he makes.

> Didn't like decision on imputation for home ownership; $2.50 too little to go through trouble of answering questions, etc.

> $2.50 is insult—volunteered to file for nothing but office manager doubts seriousness of offer.

Distrust of the experiment:

> In enroller observation sheet it is noted that the family has a general distrust of anything run by or connected with the government . . . especially in financial dealings with the government.

> Suspicious of source of funds—afraid he would have to pay them back.

> Never cashed any checks because he was afraid he would have to pay money back.

Dislike of receiving unearned income:

> "My son works steady . . . we don't need no help . . . I'm starting a business of my own . . . we take care of ourselves. . . . I'll send the checks back."

> "My future is good. I can depend on myself to take care of our needs. I never got anything for nothing and don't expect to now. . . . You are trying to eliminate poverty but why do you include me in this experiment?"

> Mr. _____ is in the junk business and enjoys it. His daughter wants him to quit the junk business, take a janitor's job, and live with her and her husband. She didn't understand, he said, that he wants to work, enjoys the men who visit, whom he can help with little favors or car parts. The program is a threat to his working, he feels, for we are guaranteeing only $1000 less per year than he now earns. And that amount, if accepted, plus the pressure his daughter is now presenting might be enough to force him to leave a life he enjoys.

Given the importance of maintaining the sample population, we contacted refusals for two consecutive interviews before we dropped efforts to persuade the families to continue. As mentioned above, experimental families who failed to file their income report forms were contacted by letter or by phone or, if these failed, by a house call, to ascertain the reason for dropping out and to try to persuade the family to continue.

Methods used by the field offices for finding families who had moved and left no forwarding address included the following: questioning of new tenant, landlord, superintendent, or other tenants in apartment building for family's new address; questioning of neighbors; questioning of authorities at children's school; checking with welfare, unemployment, and manpower offices; if one member of the family was in jail, checking with police and prison authorities for a recent address; checking neighborhood stores and bars; for families with uncommon names, calling persons in local telephone directory with the same name; sending a self-addressed card to the last known address, asking the family to return the card with their new address; asking the post office for a forwarding address; checking with state migrant authorities; and checking with the county clerk's office. Although we did not keep quantitative records of the relative effectiveness of each method, it was generally felt by the field staff, and later verified by the "search" staff (see Chapter 8), that the most effective methods of locating lost families were questioning persons living at the family's last known address and questioning neighbors.

In addition to actively pursuing families who had dropped out, the research and administrative staff took several major actions to inhibit additional attrition. The first attempt to cut down the rate of attrition was made in late 1968, shortly after families in Trenton were enrolled, on the assumption—which turned out to be mistaken—that attrition would be less if the burden of filling out forms were lessened. The payments department had noticed that families receiving the minimum biweekly payment of $2.50 (later changed to $10.00) comprised most of the late-filing and attrited samples. In the November report period, for instance, eleven of the sixteen late filers and all seven of the families who did not file for that period were receiving the $2.50 minimum payment. In an effort to minimize the filing burden for these families and to encourage them to remain in the experiment, provision was made for a twelve-week reporting period for families regularly receiving the $2.50 payment. They would continue to receive $2.50 biweekly but would be required to report their income and send in their paystubs only once every twelve weeks. Twenty-seven families in Trenton qualified for this treatment (no other cities had yet been enrolled). However, the minimized contact with the families, the task of saving paystubs for twelve weeks rather than four, and the problems of recall over such a long period, made the twelve-week reporting system worse than the four-week system, and it was dropped.

The second major action to check the dropout rate in the experimental group was changing the minimum $2.50 payment to a filing fee of $10.00 (in June 1969, following the Tobin judgment, as noted in Chapter 6). Comments from the families and such data as those given above made it clear that many of the families who were getting the minimum payment felt it was too much trouble to file for so little reward. An early field-office report indicated that thirty-one of the thirty-six experimental families who had dropped out were receiving the minimum payment. Jersey City and Scranton families both were enrolled under the $10.00 filing-fee provision, and their lower rates of attrition during the first few quarterlies were certainly due in part to the larger filing fee.

Control-group attrition presented even more difficult problems. The first step was to make attrition less damaging by enrolling more controls. About half of the families in Jersey City and Scranton were put into the control group and, after an additional screening and pre-enrollment effort, 141 new controls were added to the Trenton and Paterson–Passaic samples in the fall of 1969.

The second step to counter attrition among controls was to maintain more frequent contact with the control families and to provide them with some additional financial incentive for staying in the experiment. We generally agreed that some financial incentive was less dangerous to the experiment than excessive and self-selected attrition. We decided upon an address verification system for which the control families would be paid. Beginning in the fall of 1969, we sent each control family a monthly postcard asking for the family's current address. Upon receiving the return card in the Princeton office, we mailed the family an $8.00 check. It is difficult to say whether the measure was effective, since the rate of attrition after the monthly address card system was instituted showed no major change from previous quarterlies.

In sum, major efforts were made to encourage those families who wanted to drop out of the experiment to remain and to prevent further attrition in both the experimental and control groups. The ultimate overall attrition rate, as mentioned above, reached 20 percent. In order to ascertain what effects, if any, this had on experimental results, an extensive effort was made to find and interview a sample of the families whom we could not keep in the experiment. This effort is described in detail in the following chapter.

8

Recovering data
on lost families

As indicated in the previous chapter, about 20 percent of the families enrolled in the income-maintenance experiment had dropped out by the end of the three years. The potential problem this created for data analysis is part of the general problem of nonresponse, which affects analyses in two ways.

First, it causes a reduction in sample size and a resulting loss in the efficiency of the estimates of parameters of interest; that is, the confidence that can be placed on any estimate decreases with the size of the sample. This problem was not serious for the experiment because the original sample was designed with a predicted attrition rate of 20 percent.

Second, the critical consequence of nonresponse is that estimates of parameters may be biased if the attrited group is different from the nonattrited group in some unknown way. The people who drop out of the experiment may be the same as those who fail to be included in a national program (those who fail to register and those who fail to report their income or in other ways fail to maintain their right to benefits). To the extent that this is the case, the behavioral responses measured in the experiment will be a good measure of the

Locating and interviewing families that had moved was undertaken by a special group of "searchers" under the immediate supervision of Audrey McDonald, who contributed parts of this chapter.

117

responses that may be expected in the population as a whole. To the extent, however, that the people who drop out of the experiment differ significantly from those that remain and to the extent that they could be expected to be included in a national program, the estimates will be biased in a way that will impair the usefulness of the experiment as a guide to a national program.

REASONS FOR ATTRITION
THAT PRODUCE SYSTEMATIC BIASES

The benefits of continuing (as of enrolling) in the experiment were mainly the financial benefits of the cash transfer payments made to the experimental group. In addition, there was the economic security of knowing that if family income went down, transfer payments would increase. Neither of these benefits were enjoyed by the control group, and it could be expected, therefore, that the control group would have a higher rate of attrition than the experimental group. This was borne out, as indicated in Chapter 7.

Within the experimental group, in addition to the plan, the family's own income affected the size of the payment. Controlling for experimental plan, the more income earned by the family the lower would be its payments and the more likely the family would be to drop out, other things equal. It could be expected, therefore, that the rate of attrition would be higher for high-income families, with consequent important implications for interpreting the results.

An additional hypothesis suggests that all characteristics correlated with a family's normal income[1] would be positively associated with attrition. That is, the incomes of those persons who usually earned more than they were earning during the enrollment period could be expected to increase over the period of the experiment simply because they would be rising again to their long-term average. As their incomes rose, the experimental payments of such persons would decrease. Their expected gains from continuing in the experiment, therefore, would be less than the gains of those with a lower normal income. Thus, the less educated, the very young, the very old, and those who were Spanish-speaking or black, were all expected to have lower attrition rates insofar as the expected monetary gain from the experiment was the controlling factor.

Another factor expected to affect attrition was the experimental site in which the family lived. The site variable represented, in part, improvements in administrative policies (because the experiment began at different times in the four different sites) and, in part, the quality of the administrative staff as it varied across sites.

---

[1] "Normal income" is the expected or average income of a person over a long-term period and can be predicted by relating such characteristics as age, family size, education, and ethnic group.

Other factors that caused families to be "attrition prone" were personal characteristics or personal events that were wholly or partly noneconomic, for example, family breakups. The departing male head was often ineligible for cash benefits from the experiment when he became a separate unit by himself, because his earnings were likely to be high relative to the reduced transfer payment to which he became entitled. In these situations, the female head was typically left behind with the children but without the earnings; she often found Aid to Families with Dependent Children (AFDC), with Medicaid and other social-service benefits in addition to cash payments, more beneficial to her and her family than the experimental payments, causing her to drop out of the experiment.

Another personal event that often made participation in the experiment more trouble than it was worth was moving, particularly long-distance moves. Although eligibility for benefits was maintained as long as a person or family moved within the continental United States, it was more difficult for both the participant and the administrative staff to maintain communication. In addition, families who moved Puerto Rico were no longer eligible for payments.

Preliminary regression analysis of the available data on attriters and nonattriters explained less than 10 percent of the variation in attrition status. If all of the unexplained variation was attributable to various random or chance events uncorrelated with the behavior being studied, then the inability of the regression model to explain more variation was harmless. If, on the other hand, the unexplained variation was attributable to unmeasured motivational or attitudinal characteristics that were related to such factors as earnings abilities and work, the low explanatory power of the regression analysis was cause for concern. The latter possibility led to the decision to locate and interview as many of the dropouts as possible.

THE ATTRITION INTERVIEW

The attrition interview was designed to measure those characteristics of attrited families that could be expected to differentiate them from nonattrited families, with respect to the parameters of interest. Since there was the distinct possibility that some of the respondents, especially those who had previously refused to be interviewed, would be hostile to another interview, the instrument was somewhat reduced in time from the regular interview, with the questions arranged in descending order of importance. Topics included[2] changes in family composition since the family's last interview; the status of the labor-force involvement of the male and female heads of household; 1971 annual income;

[2] See Chapter 10 for a more detailed discussion.

job history for the head of household (data on longest-held job and on jobs held during last three years); the most recent occupational status and the occupational status at the time of attrition for both male and female heads (including labor-force participation status since the family was last interviewed); welfare status since the family was last interviewed; geographic mobility since the family was last interviewed; reason for attrition. The questionnaire contained roughly 150 questions and took about forty-five minutes to administer.

LOCATING ATTRITED FAMILIES

We began a pilot attempt at locating and interviewing attrited families in Trenton in the spring of 1972, nine months after the experiment ended in that city. Using a small number of the best interviewers, we first employed regular field techniques for locating and interviewing lost or dropped families but found few families by this method. Analysis of the field operation revealed that the main difficulty came from using only part-time interviewers. Regular interviewers, all of whom had other nine-to-five jobs, could not devote the amount of time and effort needed to trace missing families. The interviewer, or searcher, also had to be available in both daylight and evening hours, in order to follow the many different leads that made locating families possible. Given these considerations, the task of locating attrited families was transferred from the regular interviewing staff to a special group of searchers.

Including split family units, there were fifty-five attrited families in Trenton. Twenty-three of these units were located and interviewed; nine units were either deceased or institutionalized; four units refused to be interviewed; six units were not interviewed because they were receiving welfare and appeared to be frightened of answering the questionnaire; and thirteen units were not located. Excluding deceased and institutionalized units from the base, the completion rate was 50 percent (Table 8.1).

Several families who refused the attrition interview gave fear of the welfare authorities as their reason. We therefore decided not to try to trace Trenton families known to be on welfare if it proved difficult. After we had made a reasonable effort to locate and interview them, but without success, we discontinued the search and collected data on their family composition, work history, and residential mobility from the Mercer County Welfare Board records.

Since the characteristics of attrited families could have varied according to the date of attrition, it was important that interviews be obtained on at least a fraction of families who attrited at each stage of the experiment. Fortunately, as can be seen from Table 8.1, families who completed the interview were fairly evenly distributed with respect to the date at which they dropped out. Forty percent of those who attrited before the first quarterly interview completed the

Table 8.1 Number of Families Attrited and Number Completing Attrition Interview, by Period of Attrition: Trenton (Pilot Site)

Group	Present at Pre-Enrollment Interview but Not at 1st Quarterly	Present for 1st Quarterly Interview but Not for 5th	Present for 5th Quarterly Interview but Not for 9th	Present for 9th Quarterly Interview but Not for 12th	Total
Experimental					
Number attrited[a]	5	7	5	6	23
Number completing attrition interview	4	5	4	3	16
Percentage completed[a]	80.0	71.4	80.0	50.0	69.5
Control					
Number attrited[a]	5	7	7	4	23
Number completing attrition interview	0	3	3	1	7
Percentage completed[a]	0	42.8	42.8	25.0	30.4
Experimental and Control					
Number attrited[a]	10	14	12	10	46
Number completing attrition interview	4	8	7	4	23
Percentage completed[a]	40.0	57.1	58.3	40.0	50.0

[a]Deceased and institutionalized units not included in base.

attrition interview, as did 57 percent of those families who were present for the first quarterly interview but not for the fifth, and 58 percent of those who were present for the fifth quarterly interview but not the ninth. Forty percent of those families who dropped out after the ninth quarterly completed the attrition interview. As was expected, the completion rate was not evenly divided between the control and experimental groups. Fewer than one-third of the control families were interviewed compared to two-thirds of the experimental families. Given the completion rate in Trenton, we decided to extend the search effort to the other sites.

The general search procedures were as follows. We began by examining all records on the attrited families—interviews, payments records, field memos—to obtain last-known addresses, telephone numbers (if any), and other leads. In our efforts to contact families, we telephoned those with telephone numbers, but had little success since most of the numbers were out of date. Then, to families for whom a recent address was available, we mailed letters requesting the family to call the Princeton office concerning a final interview. This met with little success despite the promise of a $10 payment.

Real progress was made only when the searchers went into the field. They concentrated their efforts in one city at a time—with the exception of Scranton, where the search was run simultaneously with the other cities.[3] Some of the sources used in tracking the families included post office change-of-address cards, election boards, motor vehicle registration offices, welfare boards, county and state prisons, last known places of employment, and such community groups as the Puerto Rican Council or the Community Center. Although the persons contacted were often willing to cooperate, these sources were not very useful.

The most successful means of locating lost families was face-to-face questioning of neighbors, relatives (especially former spouses), storekeepers, and bartenders. They were assured that (1) the searcher was not a bill collector, (2) the searcher was not from welfare, (3) some money would be in it for the interviewee, and (4) as a last resort, some money would be in it for whoever supplied a good lead (euphemistically called "discretionary payments").[4] Through these sources the searchers made considerable progress in locating and interviewing families who had remained in town and in getting good leads on families who had moved out of town and to Puerto Rico. One of the best descriptions of the

---

[3] Scranton was different in many respects from the other sites. Far fewer families attrited (5 percent compared to about 25 percent for the rest of the sample); of those that did attrite, most stayed within Scranton and were able to be contacted by telephone.

[4] A total of only $17.88 in "discretionary payments" was actually paid out in the recovery operation. The sum was composed of one $10.00 payment and a bouquet of flowers ($7.88, including tax).

search effort is contained in excerpts from a progress report written by one of the searchers after the first week's efforts:

> The first interview turned out to be the norm for the families we were able to contact. With only three exceptions the respondents were all extremely pleasant and quite willing to take the interview. The first interview was with Mrs. _____. Mrs. _____ is a warm, extraordinarily sensitive woman, who was cleaning fish when we knocked. The interview—interrupted occasionally by casual chats about fish, the price of groceries, and delicate family problems—took nearly an hour and a half but it taught me an important first lesson. The lesson is that an interviewer, no matter how much he or she emphathizes with a family's situation and feels inside of himself their own desperation, must, nevertheless, remain a distant, almost irrelevant entity with a ten-dollar check and a "Thank you—Good Night."

> The next several days were spent searching out additional families. Since many of the people had never changed addresses, finding them was mostly a matter of being at their house when they were home (a time-consuming, backtracking, crosstracking task). But on the other hand, since many of the families had not been interviewed since 1969, and existence in a ghetto is tenuous at best, some of them had long ago disappeared, and digging them out from obscurity would require eight soothsayers and a pound of hocus-pocus.

> For instance, while we were looking for Mr. _____ the warmest clue we got as to his whereabouts came from a very alert elderly woman who is now living at the address we have for Mr. _____. She told us that quite a few months ago, while she was standing on her second-floor porch, a guy walked by and shouted up to her how could she stand it up there with all those roaches. The woman seems to think that was Mr. _____. For a lack of anything better to think we think it was too.

> Another "warm" clue to another lost face came from the wife of a man who had packed up and split. She said, "I heard he came here about a year and a half ago driving a moving van truck." She is as close to him as we are.

> The ideal time to catch someone is after dark, in their homes. But this can run into problems—especially if word gets around that some cats are walking around after dark with all this money and checks in their pockets. One way to minimize post-sunset harassment is to contact families during the day, if possible, arrange for an interview, and return at night. Most of the respondents were either not home during the day or advised us to return at night. Six o'clock is dinnertime, so seven o'clock would be better.

> Three respondents contacted were adamantly opposed to the interview. One, Mrs. _____, had been intimadated by the Passaic County Welfare Board enough that it was clear our presence in her house caused great anxiety and, to her, we represented Danger. She was plain scared. Consequently, the attrited families who have been getting static from the welfare people have been withdrawn from our list of families being sought.

> The other reluctant respondents (Mr. _____ and Mrs. _____) said that the interviews were too damned personal and they're tired of answering questions. Although it's fairly obvious that _____ and _____ won't come through with the final interview, it seems to be a good idea to make it clear to ALL respondents that this *is*

the final interview and the questions are about recent work experience and nothing else. Many many people we interviewed resented the personal nature of many of the questions asked in previous interviews. They wanted nothing more to do with those kinds of questions; consequently, they were angry at us before we even opened our mouths.

About the discretionary payments, the searcher wrote:

This maneuver worked to perfection in the case of Mrs. ____. After verbally sparring with some of Mrs. ____'s neighbors and having them scrutinize me with deft, feline caution, I was directed to the candy store on the corner where another person would supposedly help me out. While talking with the woman at the candy store it became quite apparent that she wasn't going to say anything until I whispered, "I'll take care of you if Mrs. ____ calls me." Ten minues later Mrs. ____ called. Shopkeepers are in it for the money.

But it is mostly tenacity that's the key to locating lost families; tenacity, knowledge of the turf, rapport, and finesse. And, oh yes—greenbacks.[5]

A total of 138 attrited units was traced during the within-site search. This task took six searchers five months to complete. When it was finished, the search team began the job of following up leads on families who were alleged to have moved, either out of town but within the continental United States or to Puerto Rico.

Excluding families who had moved to Puerto Rico, we estimated that about forty-eight (10 percent) of the attrited families would be found to have moved outside the original sites and that interviews could be obtained on about twenty-five of these families. In fact, forty-four families turned out to be "known" to have moved out of town, but most of these leads were tenuous at best. Leads on the families' whereabouts consisted of such statements as, "They have gone to Florida (Connecticut, Philadelphia, California, somewhere in Pennsylvania, down South)."

Given the small number of out-of-town families whose whereabouts were even vaguely known, it was not economically feasible to send searchers routinely on an extended lead. If a family could be located within a day's driving time of the original site, the interview was administered by a member of the regular search staff. Families believed to be living at a considerable distance from the original sites were located and interviewed by a Seattle—Denver experiment task force, already scheduled to make trips that would take them to most areas of the country. For the families outside even these areas, interviews by phone were attempted. Only four telephone interviews were made, but all were successful. The respondents in each case had a reasonably high degree of literacy, and the

[5] Pannell, Internal Report, October 1972, Data Center Archives, Institute for Research on Poverty, University of Wisconsin-Madison.

interviews were completed with a minimum amount of effort and time. In total, interviews were completed on only eight of the families thought to be out of town but within the continental United States.

According to the leads obtained during the intercity search for attrited families, seventy families were thought to have moved to Puerto Rico. The leads varied in detail, ranging from "probably gone back to Puerto Rico" to an exact address. Two searchers were dispatched to Puerto Rico, each for two weeks, and their efforts resulted in a total of sixteen completed interviews.

Completed interviews were thus obtained on 162 of the 449 attrited units. Excluding from the base those units who were found to be institutionalized or deceased (56 units), the overall completion rate for the attrition interview was 41 percent (see Table 8.2).

The effort involved in locating and interviewing attrited units was in all cases considerable but varied greatly by type of contact. The type of contact and the approximate time taken to locate a family and administer an interview are given in Table 8.3 and 8.4, respectively.

The searchers were told to spend no more than one day looking for an individual or family unless enthusiasm and a warm trail caused the searcher to try longer. The reasons for not obtaining an interview with 288 of the attrited families are summarized in Table 8.5.

Of the families who were contacted, 14 percent (twenty-seven) refused to take the interview. In these cases, the interviewers observed as much as possible and made notes about the family composition and the condition of the house.

Refusals were not always straightforward. Many were "refusals by avoidance." Instead of refusing outright, the respondents gave false addresses and false telephone numbers, and failed to keep scheduled appointments. Those families who refused directly gave many reasons for doing so. Examples of reasons for refusing to be interviewed (as described by the searchers) are given below:

> Respondent said wife had told him right at the beginning not to get involved in statistical or research things. "And you know how that is, I've got to live with her."

> Cannot afford another problem with welfare.

> Frightened off by publicity given to families in Mercer County Welfare Fraud case.

> Refusal based mainly on machismo. He is the man of the house and no one can do anything in the house without his permission. It seems that enrolling was done through the wife—that's why he feels that he will not answer the questions.

> Called our efforts to interview her "an invasion of privacy. I just don't want to be bothered. You could give me a hundred dollars, I won't do it."

> Refused. Dark stairwell and vicious dog did not allow interviewer to make notes on dwelling or occupants.

Table 8.2 **Number of Families Attrited and Number Completing Attrition Interview, by Period**

	Present at Pre-Enrollment Interview but Not at 1st Quarterly			Present for 1st Quarterly Interview but Not for 5th			
	Number Attrited	Number Completing Attrition Interview	Percentage Completed[a]	Number Attrited	Number Completing Attrition Interview	Percentage Completed[a]	Number Attrited
Trenton							
Experimental	5	4	80.0	7	5	71.4	5
Control		0	0.0		3	42.8	7
Total		*4*		*14*	*8*	57.1	*12*
Paterson							
Experimental	10	2	20.0	19	7	36.8	32
Control	5	2	40.0	8	1	12.5	18
Total	*15*	*4*	26.6	*27*	*8*	29.6	*50*
Passaic							
Experimental	2	0	0.0	20	10	50.0	11
Control	3	0	0.0	12	2	16.6	13
Total	*5*	*0*	0.0	*32*	*12*	37.5	*24*
Jersey City							
Experimental	6	2	33.3	8	4	50.0	10
Control	12	0	0.0	13	3	23.0	23
Total	*18*	*2*	11.1	*21*	*7*	33.3	*33*
Scranton							
Experimental	1	1	100.0	5	3	60.0	3
Control	2	2	100.0	4	2	50.0	7
Total	*3*	*3*	100.0	*9*	*5*	55.5	*10*
All cities							
Experimental	24	9	37.5	59	29	49.1	61
Control	27	4	14.8	44	11	25.0	68
Total	*51*	*13*	25.4	*103*	*40*	38.8	*129*

[a]Deceased and institutionalized units are not included in base.

126

Present for 5th Quarterly interview but Not for 9th		Present for 9th Quarterly Interview but Not for 12th			Total		
Number Completing Attrition Interview	Percentage Completed[a]	Number Attrited	Number Completing Attrition Interview	Percentage Completed[a]	Number Attrited	Number Completing Attrition Interview	Percentage Completed[a]
4	80.0	6	3	50.0	23	16	69.5
3	42.8	4	1	25.0	23	7	30.4
7	58.3	10	4	40.0	46	23	50.0
15	46.8	23	8	34.7	84	32	38.0
7	38.8	21	13	61.9	52	23	44.2
22	44.0	44	21	47.7	136	55	40.4
6	54.5	9	1	11.1	42	17	40.4
6	46.1	15	6	40.0	43	14	32.5
12	50.0	24	7	29.1	85	31	36.4
6	60.0	10	6	60.0	34	18	52.9
13	56.5	18	4	22.2	66	20	30.3
19	57.5	28	10	35.7	100	38	38.0
2	66.6	1	0	0.0	10	6	60.0
5	71.4	3	0	0.0	16	9	56.2
7	70.0	4	0	0.0	26	15	57.6
33	54.0	49	18	36.7	193	89	46.1
34	50.0	61	24	39.3	200	73	36.5
67	51.9	110	42	38.1	393	162	41.2

Table 8.3 Number of Families Completing Attrition Interview, by Degree of Difficulty in Obtaining the Interview

					Degree of Difficulty						
	1	2	3	4	5	6	7	8	9	10	Total
Trenton											
Experimental	0	3	8	4	0	0	0	1	0	0	16
Control	0	5	0	1	0	0	0	1	0	0	7
Paterson											
Experimental	1	15	4	4	0	0	4	1	2	1	32
Control	2	10	1	6	0	0	1	1	2	0	23
Passaic											
Experimental	1	8	2	4	1	0	0	0	1	0	17
Control	1	6	4	2	0	0	1	0	0	0	14
Jersey City											
Experimental	0	10	1	3	0	1	2	0	0	1	18
Control	3	8	5	1	2	1	0	0	0	0	20
Scranton											
Experimental	0	3	3	0	0	0	0	0	0	0	6
Control	1	3	4	1	0	0	0	0	0	0	9
All cities											
Experimental	2	39	18	15	1	1	6	2	3	2	89
Control	7	32	14	11	2	1	2	2	2	0	73
Total	*9*	*71*	*32*	*26*	*3*	*2*	*8*	*4*	*5*	*2*	*162*

NOTE: Numbers in column heads correspond to the following steps taken to find and interview attrited families, graduated by degree of difficulty:

1. Responded to mailing or was located by phone from Princeton
2. Was located at last-known address
3. Had moved, but address easily obtained
4. Intensive search in city needed to locate
5. Had moved but left forwarding address
6. Search in original city yielded out-of-town address within continental U.S.
7. Search in original city yielded definite Puerto Rican address
8. Search in original city fruitless, but family located after intensive search out of town
9. Search in original city fruitless, but family located after intensive search in Puerto Rico
10. Someone (friend or relative) other than attrited unit answered interview questions

Table 8.4 Number of Families Completing Attrition Interview, by Approximate Time Taken for the Search and Interview

	Number of Hours										
	1 1/4 (a)	2 (b)	4 (c)	4 (d)	4–6 (e)	8 (f)	8 (g)	4–6 plus Travel (h)	4–6 plus Travel (i)	8 plus Travel (j)	Total
Trenton		4	4		12	1		2			23
Paterson		14	9	2	15	3	1	1		10	55
Passaic		19		1	5	3			1	2	31
Jersey City	3	19	2	2	5	3			4		38
Scranton	1	4	2		8						15
Total	*4*	*60*	*17*	*5*	*45*	*10*	*1*	*3*	*5*	*12*	*162*

NOTE: Types of activity required for the search and interview are listed below. Approximate time for a straight visit and interview is 2 hours.

a. Telephone interview	1¼ hours
b. Found at last-known address, took attrition interview on first request	2 hours
c. Thought to be at last-known address but difficult to catch at home	4 hours
d. Found at last-known address, reluctant to take interview	4 hours
e. Moved once and traced (intercity)	8 hours
f. Moved several times and traced (intercity)	8 hours
g. Moved out of town but not out of state, left forwarding address	4–6 hours
h. Moved out of town and state, left forwarding address	4–6 hours plus 1-day traveling time
i. Moved to Puerto Rico, left forwarding address	4–6 hours plus 2-day traveling time
j. Moved out of town or to Puerto Rico, only general area or barrio known	8 hours plus 2-day traveling time

129

Table 8.5 Number of Families Not Interviewed, by Reasons

	Reasons									Total
	(a)	(b)	(c)	(d)	(e)	(f)	(g)	(h)	(i)	
Trenton										
Experimental	0	2	1	1	1	0	6	1	2	14
Control	0	4	0	4	0	4	1	1	4	18
Paterson										
Experimental	2	8	2	16	10	3	5	0	11	57
Control	2	10	1	5	5	6	4	1	0	34
Passaic										
Experimental	1	5	1	9	7	0	2	2	1	28
Control	1	6	0	13	6	4	1	1	0	32
Jersey City										
Experimental	1	4	0	9	3	0	4	1	0	22
Control	3	3	6	25	2	6	7	0	0	52
Scranton										
Experimental	0	2	1	0	0	1	6	5	0	15
Control	0	4	0	0	0	3	7	1	0	15
All cities										
Experimental	4	21	5	35	21	4	23	9	14	136
Control	6	27	7	47	13	23	20	4	4	151
Total	*10*	*48*	*12*	*82*	*34*	*27*	*43*	*13*	*18*	*287*

NOTE: Reasons households were not interviewed are keyed to letters used in column headings:

a. Moved before first quarterly interview, no leads
b. Moved, new address unknown
c. Moved, located new address, investigated, but lost trail
d. Moved out of town or to Puerto Rico, address unknown
e. Moved, followed out of town, and lost
f. Refused
g. Deceased
h. Institutionalized
i. On welfare, no attempt made to interview

Very delightful woman who refused with a gigantic smile, said we come back to her house all we want but she's not going to answer any more questions. Mr. _____ does not want to answer and she has to live with him. She doesn't want anyone writing a book about their lives. Questions too personal.

The effort made to locate and interview attrited units, thus, met with considerable success. It was initially estimated that completed interviews could be obtained on one-fourth of the attrited units; instead, more than one-third of the attrited units were located and interviewed.

9 Development of the survey instruments

During the course of the negative-income-tax experiment, twenty-two separate survey instruments were developed. These instruments included two sample-selection baseline instruments; twelve quarterly interviews, to be administered every four months during the three-year period; and eight special interviews. This chapter discusses the general procedure for developing the instruments, certain major problems encountered in that development, and the reasons for the special interviews. The subject matter of the quarterly interviews is discussed in Chapter 10.

THE INTERVIEW DEVELOPMENT PROCESS

Three major groups contributed to the development of the interviews: (1) the research staff, both at Mathematica and at the University of Wisconsin, whose principal concern was the specification of experimental hypotheses and data needs; (2) the operational staff whose concern was ease of administration; and (3) the interview development staff, whose task was to reconcile research needs

Survey instruments were developed under the direction of Cheri T. Marshall, who wrote the major part of both this chapter and Chapter 10.

131

with operational requirements, in order to create a useful and usable survey instrument.

The Questionnaire

The flow chart shown in Figure 9.1 illustrates the sequence of events by which a questionnaire was produced. Each questionnaire went through the same general process of development. The first step was to develop working hypotheses concerning experimental outcomes; the second was to incorporate these into analytical models; the third was to examine the survey literature for relevant batteries of questions and to prepare drafts or descriptions of the questions or variables to be included in each interview. These three steps were performed by the senior research staff. The first draft of the questionnaire was then prepared by the interview development staff.

For topics to be repeated annually, the interview development staff merely inserted the original questions in the new instrument. If, however, any parts of a section had caused major problems in the field, they were submitted to the research staff with suggestions on how the section should be rewritten.

When a new topic was to be included in an interview, the interview development staff constructed questions designed to cover the topics submitted by the research staff. In order to do this, they first clarified with the researcher the precise nature of the information desired. The more general topics or variables were frequently broken down into a series of questions, with each question designed to obtain a well-defined single piece of information. For example, to obtain information on wages and work effort, the following questions would be too general: How much did you make at your job? How many hours did you work? Instead, these two questions might be made into the following series:

1. Over what time period are you paid on your job with [COMPANY]? Is it weekly, bimonthly, monthly, piecework rate, or what?
2. What is your average rate of pay befores taxes and other deductions for [A TIME PERIOD IN Q.1] on your job with [COMPANY]?
3. For that rate of pay, how many hours do you normally work?
4. Do those hours include hours of overtime? How many hours of overtime are usually included?
5. What is your hourly overtime rate of pay? If hourly rate is not known, what is your fractional overtime rate? For example, time-and-one-half, double time, etc.

Once the first draft of an interview had been prepared, it was sent to the Wisconsin research staff and to an interview review committee.

The Review Committee

The review committee was composed primarily of persons on the Mathematica staff and represented a broad spectrum of viewpoints. On the committee were a staff sociologist, the interview development coordinator assigned to the project, the field administration supervisor, the interview training supervisor, the coding supervisor, and a member of the data quality control staff. The major stages through which the interview passed, on its journey from conception to data bank, were represented by members of the committee.

Each member of the committee made suggestions to the group and worked through any problems in the interview until general agreement was reached. Throughout these meetings, it was the role of the interview development staff to take notes, remind the committee of the intent of the interview, and devise on-the-spot working formats for revisions in the questionnaire.

After each meeting of the review committee, the interview development staff prepared a new draft incorporating the suggestions the committee had made, rewriting questions or complete sections, and paying particular attention to the effect of these changes on question logic, skip logic, and longitudinal consistency. All proposed revisions, along with justifications for the revisions, were then presented to the researchers for their approval. On the average, seven drafts of each interview were prepared before a final draft was completed. The final draft was then sent to the Office of Economic Opportunity (OEO) and the Office of Management and Budget (OMB) for the formal approval necessary for all survey instruments used in federally funded projects.[1]

Pretesting

During the early part of the experiment, new interviews were pretested on a sample in New Brunswick, New Jersey. The sample consisted of eighteen families, mostly in public housing, and included blacks, whites, and Puerto Ricans. All were two-parent families, and their income levels were well within the range covered by the experiment. They were paid $5.00 for each interview. After the sixth quarterly, almost no new material was introduced. The New Brunswick sample was dropped, and all additional pretesting was done on an ad hoc basis in Princeton or Trenton.

While both these groups served well for pretesting, it probably would have been better to enroll and interview the same pretest group throughout the

---

[1] Executive Order #10253, 11 June 1951, provides that all data instruments administered to more than nine persons as part of a project funded by the federal government must have formal approval from OMB in the form of a number printed on the first page of the instrument.

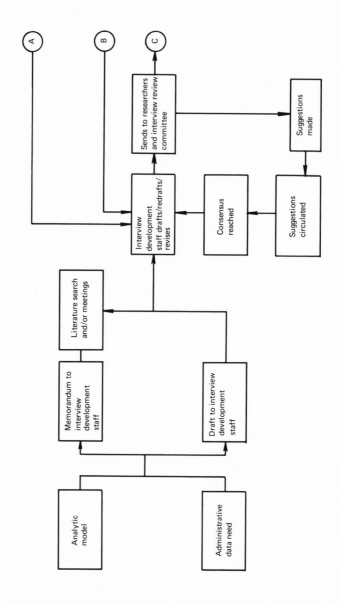

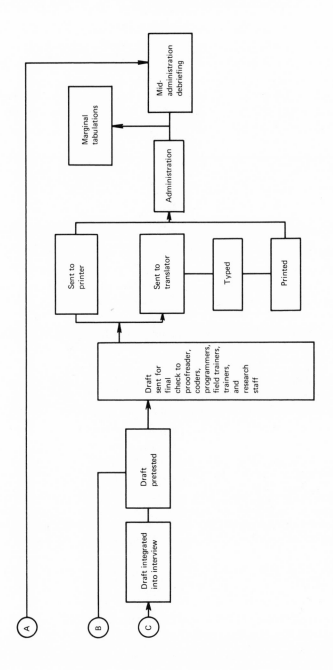

Figure 9.1 Interview development process.

experiment. This would have provided a continuous, longitudinal data file on pretest families and enabled us to estimate panel fatigue and attitudes toward the length and content of the interviews by panel members. (Longitudinal panel members, of course, view an instrument differently from cross-sectional survey respondents.) Had a data-processing system with more rapid turnaround been operating at the beginning, there would have been the additional benefit of longitudinal analysis of repeated batteries as well.

The Midquarterly Meeting

After an interview had been sufficiently revised and pretested, it was adminis- tered in the field. Halfway through the administration of an interview in each city, a meeting was held to discover what problems there might be with the interview.

The midquarterly meeting was attended by the interview development staff and the research staff in an effort to learn from the interviewers what they thought were the problem questions. This interviewer debriefing was particularly important in Trenton, because that city was used as a pilot site, where major instrument problems could be corrected for subsequent cities. In some instances, problems could be cleared up with new training instructions. In other instances, entire sections had to be revised. This happened, for example, with a section of the tenth quarterly interview, designed to obtain job history over a five-year period. The interviewers reported severe recall problems and evident hostility to any serious probing. The hostility in some instances flowed over to other sections, jeopardizing the entire interview. We decided, therefore, to eliminate the job-history section from the tenth quarterly interview for the rest of the sample, to shorten that section to cover three years only and add the shortened version to the eleventh quarterly interview.

Between the ninth and tenth quarterly interviews in Trenton, the interview doubled in length from the originally planned length of one hour, and subse- quent quarterly interviews grew even longer, as the researchers became acutely aware of the approaching end of the experiment. The attrition rate increased, and some of the interviewers complained about the length of the interviews. In consequence, we cut down the final interviews for the remaining cities, omitting entire sections and reducing others in size, which did reduce panel hostility and refusals. For example, a major part of the twelfth quarterly interview in Trenton concerned children's health and their medical expenses. In the fourth and eighth quarterly interviews, this information was asked for every child in the family. For the twelfth, in the remaining cities, we cut the section down to obtain information on the oldest and youngest child only. Every effort was made not to alter interviews after the Trenton revision.

Problems and Lessons

Any new research effort produces new expertise gained through making mistakes or learning from unforeseen problems and issues. This section describes some of the more important lessons learned in the course of developing the interviews. They may serve as a guide to those interested in the efficiency of future experimentation.[2]

INITIAL MISSPECIFICATIONS OF DATA NEEDS

While for the most part data needs were accurately perceived at the outset, there were several areas requiring midstudy revisions. The most crucial of these was in the area of work response and income data.

The experiment began collecting labor-force and income data using sets of questions from the Current Population Survey (CPS).[3] We felt that the use of a standard and well-known set of questions would minimize the risk of producing unusable data. Another reason for using existing CPS questions was that we could then compare our findings to national figures. Alternative questionnaire batteries that we might have considered elicited too little information. It was clear by the end of the first year, however, that the CPS questions were inadequate for the purposes of the experiment: (1) They did not provide a complete and continuous work history and income picture (labor-force participation was ampled for only one week out of every quarter). (2) Income data derived from CPS could not easily be compared to income reported on the experiment's four-weekly income report forms. (3) The CPS questions omitted several stages of questioning needed to check the data for quality and consistency (such as direct questions on hourly wage rates). (4) The CPS questions did not address the issue of hours of nondiscretionary over- or underemployment. On many jobs hours are not, in fact, optional; a worker must work the number of hours preferred by his employer or not work at all. Work-response estimates would, therefore, be biased to the extent that nondiscretionary work variations were not isolated. (5) The CPS questions did not adequately measure the time spent on job search. The "reservation wage hypothesis"[4] could not be adequately tested without such information. Several questions dealing with the

---

[2] See Marshall, "Interview Development in the Health Insurance Experiment," Internal Paper, August 1972, Data Center Archives, Institute for Research on Poverty, University of Wisconsin-Madison.

[3] A battery of questions administered to a national sample on a quarterly basis by the Census Bureau.

[4] The theory that workers may forgo immediate employment in order to search for a better job.

extent and nature of job search and bargaining with employers were needed to clarify this phenomenon. (6) For the New Jersey sample, the CPS questions occasionally picked up large portions of the sample in atypical weeks, such as Christmas and other holidays. (7) The CPS questions did not obtain thorough data on work-related expenses and nonwage benefits.

The most severe of these problems—that of having only "snapshots" of income and work response—was recognized early in the experiment. It was proposed that the section be revised, taking care that it did not lose comparability with previous quarterly interviews. The number of problems caused by trying to maintain the CPS series while also expanding to a continuous work history necessitated compromise that called for expanding the "last week" set to "last month by weeks." The definition of "last month" was associated with pay periods, which simplified the interview, increased accuracy, and aided the matching of interview income data with IRF (income report form) data. Since then, the Seattle—Denver experiment has been highly successful in using a continuous history method and has incorporated some questions dealing with under- and overemployment and the reservation-wage phenomenon.

PECULIARITIES OF THE SAMPLE

As the study progressed, some concessions had to be made to the particular socioeconomic and ethnic characteristics of the sample in terms of question construction.

For example, interviews in Spanish were needed for about 8 percent of the sample (about 25 percent of the Puerto Rican sample). Although a number of interviewers were bilingual and capable of ad hoc translations, it was decided at the screening stage to translate the interviews, because standardization of translation was vastly preferable to on-the-spot translations by each interviewer. While the translations were generally recognized as indispensable, a few unexpected issues emerged.

Problems with idiomatic translations were dealt with by hiring a Puerto Rican translation reviewer. However, concepts did not translate well. Particularly in sociological and attitudinal questions, there seemed to be strong cultural biases and influences. For example, in the series on liberalism—conservatism, the respondent was asked to agree or disagree with a series of statements. One of these statements was to the effect that the government should not nationalize public utilities. For a sizable group of families who were newly arrived from Puerto Rico (where public utilities are nationalized) or who were unacquainted with the system in the United States, the question had no meaning. Similar cultural differences provided problems of comparability across the sample.

Since the interviewers were also Spanish-speaking, responses to questions were often written in Spanish. While the interviewers were instructed to make literal translations, some responses could not be translated easily, such as open-ended questions that were answered in Puerto Rican aphorisms. Since a number of these appeared, the coding department had to develop a rather extensive list of aphorisms along with literal translations and meanings. One question dealing with reasons families did not trust the news media generated the following list:

Con baila plata el mono.
Lit. trans.: "With silver the monkey dances."
Interpretation: People will sell themselves for money.

Perro que ladra no muerde.
Lit. trans.: "A dog that barks does not bite."
Interpretation: Those who talk do not act.

El que ha de morir a oscuras que no ande vendiendo velas.
Lit. trans.: "He who is to die in the dark, let him not go selling candles."
Interpretation: He who wants things to go his way must not go about hindering them.

Radio BEMBA dice mas.
Lit. trans.: "Radio LIPS says more."
Interpretation: One can get better information by word of mouth.

La mona, aunque se vista de seda, mona se queda.
Lit. trans.: "The monkey, whether or not dressed in silk, remains a monkey."
Interpretation: [self-explanatory]

El papel aguanta todo lo que le pongan.
Lit. trans.: "Paper will hold anything put on it."
Interpretation: "Paper" in such usage generally means toilet paper.

Hay quien habla por boca del ganso.
Lit. trans.: "There are some who talk by mouths of geese."
Interpretation: There are some who talk by using others and the mouth of others.

Another problem was difficulty with wording. Although many of the questions used in the experiment had been developed elsewhere for other batteries, pretesting and field experience provided ample evidence that for the families in our sample many polysyllabic words in the batteries had to be reduced to simpler ones. While conserving original wording is strongly supported by survey researchers, the percentage of families with limited vocabularies necessitated certain changes. If a wording proved particularly difficult to a family, the interviewer was forced to paraphrase. Preserving internal consistency required generally usable wording at the outset to forestall interviewers having to paraphrase individually.

Special Interviews

A number of special interviews were given to provide the answers on particular issues or to collect data that were not covered in the regular quarterly interviews.

THE SPECIAL PRE-ENROLLMENT AND MAKE-UP INTERVIEWS FOR NEW CONTROLS

When we decided to locate and enroll new control families in Trenton and Paterson–Passaic, special interviews had to be developed. The original screening interview was considered sufficient for screening purposes but the pre-enrollment interview was modified. Questions necessary to replicate the eligibility verification and stratification process used for the original sample, and all historical data collected on the original pre-enrollment interview, were retained, but data relating to current information were omitted unless time of administration coincided with on-going quarterly interviews. In addition, the family history sections from interviews that had already been administered in the respective cities were added to the special pre-enrollment interview (with the exception of a section on educational background which, due to the length of the special pre-enrollment interview in Paterson–Passaic, was administered later as a supplement to the regular sixth quarterly interview).

THE IN-DEPTH INTERVIEW

During January and February 1970, this interview was administered to a 10 percent subsample of experimental families, drawn at random in each of the five cities, to explore the question of program knowledge and to ascertain how certain administrative and methodological problems were viewed by the families. It was administered by members of the research staff, rather than by regular interviewers. Topics were discussed in an open-ended, conversational manner and included clarity of enroller's explanation of the program; timing, ease of filling out, and understanding of paystub and other requirements; the income report forms; understanding of payments calculation; reasons for attrition, if attrited; knowledge of maximum payment, breakeven point, length of program, affiliation and funding of the experiment, and effect of mobility on eligibility; attitudes toward experimentation; attitudes about need for program; and attitudes toward interviews.

ANNUAL-INCOME SUPPLEMENTARY INTERVIEW

Due to the lack of continuity in the income and work-history data gathered in the quarterly interviews, an annual-income questionnaire was developed. The purpose of the annual-income supplementary interview was to trace the work stream of each potential worker over the previous calendar year; to get an estimate of annual earnings; and to reiterate questions concerning outside sources of income—such as transfer payments, rental income, and windfalls (insurance benefits, for example). The supplement was administered every calendar year, along with the first interview of the year.

FAMILY COMPOSITION INTERVIEW

Near the end of the experiment, a special questionnaire was administered to pick up any within-quarter family composition changes that had been missed (particularly important for the control families, who did not report family composition every four weeks as did the treatment families on the income report forms).

TERMINATION INTERVIEW

An attempt was made to interview all experimental families who decided to leave the experiment. This interview was given immediately after the family dropped out, and was done by the local office manager. It was unstructured and covered such topics as the family's understanding of how the experiment worked, the family's opinion of the income-reporting and payments systems, their reasons for quitting, their views on a guaranteed income, and their opinions about the interviews and about experimentation in general. This interview was dropped in late 1970 for two reasons. Most families had made clear their reasons for leaving the program when contacted by the office managers in the regular course of events; and, further, many families were irritated about being interviewed yet again after they had made it clear they no longer wanted to participate.

THE THIRTEENTH QUARTERLY INTERVIEW

Based both on findings in the in-depth interview and on methodological questions not addressed in that or other interviews because of possible interactive effects, the thirteenth quarterly interview was developed to be administered approximately three months after cessation of payments. This interview was also designed to determine at least the short-run impact of the end of the experiment on families in the payments group. Three major topics were covered: (1) level of knowledge about the following experimental parameters—requirements for eligibility of payments, maximum payment possible under family plan, minimum payment possible under family plan, breakeven point, guarantee level, and effect of family composition on grant level, tax rates, and welfare rules; (2) effect of program on family—treatment of experimental money, budgeting patterns, problems caused by participation in experiment, perception of promptness and correctness of payments, demand for noncash services from experiment, communications with experimental staff, attitudes toward questionnaires, attitudes and activities related to end of experiment, and long-range effect of participation in experiment; and (3) reliability of reported income.

ATTRITION INTERVIEW

After the Trenton operation had been phased out, as described in Chapter 8, plans were made to locate and interview all families who had dropped out of the experiment. The attrition interview was begun in Trenton in May 1972, and in the other sites closely following the thirteenth quarterly interview. It covered income, work history patterns, and family composition during the period since the last completed interview. These were the factors expected to bias the results of the experiment most severely if the attrited group were found to differ significantly from the active group.

THE QUESTIONNAIRE-PROCESSING SYSTEM (QUEST)[5]

Much of the experimental budget and the energy of the staff were devoted to the processing of the questionnaires. The system developed in the experiment to process, store, and manipulate the data gathered on the various questionnaires required the employment of approximately five full-time data-processing professionals, four coders, four editors, and the use of an in-house IBM 1130 computer and remote terminals to enable the staff to work directly with the data stored on an IBM 360—65. This section contains an overview and brief description of the data-processing system.

Coding

The coding operation was an integrated system combining manual coding and keypunching operations. A Friden Flexowriter equipped with both a paper-tape reader and a paper-tape puncher was used. This system helped to guide coders through the coding of a questionnaire by a prompter tape prepared previously and positioned in the paper-tape reader. During this process, the information contained on the paper tape was typed by the Flexowriter, one line at a time.

---

[5] The QUEST system was designed and developed by Frank Mason, who led the data-processing team throughout the experiment.

Two types of information were contained on the line: (1) prompting information specifying to the coders what information to enter on the line and (2)
identifying information telling the processing programs what pieces of data were
on the line (the prompter number or list entry number described above).

By this process, the coding and punching operations were speeded up and
accuracy was increased. The machine paced the coder, controlling the work
flow. The coder observed the answers on the hard copy as they were typed, and
thus had an opportunity both to check them and to correct previously entered
information simply by re-entering it. This physical process of transferring accurate information to paper-tape—as opposed to transferring it to keypunched
cards through the traditional process of coding, keypunching, and verification—is
relatively cheap, allows easy retrieval of raw data, and minimizes storage space.
Figure 9.2 illustrates the data-entry and checking process employed in the
experiment.

Checking

A series of checking procedures was then undertaken: syntax checking, validity checking, logical-structure checking, and consistency checking.

SYNTAX CHECKING

This is performed for free-format input lines entered on paper tape or in the
interactive mode. If alphanumeric data are not enclosed in ampersands, the rest of
the input line is ignored. If ampersands are not paired, the entire input line is
ignored. If more answers are entered than are expected, the extra answers are
not processed. If more than the expected number of digits are entered for a
numeric answer, the rest of the line is not processed, assuming that a missing
comma might be the cause. Similarly, if an invalid character is processed, the line
is ignored. The syntax routine also verifies that the questionnaire header, which
relates the entire set of data to its internal description, has been processed;
otherwise, the program will not process the other lines.

VALIDITY CHECKING

Validity-error messages cause the answer in question not to be entered in the
data base. The validity limits are used to flag incorrectly coded answers (which
are not stored). They do not check for statistical outliers. For numeric answers,
any number of ranges may be specified (that is, an answer value should be
between zero and one or between nine and ten). Limits are always considered to
be closed intervals. For alphanumeric strings, a maximum number of characters

is the only validity check unless the answer is to be translated, as described below.

LOGICAL-STRUCTURE CHECKING

The logical-structure checking routine can begin at any point in the question-naire and continue checking up to any other point. It diagnoses whether or not all items that should be present are, in fact, present and spotlights items that are present but should not be. A code is available to accommodate questions that have no response but that should have been answered. Erroneously entered data can be removed from the record both during coding and in updating.

CONSISTENCY CHECKING

This level of error checking does not stop data from being inserted in the record but is used as a quality-control function to catch further errors and to

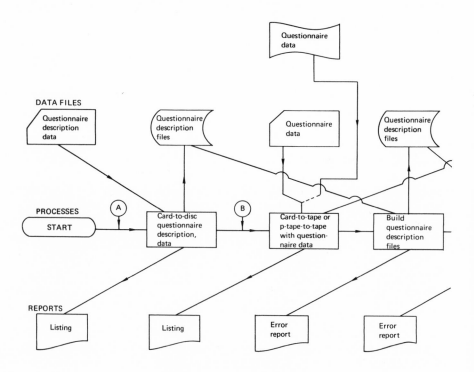

Figure 9.2 Data entry program.

provide researchers with estimates of error rates and outliers in the data. Any arithmetic expression combining answers, list entries, or constants may be included. Lists may also be operated on with the special operator "SUM." Logical expressions may be used to enhance further the checking ability.

Data Description

The programs in the system are controlled by a set of tables that describe the data. These tables include the following: (1) prompter table—indicates which answers are found in each line of answers in each prompting tape, and in what order they occur; (2) format table—describes the record types and the beginning and ending columns of each piece of data; (3) process table—describes each answer (whether it is numeric or alphanumeric; if numeric, the range limits for the acceptable values; if alphanumeric, the number of characters allowed); (4) skip table—defines the logical structure of a questionnaire (whether an answer is a simple answer, header, or part of the body of a list; whether the answer is a

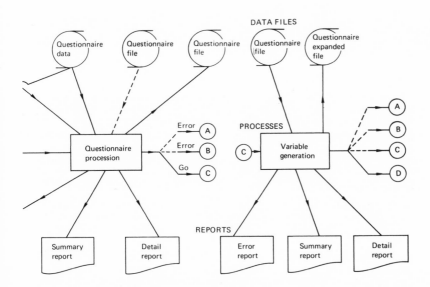

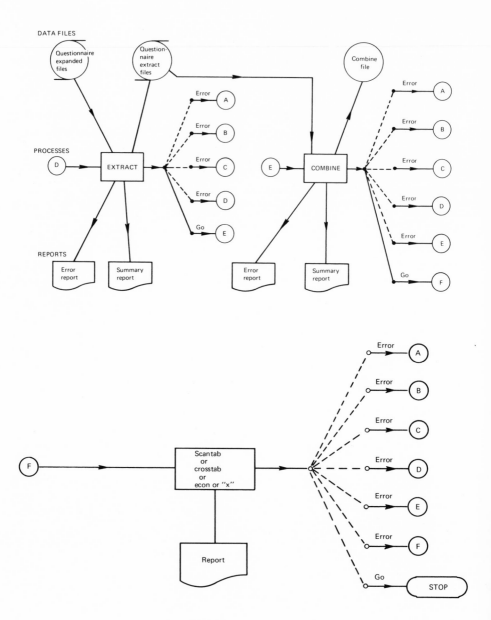

Figure 9.3 Data extract program.

146

multiple answer; whether, following any answer, it is possible to skip forward to another place in the questionnaire, and on what conditions); and (5) translation table—specifies whether or not, before processing is begun, the answers to any question are to be translated from alphanumeric strings into numeric codes or certain numeric codes are to be substituted for others.

After the data were entered and cleaned, they could be extracted for manipulation by a set of programs designed for report writing, cross-tabulation, and regression and other forms of analysis. Figure 9.3 illustrates the main elements of the extract system.

10

Contents of the survey instruments

The survey instruments used in the experiment consisted of a core of questions that were repeated at each quarter; a rotating group of questions, some of which appeared on an annual basis and some of which appeared semiannually, a few topics that appeared only at the beginning and end of the experiment, and some "once-only" topics. The questionnaires covered a wide range of economic and sociological topics. The key elements of the instruments are reviewed briefly here.

The topics are arranged within five major categories: work and income patterns; debts and assets; family life and background; political and social life; and scales and indicators covering various social, psychological, and political attitudes. Some topics in these categories overlap. Table 10.1 shows when the various sections were administered.

WORK AND INCOME PATTERNS

This area of questioning consisted of several topics: current labor-force status, income, job training, job history, wife's labor-force patterns, child care, and welfare history.

149

Table 10.1 Information Sought in Pre-Enrollment and Twelve Quarterly Interviews

	Pre	1	2	3	4	5	6	7	8	9	10	11	12
Work and income patterns													
Core (current labor-force status and earnings)	X	X	X	X	X	X	X	X	X	X	X	X	X
Cash benefits					X	X	X	X	X	X	X	X	X
Job training					X				X				X
Job history			X									X	
Wife's working pattern					X				X				X
Child care					X			X	X				X
Welfare history													X
Debts and assets													
Net worth	X	X		X			X	X			X		
Property ownership	X												
Insurance ownership	X		X^a		X^b				X^b				X^b
Cost of housing					X		X	X	X	X	X	X	X
Home improvement expenditures			X				X					X	
Meals and food expenditures			X					X				X	
Clothing and clothing expenditures			X					X				X	
Child-support paid out					X		X	X	X	X	X	X	X
Family life and background													
Family composition													X
Marital history												X	
Ideal family size, family planning, and fertility	X^c												X
Family integration	X			X		X		X		X		X	
Residential mobility					X				X		X		
Educational and occupational background of family and siblings		X^c										X^c	
Children's education		X			X				X				
Homework and chores			X					X					
Division of financial responsibility													X
Religion								X					

150

Table 10.1 (continued)

		Quarterly Interview											
	Pre	1	2	3	4	5	6	7	8	9	10	11	12
Hobbies, vacation, and leisure								X				X^c	
24-hour time budget				X									
Medical history		X				X^d			X^e		X^d		X^e
Family background								X			X		
Political and social life													
Political awareness and political integration	X^c	X^c				X^c				X^c			
Organizations	X			X		X				X			
Social network	X				X				X				X
Ethnic and racial composition of neighborhood								X					
Attitudinal scales and indicators													
Subjective social status and perceived social mobility	X				X^c				X^c				
Social desirability									X				
Self-esteem									X			X	
Conservatism–liberalism	X					X				X			
Worry and happiness	X					X				X			
Anomie–future control	X					X				X			
Time-horizon and future events								X					
Indicators of psychological instability										X			
Ammons and Ammons Quick Test (IQ)													X
Attitudes toward work	X				X				X				X
Job satisfaction					X				X				X

[a]Medical.

[b]Life.

[c]Subset of questions asked in this interview.

[d]Of husband and wife.

[e]Of children.

Current Labor-Force Status and Earnings (Core Questions). The core questions appeared in every quarterly interview and solicited detailed information on the current labor-force status of each adult. Data from these formed the backbone of the labor-supply analysis and cost projections. This battery originally replicated the Current Population Survey (CPS), which covered the following general areas: whether or not the person was in the labor force; if not in the labor force, what the reason was (for example, ill, taking care of children, student); if in the labor force, whether or not the person held a job; if not holding a job, the methods and intensity of the job search; if holding a job, the place and type of employment, hours supplied, wage income, and method and cost of transportation to work.

These questions, originally, were asked only for the week preceding the interview. Converting the CPS "snapshot" labor-supply and income data to an annual basis, however, gave no information on how the person's income flow was changing over time. Later, the experiment focused attention on the dynamics of labor supply, which necessitated an overhaul of the CPS battery in the middle of the experiment, as described in the previous chapter. One important issue that emerged during the experiment, for example, was that of the time period over which income should be counted in calculating the transfer payment.[1] It was recognized for the first time that patterns of earnings over a year can enormously affect the patterns and amounts of transfer payments due families, which in turn have major implications for the costs of a national program.

Cash Benefits. In addition to labor supply, a short section of each quarterly questionnaire was devoted to cash benefits. This section asked questions about the amounts and sources of income other than wages, such as Aid to Families with Dependent Children (AFDC), other public assistance, Workmen's Compensation, Unemployment Insurance, and Social Security. This information was needed to compare income levels, assess additive tax problems, and discover the extent to which families were dependent upon wage income.

Job Training. A rotating section on job training (type, length, intensity, and cost) was added to discover the extent to which earners trapped in dead-end or unskilled-labor jobs would use the security offered by the experiment to train for higher-paying or better jobs.

Job History. Questions regarding the total length of time people had spent in the labor force and eliciting descriptions of jobs they had held longest, liked

---

[1] See Chapter 4 of this volume.

best, and were paid the most for, were used to provide information on normal (or usual) income, previous job mobility, and education and training. These questions were modified from work history batteries currently in use by the Census Bureau.

Wife's Labor-force Pattern. While the experiment was too short for us to learn much about its long-term effects on female labor supply and our sample prevented us from collecting information on the behavior of female family heads, we thought it important to get some information on married women's working patterns prior to the experiment and during it, to assess the degree of change induced by the experiment. Questions about the extent to which a woman had worked before marriage, after marriage but before the first child, and between children, and about any special restrictions on working hours related to children's ages, provided this background information.

Child Care. The cost and availability of adequate child-care arrangements were felt to be extremely important to women's labor supply. Lack of acceptable care might be a factor inpeding entry into the labor force, and the cost of acceptable care would raise the cost to the woman of working as opposed to staying at home and looking after the children herself, particularly when women's earnings were also taxed by the experiment.

For women committed to working, it was felt to be of interest to know whether experimental payments would be used to purchase better child care; thus, questions about the type of care utilized and about expenditures on care were also asked.

Welfare History. Families that had had experience with welfare were felt to be of special interest for several reasons. First, the experimenters wanted to determine the extent to which "welfare families" had an intrinsically different behavioral response to the treatment. That is, were families with extensive welfare experience self-selected into or affected behaviorally by a welfare system that treated work effort unevenly and unpredictably, or would they respond "normally" to the payments? Second, did experience in dealing with a bureaucracy help or hinder welfare families in dealing with the experiment in terms of income reporting and adherence to rules affecting eligibility and payments levels?

DEBTS AND ASSETS

Items in this area were included for three broadly defined purposes: (1) to help determine the extent of any "time horizon" problem by seeing whether families treated experimental payments differently from regular income; (2) to see what kinds of decisions were made in regard to expenditures and savings; (3) to assess the extent to which families might be financially hurt by cessation of payments.

Net Worth. This section consisted of an accounting of consumer durables owned by families, and their equity in the items. The section was used to see whether families treated experimental payments as "funny money," that is, by making purchases of goods that they would not normally buy and that control families at comparable income levels did not buy. It was anticipated that this section could be used as a method of auditing income-reporting accuracy. Such an audit was later rejected since the amounts of net worth were too small to detect any marginal increases that might be due to unreported income; and in any case there was considerable guesswork involved in estimating the value of items and in recalling their prices and the amounts still owed on them.

Property Ownership. This battery estimated equity and debt service on real property.

Insurance Ownership. Insurance purchasing is simply another form of savings—one that is common and important among low-income families. Data on insurance ownership were necessary for "closure"[2] on debts and assets data.

Cost of Housing. This section included questions on rental contract amounts, utilities and furniture, number of rooms, and subsidies. There were two reasons for asking these questions: first, to help obtain closure on expenditures data and, second, to provide sufficient information on the cost of housing to make rent imputations for homeowners and those in subsidized housing (as described in Chapter 4).

Home-Improvement Expenditures. These data were used to update the value of owner-occupied housing and to help obtain closure on expenditures data. They included descriptions of major improvements and their costs.

Meals and Food Expenditures. This section rounded out expenditures data and provided information on the purchase of leisure and on family organization. Questions concerned the frequency of eating out, estimates of food expenditures, the numbers of family members regularly eating at home, and the roles of

---

[2] "Closure" refers to obtaining a completely closed system, that is, accounting for all income reported in the sum of expenditures and savings.

various members in meal preparation. (The latter tied into other sections to provide data on changes in family roles and responsibilities during the experiment.)

Clothing and Clothing Expenditures. These questions related to the general distribution of expenditures and family roles. They asked about overall levels of clothing expenditures for male head, female head, and children, as well as which members had main purchasing responsibility.

Child Support Paid Out. Child support and alimony paid to people outside the family were treated as "deductions" from income.

FAMILY LIFE AND BACKGROUND

Most family life and background questions were designed to provide "intervening variables"[3] for various sociological analyses, and to assess the impact of the experiment on family organization and purchase of leisure time.

Family Composition. At each quarterly interview, families were asked to bring us up-to-date on the movement of people into and out of the household. This information was needed for administrative purposes and to provide data on the impact of experimental payments on family stability. (There were conflicting hypotheses regarding family stability: One was that families would tend to remain together during times of financial crisis because the experiment, unlike welfare, would make payments to families with adult males present; the other was that families would tend to break up because the experiment provided support for remaining members and relieved the financial strain of breaking up.)

Marital History. Previous marital patterns were assumed to be a strong influence on current and future marital stability; the experiment wanted to measure any differential in marriage breakups during the payment period, because such an effect could have a major impact on the costs of a national program.

Ideal Family Size, Family Planning, and Fertility. One concern in any transfer program conditioned on family size is the impact of the treatment on decisions to bear children. In a short-term experiment, there was also concern with the extent to which the *temporarily* lowered opportunity cost of child-

---

[3] An "intervening variable" is one that, because of its effect on a respondent, changes his response to the treatment. For example, the different levels of education of experimental respondents could be expected to cause differential responses to the same treatment.

bearing might inflate the actual effects of a national program. That is, adding an extra child to the family raised the experimental payment to the family, but only, of course, over the period of the experiment. This might lead women to shorten the space between children and bear a child—a child they would in any case have planned—at some time during the experimental period, rather than after. Such an effect would lead the experiment to overestimate the effect of the income-maintenance program on total family size, because, in fact, extra children were not added to households; expected children were simply added earlier. The questions in this section were drawn largely from a Princeton study[4] and asked about the number of additional children desired by sample families and birth-control patterns before and during the experiment, as well as inquiring about fertility, using such standard measures as total live births and total miscarriages.

Family Integration. This section asked about the frequency with which families enjoyed leisure activities together. It was hypothesized that earners whose general wage rates were low might use the payments to replace second jobs or overtime hours. If they did, it was of interest to learn how families spent these extra hours. Investment in either human capital or increased family recreation time were considered "beneficial" social outcomes.

Residential Mobility. Questions regarding the region and type of place (such as large city, farm) in which respondents grew up, and the frequency with which they moved, provided information valuable in controlling for experimental effects. For instance, region of origin could be an important factor in interpreting the relationship of educational level to earnings, because the quality of education varies by region. A second reason was to provide an additional control for mobility during the experiment. Would payments "free up" labor mobility— that is, would they allow people to move where better employment opportunities exist? Would they encourage families to move for noneconomic reasons because the families would be supported by the program even in a poor labor market? Or would payments have no effect? To answer these questions it was essential to know the mobility patterns of the families before the experiment.

Educational Background, Siblings' Education and Occupation. Several well-known studies have found that the educational and occupational success of a person's parents and siblings are often strong influences on his or her own occupational success. These variables were measured in order to control for exogenous factors in wage-rate differentials.

[4]C. Westoff, R. Potter, Jr., P. Sagi, and E. Mishler, *Family Growth in Metropolitan America* (Princeton, N.J.: Princeton University Press, 1961).

Children's Education. This section consisted of a few questions about the aspirations of parents for their children in regard to education and occupation. One sociological hypothesis regarding the impact of a negative tax system was that the nonjudgmental, regular nature of the payments would result in an increased feeling of control over one's life. Change in aspirations would be one clue that this outcome had occurred.

Children's Homework and Chores. It was crucial to try to determine the extent to which people actually made changes in behavior when they had expressed verbally their intention of doing so. These questions were intended to indicate whether or not families set up situations conductive to attaining their goals. The questions asked whether place and hours of doing homework had changed, and how, and about changes in the regularity and extent of chores.

Division of Financial Responsibility. Changes in the extent to which both partners participated in the financial affairs of the household were considered useful indications of work and expenditure patterns induced by the experiment.

Religion. A few questions were asked concerning religious preferences, to determine the impact of this facet of culture on propensity to work. For example, did people reduce work effort less when their religion strongly emphasized the work ethic? The attitude of the particular religion toward birth control was also expected to influence fertility behavior.

Hobbies, Vacations, and Leisure. Data about the purchase of leisure time and the structure and direction of leisure-time activities were of major sociological importance in shedding light on family cohesiveness and stability. There were even broader implications if people who traditionally had not been able to afford it, now permitted themselves significant amounts of leisure time.

Twenty-Four-Hour Time Budget. The primary purpose of the comprehensive measurement of the use of time by various family members was to get a "true" labor-supply response—that is, the time spent not only in paid work at the job, but also in work around the house. A secondary reason for these questions was to gain additional information on family cohesion. Initially tested measures of family cohesion had two flaws: They did not adequately show *which* members of the family were spending time together and, more importantly, they made no progress toward understanding the *quality* of time spent together. That is, a parent might say that several hours a day were spent with the children but not distinguish the proportion of time spent in active communication versus simply being in the same house. Several alternate methods of tapping quality were pretested, but none proved to be satisfactory. The answer seemed to be a time budget that accurately measured the activities of each individual. With this it would also be possible to determine which other individuals were present during any activity.

Medical History. The impact of health upon labor supply was a potentially major intervening variable. Moreover, medical expenditures accounted for a sizable portion of total expenditures and were therefore essential to the expenditures breakdown.

Questions included the nature and extent of disabilities; numbers, lengths, and costs of hospitalizations; numbers of physician and dental visits and their costs; and such general indicators of health status as work-loss days and bed days due to sickness. These questions were adapted from standard disability indicators on the National Health Interview Survey.[5] They proved too lengthy and were truncated in the tenth and twelfth quarterly interviews to include only the most important cost and health-status indicators for the male and female heads and for the oldest and youngest children.

Family Background. This section consisted of standard measures of parental contact: whether the respondent grew up with either or both of his natural parents, whether he grew up with a male or a female guardian present, and the number of his siblings. These correlate with sociopsychological characteristics manifested in later life.

POLITICAL AND SOCIAL LIFE

The extent to which people spent more time with their families as a result of the tax payments was one of two indicators of "social good" that might be derived from expanded leisure time. The other was greater participation in the community. Several sets of questions dealt with the type of participation exercised in community affairs.

Political Awareness and Political Integration. These two scales were designed to measure changes in political participation over time. A political awareness scale asked respondents to identify local, state, and national public figures. (It showed some differences by city but was unsuccessful in general since the number of correct responses in all cities was extremely low.) Political integration was measured by an attitudinal scale of items designed to elicit in what ways the respondent thought political power was achieved and whether the respondent

[5] A series of annual surveys conducted by the Census for the National Center for Health Statistics, Department of Health, Education, and Welfare.

felt that he and people in his neighborhood could influence decisions if they got together.

Organizations. Organizational participation has been used as an indicator of social participation for middle-class families for some time. Whether organizational memberships would increase, decrease, or remain the same for the experimental sample was, therefore, of some interest. The questions were not successful because there was never much formal membership for our sample, other than in PTAs and church groups. Unfortunately, neither the existence of informal community groups nor the barriers to group participation by low-income people were anticipated to be important, and they were not adequately addressed in the instruments.

Social Network. Extended families and close ties with friends were also chosen as indicators of stability, both family and residential. Families were asked how many people in the area they knew on a first-name basis, how many of their relatives lived in the area, and the frequency with which they visited with relatives, friends, and colleagues.

Ethnic and Racial Composition of Neighborhood. Families were asked their perceptions of the proportion in their neighborhoods of various ethnic and racial groups. They were also asked their perceptions of changes in the proportions of these groups over time. The purpose of these questions was to serve as a proxy for actual change and to determine the extent to which the changing characteristics of their neighbors influenced a family's participation in neighborhood or community groups.

ATTITUDINAL SCALES AND INDICATORS

A wide variety of sociopsychological scales was administered, both to provide descriptive data on the effect of poverty upon attitudes and to assess change in attitudes over time as a result of the experiment.

Subjective Social Status and Perceived Social Mobility. Many of the scales and indicators were directed toward providing alternative measures of efficacy and fate control. The Subjective Social Status Scale asked people to describe their social class (upper, upper-middle, middle, working, or lower). The scale was not repeated because very little variance was found. The Perceived Social Mobility Scale asked people to picture a ladder of ten steps, the first representing the worst way of life and the tenth representing the best. They were then asked the step they were on now, five years ago, and when growing up; what step they expected to be on in five years, and what step they expected their children to be on.

Social Desirability. One of the problems in using questionnaire data is that people often try to respond, consciously or unconsciously, in a way that they think will enhance, or at least not damage, their image. This is a phenomenon that psychologists refer to as social-desirability response bias. To attempt to control for this type of bias, ten items from the Crowne–Marlowe social-desirability scale were used.[6] This scale includes two types of items. The first consists of negatively regarded traits that are true of almost everyone, such as, "There have been times when I felt like smashing things," and "There have been times when I was very jealous of the good luck of others." The second consists of positively regarded traits that are literally true of almost no one, such as, "I always like everyone I meet," and "I'm always willing to admit it when I make a mistake." If an individual says that the first type of item is false in his case and that the second type of item is true, there is a strong possibility that his answers are distorted by social-desirability bias.[7]

Self-Esteem. This scale was one of the measures of efficacy. The scale asked respondents to agree strongly, agree, disagree, or disagree strongly with a short series of statements like "I feel I am a person of worth." It was hypothesized that high self-esteem would correlate with such behavioral factors as success in the labor force and family stability; also, that self-esteem might tend to increase among former welfare recipients because of the nondiscretionary nature of the experimental treatment and, for poor families not previously eligible for any financial assistance, because of the increased income at their disposal.

Conservatism–Liberalism. This scale, which consisted of agree–disagree statements on the role of government, was intended to assess the impact of basic political beliefs upon work ethic (and, therefore, work response), and upon attitudes toward the experiment. The scale met with difficulty among recent immigrants, who did not understand the questions, and seemed outdated—decentralization, for example, has come to seem more "liberal" than "big government."

Worry and Happiness. The worry scale asked people to respond (worry a lot, a little, not too much) to a brief list of reasons for worry (money, bringing up children, health, and jobs). The intent was to discover shifts in the problems of

[6] D. P. Crowne and D. Marlowe, "A New Scale of Social Desirability Independent of Psychopathology," *Journal of Consulting Psychology* 24 (1960): 349–354.
[7] See Russell Middleton, "Initial Social Psychological Outcomes in the Rural Experiment." Paper presented at the Meeting of the American Sociological Association, August 1972.

experimental families. Were money or jobs replaced by other issues as reasons for worry? To what extent did the experiment provide enough financial stability to shift these patterns?

The happiness scale consisted of a single question asking whether respondents were very happy, fairly happy, or not too happy. Replies of unhappiness may be considered as one component of alienation from the social system. The attempt was to see whether people whose incomes had increased as a result of the treatment attained higher levels of happiness or personal satisfaction with their lives.

Anomie and Future Control. The McClosky and Schaar anomie scale was used.[8] It consisted of agree–disagree statements concerning whether or not the respondent felt "untied" from society or confused by changes in social structure. Again, the focus was on efficacy—the respondent's confidence in his or her ability to deal with the world. The scale, which was drawn from older studies, was less than satisfactory—shocking, for example, some black participants with statements like, "People were better off in the old days when everyone knew just how he was expected to act."

The future-control scale dealt with a person's attitudes concerning his or her ability to plan ahead and the extent to which circumstances were perceived to be arbitrary and impossible to predict. It consisted of agree–disagree items such as, "Nowadays, a person has to live pretty much for today and let tomorrow take care of itself."

Time Horizon and Future Events. One potential source of bias in the experiment was the fact that participants might react differently to a three-year experiment than to a lifetime program. They might, for instance, remain in the labor force during the experiment in anticipation of having difficulty finding a job when the study ended. In a national program, they might never have to look for work again. These two scales were designed to determine whether the three-year period of the experiment extended beyond the "planning horizon" of families in the study. The questions dealt with what events families were looking forward to and planning for. To the extent that their horizon approached three years or extended beyond three years, the length of the study could be expected not to bias results.

Psychological Instability. The Mid-Town Manhattan Study[9] developed a series of physical (psychosomatic) symptoms that correlate with mental illness.

---

[8] H. McClosky and J. Schaar, "Psychological Dimensions of Anomy," *American Sociological Review* 30 (1965): 14–40.

[9] L. Strole et al., *Mental Health in the Metropolis: The Mid-Town Manhattan Study* (New York: McGraw-Hill, 1962).

Questions from this study were incorporated into the experimental questionnaires to enable us to assess the prevalence and intensity of psychological problems in the sample and to determine the effect of these problems on work patterns and family stability and their relationship to poverty.

Ammons and Ammons Quick Test. This vocabulary test has been validated on standard IQ tests and was used to provide an additional proxy for education, given the regional and language differences in our "years of education" measure. The test consisted of the respondent's associating a graduated series of words read by the interviewer with four pictures on a card. Despite its validation, some cultural biases were identified. For instance, one of the words on the test, "respectful," was frequently associated by families with a picture of people dancing *very* far apart, rather than with a picture of a traffic policeman, which was the "correct" answer. The test had several administrative problems. Some respondents were aggravated by "game-playing" or "testing"; and there was some ambiguity concerning reasons for lack of comprehension. Pronunciation practice was conducted with interviewers to ensure that all words were pronounced the same way to all respondents, although it was suspected that, even so, some respondents missed words that they would have understood in their own accents.

Attitudes toward Work. This agree–disagree scale was designed to test the strength of the "work ethic" among respondents. It was used to determine what factors held people in low-paying or unrewarding jobs, and whether people who were not able to find jobs felt committed to working.

Job Satisfaction. This scale asked respondents to rate the facets of work—such as job security, high pay, and interesting work—that were most important. It was used for two reasons: (1) to determine whether or not, over time, people in the experiment found more satisfactory work (perhaps by using experimental payments to cushion the expense of job search); and (2) to determine whether people's definitions of job satisfaction changed in the course of the experiment. The former might result in temporary reductions in work effort; the latter would be reflected in changes in the rating of factors considered most important in a job.[10]

---

[10] See A. Kornhauser, *Mental Health of the Industrial Worker* (New York: John Wiley, 1965).

part III
Administrative issues

11

Auditing and verifying reports from families

There were four major types of audits performed throughout the experiment: (1) the operational audit, (2) the welfare audit, (3) a comparison of the payments data with federal tax returns, and (4) a comparison of the quarterly data with Social Security records on each family. The first three audits were applied to the experimental group only and were designed to deter as well as to detect and measure misreporting. The Social Security audit applied to both the experimental and the control groups and was designed to measure misreporting on an aggregate basis.

THE OPERATIONAL AUDIT[1]

The central consideration in the operational audit was that it be conducted with only those tools available in a national income-maintenance program. Specifically, this meant that instruments or persons related strictly to experimental research (that is, interviews or interviewers) were not valid sources for evidence of fraud.

[1] The "operational audit" was conducted by Kathleen Roche, Michaelyn Olsen, and Anne Freeman, and results were tabulated by Anne Freeman.

Legitimate sources of potentially incriminating information were considered to be (1) a suspicious entry or omission on an income report form (such as the sudden omission of a regularly received source of income), (2) a report from a public official that one of the families had defrauded the experiment (usually the observation of unreported income), (3) an observation by field staff (*not* interviewers) that a participant had broken the rules (such as working or wearing a working uniform while reporting no job), (4) public information (such as a newspaper article), and (5) data from the Internal Revenue Service (IRS) (W-2 and/or 1040 forms).

Sources considered *not* legitimate under any circumstances included the following: (1) observation of fraud by interviewers or other research personnel and (2) compromising information on the interviews.

Sources treated on an ad hoc basis were complaints from neighbors or members of the general public about a family. In these cases, the office manager or a staff member in Princeton examined the complaint in detail before deciding whether or not to take action.

Cases of suspected fraud were reported to the field-office manager for further inquiry. If upon investigation it appeared that nothing was wrong, the manager filed a brief report and the case was dismissed. If there was evidence of misreporting, a more detailed report was filed with the secretary of the audit-review panel.

The panel had five members—the project director, the project administrator, the field supervisor, the payments supervisor, and a member of the research staff. The panel convened approximately every six weeks. Prior to the meeting, the files on the cases to be presented were circulated among the members of the panel. At the meeting, the payments assistant and office manager from the relevant site were available for consultation. If more information was needed, the case was referred back to the field. Otherwise, a vote was taken, with a three-vote majority required for a ruling. The five designations that a case could be assigned were the following: (1) audited and dismissed; (2) filing problem; (3) possible fraud; (4) probable fraud; or (5) confirmed fraud.

When the designation indicated the need, one of the following actions was then taken: Future payments were reduced until all overpayments were recaptured; overpayments were added onto the family's income so that future payments were lowered accordingly; or the family's relationship with the experiment was terminated—very rarely done.

A major drawback to all these corrective procedures was the potential damage to the experiment. There were three main concenrs about reducing payments: first, that it meant interfering with the treatment; second, that it might eliminate the incentive for families to remain in the experiment; third, that families with no outside income might be forced onto welfare. Any of these outcomes would leave the experiment with less information on the families.

Thus, the action finally decided upon when a case was judged to be a confirmed fraud was to reconstruct the correct information for the past and threaten the families with expulsion for a second offense. Only after a proven second offense for the same type of misreporting was the more punitive action of a reduction in payments taken. Even then, families could appeal the decision of the audit-review panel by taking their case to the review board.

This three-member panel was set up to rule on disputed decisions. The operating rules of the review board—which never had to be called upon—provided that after a second offense the office manager was to inform the family of the corrective action decided upon and of their right of appeal. In the case of an appeal, all corrective action was to be suspended pending the outcome of the ruling by the review board.

The operating rules of the review board provided that the hearing was to be conducted by one member of the review board and was to be attended by the recipient, a representative of the recipient's choice, and any witness with information bearing on the case. The hearing was to be conducted informally, and the decision of the hearing officer was to be committed to writing and submitted to the other two members of the board for approval.

Results of the Operational Audit

Over the course of the experiment, 165 families were audited because of suspected misreporting. Their distribution by site and type of ruling can be seen in Table 11.1 Forty-four families were given a ruling of "probable fraud," and thirty-seven a ruling of "confirmed fraud."[2]

The number and percentage of cases of probable or confirmed fraud from the operational audit, by experimental-plan characteristics, education of head, and city can be seen in Table 11.2. There is very little variation in this percentage for most characteristics. The chi-squared test for goodness of fit was calculated for each of the characteristics. The only significant result (at the 5 percent level) was for city. It is difficult to generalize from this finding, however, since ethnic origin and age differed among cities, as did the aggressiveness of the local office manager in following up possible fraud—an important factor.

The distribution of the reason for the audit is shown in Table 11.3. The

---

[2] The confirmed fraud number will be biased and an underestimate, because the 1040 form was the primary source of fraud confirmation and certain families did not submit copies of their tax forms to us. The fraud numbers will be further underestimated for the following reasons. No operating program concerned with disbursement of collection can expect to detect every instance of dishonesty. Those who defraud in a consistent way—such that their forms show no obvious irregularities and the income source they fail to report (for example) is always omitted and has no independent source of official verification—are less likely to be conspicuous and therefore less likely to be flagged for investigation.

Table 11.1 Number of Families Audited in Each City Because of Possible Fraud, by Type of Ruling

Type of ruling	Trenton	Passaic	Paterson	Jersey City	Scranton	All Cities
Dismissed	2	1	2	1	3	9
Filing problem	6	6	5	10	10	37
Possible fraud	4	2	6	16	10	38
Probable fraud	2	8	5	24	5	44
Confirmed fraud	7	7	5	12	6	37
Total	*21*	*24*	*23*	*63*	*34*	*165*

NOTE: For families with more than one audit, each case is counted separately.

Table 11.2 Number and Percentage of Cases of Probable or Confirmed Fraud from Operational Audit, by Plan Characteristics, Education of Head, and City

	Families	
	Number	Percentage
Guarantee (percent)		
50	14	11.8
75	30	9.8
100	19	11.8
125	18	13.0
Tax rate (percent)		
30	21	13.8
50	42	10.3
70	18	11.0
Income Stratum		
I	19	10.2
II	31	10.8
III	31	11.7
Education of head (years)		
0–7	18	9.5
8	15	14.2
9–11	33	11.7
12	14	11.0
13	1	10.0
City		
Trenton	9	10.3
Paterson	10	6.1
Passaic	15	13.3
Jersey City	36	18.2
Scranton	11	6.7

168

Table 11.3 Number and Percentage of Cases Audited, by Category of Reporting Irregularity

			Reporting Irregularity			
	Change in Family Size	Interest Income	Rental Income	Male Head's Earnings and Other Miscellaneous Transfers	Female Head's Earnings[a]	Other Secondary Earner's Earnings[a]	Total
Type of Ruling							
Filing problem	3	9	7	12	2(2)	4	37(2)
Possible fraud	1	0	1	30	6(1)	0	38(1)
Probable fraud	1	0	0	35	7(5)	1	44(5)
Confirmed fraud	0	0	4	23	8(4)	2(1)	37(5)
Total	*5*	*9*	*12*	*100*	*23(12)*	*7(1)*	*156(13)*
Percentage of experimental families reporting information in relevant category[b]	25.5	3.7	4.3	93.4	19.3	12.9	
Percentage of preceeding line audited because of reporting irregularities	2.7	33.3	38.7	14.8	16.4	7.5	

[a]Numbers in paretheses indicate cases where the male head's income *and* another earner's income were *each* reported incorrectly; such cases are recorded under the category of male head's earnings and appear in the other earner's column only in parentheses.

[b]These numbers are for one year (1970), so they are underestimates for the three-year period of the experiment. The income figures are calculated from the special interview that asked for 1970 annual income. For example, 25.5 is the percentage of families reporting a change in family size in any of the quarterly interviews during 1970; 3.7 is the percentage of experimental families that reported some interest income on the annual income supplementary interview in 1970.

169

numbers in parentheses represent cases where the male head's income *and* another earner's income were each reported incorrectly; such cases are recorded under the category of male head's earnings and appear in the other earnings column only in parentheses. An estimate of the relative frequency of misreporting of various income sources is provided, thereby producing some guidelines for emphasis in future audits. It is interesting to note that the most complex aspect of the experiment's rules—the rules regarding which persons were eligible to be counted as part of the family for purposes of the payment—provided the lowest incidence of misreporting.

THE WELFARE AUDIT

A series of regular quarterly checks was instituted with the welfare boards to minimize overlapping payments. Although the procedures varied slightly by site, the basic procedure was the same. Every three months, the office manager arranged to meet with a representative of the community's welfare board to compare rosters. In cases of overlap, information on the amounts and dates of payments was exchanged. Families discovered to be misreporting receipt of welfare payments then entered the regular operational audit process described earlier. The number of families audited for unreported welfare payments is given in Table 11.4; Table 11.5 shows the number and percentage of cases of probable or confirmed fraud from the welfare audit, by plan, stratum, education of head, and city. The percentages show very little variation, and none of the differences are significant. The low rates for the highest guarantee level and the highest stratum reflect the fact that there were very few welfare families in those cells.

As in the case of city differences in the operational audit, it is difficult to make generalizations about differences by city in the welfare audit. Each county

Table 11.4 **Number of Families Audited in Each City Because of Unreported Welfare Payments, by Type of Ruling**

Type of ruling	Trenton	Passaic	Paterson	Jersey City	Scranton	All Cities
Dismissed	2	4	14	1	0	21
Filing problem	7	2	5	7	2	23
Possible fraud	0	2	0	3	2	7
Probable fraud	0	1	0	1	1	3
Confirmed fraud	9	12	20	31	12	84
Total	*18*	*21*	*39*	*43*	*17*	*138*

NOTE: For families with more than one audit, each case is counted separately.

Table 11.5 Number and Percentage of Cases of
Probable or Confirmed Fraud from Welfare Audit,
by Plan Characteristics, Income Stratum, Education
of Head, and City

	Families	
	Number	Percentage
Guarantee (percent)		
50	13	10.9
75	42	13.7
100	23	14.3
125	9	6.5
Tax rate (percent)		
30	23	15.1
50	42	10.3
70	22	13.4
Income Stratum		
I	24	13.7
II	40	14.0
III	23	8.7
Education of head (years)		
0–7	22	11.6
8	11	10.4
9–11	38	13.4
12	16	12.6
13	0	0.0
City		
Trenton	9	10.3
Paterson	13	11.5
Passaic	20	12.3
Jersey City	32	16.2
Scranton	13	7.9

was a different welfare jurisdiction, with different administrative procedures and varying degrees of cooperation. Trenton and Scranton, for example, were well-organized and cooperative. Passaic County (Paterson and Passaic sites) was uncooperative and badly organized. The intervention of the state welfare office was required to gain the cooperation of Jersey City. And, once in, we found its files were kept in a mysterious system that yielded a virtually random chance of detecting misreporting on the first check. It is to the credit of the persistence of the experiment's Jersey City office manager that cases of misreporting were detected and remedied.

COMPARISON OF INCOME REPORTED
TO THE INTERNAL REVENUE SERVICE AND
TO THE EXPERIMENT

In order for the experiment to reimburse families for certain federal income taxes paid, it was necessary for the families to file copies of their W-2 and 1040 forms.[3] This reimbursement system made possible a comparison of Internal Revenue Service (IRS) information with income reported to the experiment. If the comparison showed a family to have reported 15 percent more income for the same period to IRS, the family entered the operational audit process.

Table 11.6 shows comparative data for wages and salaries for 1970, the year used for the IRS audit and the only year for which all cities had complete income data. The data are based on the number of families with complete tax information as submitted on W-2 or 1040 forms, or both, and include families who reported zero income and said they received no tax forms, having no earnings. In 1970, less than 13 percent of units with complete tax information reported more income to IRS than to the experiment.

COMPARISON OF INCOME REPORTED
TO THE SOCIAL SECURITY ADMINISTRATION AND
TO THE EXPERIMENT

The Social Security audit was done by the Social Security Administration, using data supplied by the experiment. It was a comparison, on an aggregate basis, of earnings reported on the annual income supplement (AIS) with earnings reported to the Social Security Administration for 1970. It was done for the male and female heads of families in both the experimental and the control groups. The total sample of 1891 was composed of those individuals whose Social Security numbers were known.

We gave data on the earnings and family characteristics of these individuals to the Social Security Administration. They prepared tables showing the distribution of these individuals by characteristic: (1) those who reported the same earnings to both Social Security and the experiment; (2) those who reported more to the experiment; and (3) those who reported more to Social Security. These tables were further broken down by the percentage of over- or underreporting.

The main finding of the Social Security audit was that earnings were generally underreported to the experiment, as compared to Social Security, both for experimentals and for controls. This is not unexpected, since Social Security

---

[3] Not all families were reimbursed for all taxes (see Chapter 4).

Table 11.6 Comparison of Wages and Salaries Reported to the Internal Revenue Service and to the Experiment, 1970, by City

	Number of Completed Returns (1)	Income Reported to Experiment (2)	Income Reported to IRS (3)	Difference (3−2) (4)	Percentage Difference (4/2) (5)	Mean Income Reported to Experiment (2/1) (6)	Mean Income Reported to IRS (3/1) (7)	Difference (7−6) (8)	Families Reporting at Least 15 Percent More to IRS Than to Experiment	
									Number (9)	Percentage of (1) (10)
Trenton	58	$ 285,093.67	$ 293,129.36	$ 8,035.69	2.8	$4,915.41	$5,053.95	$138.54	8	13.8
Paterson–Passaic	181	681,031.78	722,473.36	41,441.58	6.1	3,762.61	3,991.57	228.96	31	17.1
Jersey City	143	771,349.56	810,219.09	38,869.53	5.0	5,394.05	5,665.87	271.82	17	11.9
Scranton	161	726,077.42	742,594.02	16,516.60	2.3	4,509.80	4,612.39	102.59	14	8.7
All cities	543	2,463,552.43	2,567,866.38	104,313.95	4.2	4,536.93	4,729.04	192.11	70	12.9

173

information is collected at the source, whereas the experiment collected information on a questionnaire that asked for recall data—in this case, income for the previous year. About 20 percent of the families in the sample misreported by 15 percent or more, in contrast to the more limited IRS audit described above, which indicated that only about 13 percent of the families had a reporting inconsistency as large as 15 percent.

An important finding is that the control and experimental families reported similarly across all categories. Control families obviously achieved no financial advantage from underreporting to the experiment and had no real incentive to do so. Much of the misreporting for both experimentals and controls, therefore, can probably be ascribed to error or a lack of comprehension, rather than to any intention to defraud.

Table 11.7 shows the percentage of all family heads who reported more income to Social Security than to the experiment, by sex of head and size of discrepancy. (The majority of the discrepancies were less than 10 percent, so the absolute amounts involved were small.) The numbers for female heads can be seen to be much smaller than those for males heads. This is largely attributable to the fact that there were rather few female heads who worked, and that, by definition, those with no earnings showed no discrepancy.

Table 11.8 shows, for those male heads who did have earnings, the percentage, by various characteristics, that reported more earnings to Social Security, as compared to the total with discrepancies. Female heads are omitted from these comparisons because their absolute number was small. Those who reported *exactly* the same to both are dropped from the base for this table, because they

Table 11.7 **Percentage of All Family Heads Reporting
More Income to Social Security Than to the
Experiment in 1970, by Sex of Head and Percentage
of Extra Income Reported**

	Percentage Excess			
	0–10	11–25	26–50	51
Experimental				
Male heads	27.7	13.7	8.6	7.9
Female heads	21.9	1.7	2.1	1.9
Combined	24.9	7.9	5.5	5.0
Control				
Male heads	29.1	12.1	10.7	11.6
Female heads	20.3	1.8	1.8	3.8
Combined	24.9	7.1	6.4	7.8

Table 11.8 **Results of the Social Security Audit for Male Heads of Household, by Plan Characteristics, Income Stratum, and City**

	More Income Reported to Social Security
Experimental	62.0%
Control	67.2
Guarantee (percent)	
50	52.5
75	68.0
100	67.2
125	52.6
Tax rate (percent)	
30	66.0
50	59.5
70	65.2
Income stratum	
I	60.2
II	68.6
III	63.4
City	
Trenton	63.3
Paterson	77.6
Passaic	73.3
Jersey City	61.9
Scranton	55.4

NOTE: Both experimental and control families are included except for guarantee and tax rate.

were almost exclusively those with zero earnings. Calculations were also made to determine whether the proportion discovered to have reported less to the experiment varied with guarantee level or tax rate for the experimentals, and by site for both experimentals and controls. The size of the discrepancy was found to be significantly related to tax rate and site; no readily interpretable pattern was found, however, so these relationships can probably be ascribed to artifacts of the plan—ethnic-group—site confounding caused by the way the lengthy design process forced us to fill the experimental cells.

The difference in the proportion reporting more to Social Security than to the experiment was also calculated by sex of head. Female heads were found to be significantly less likely to report more to Social Security than to the experiment, again probably because the absolute numbers were small and because the work histories involved were more straightforward.

SUMMARY

As this chapter makes clear, auditing low-income individuals is a difficult task. It is particularly difficult in the context of a program where personal contacts are limited and the concept of randomness and equity are fostered.

From an administrative point of view, the amount of fraudulent reporting detected in the experiment would not pose serious obstacles to a national program in terms either of threats to the integrity of the program or of the absolute value of the overpayments involved. The 3 to 4 percent a year figure may understate the magnitude of actual fraud, because the limited information available to the experiment probably allowed some fraud to go undiscovered. In a national program, the authority of legal sanctions and a sound, well-publicized information matching-and-verification process, well might be a more effective limitation on the temptation to misreport than anything the experiment could devise.

Both the secular upward trend in incomes as reported on the income report forms (see Chapter 4) and the lack of any interpretable relationship between the experimental parameters and differences in reports of earnings demonstrate the general absence of severe misreporting in the aggregate sense.

12

Problems of
confidentiality and early
data release

Because the New Jersey experiment was the first social-science experiment of its kind, the staff faced a number of unexpected and serious problems that, to one degree or another, threatened the continuation of the experiment. One crucial set of problems—the question of whether the information collected about families was privileged—resulted in subpoenas of experimental records, a show cause order why the director of the experiment should not be held in contempt of court, a civil suit by a welfare board, a grand jury hearing, and a number of other serious problems, all of which made the operation of the experiment more difficult. This volume would not be complete without a description of the events surrounding these incidents. Indeed, as a direct result of experiences of the New Jersey experiment, other experiments have been able to make more effective arrangements with local officials, and a number of people in government and the social-science community have begun to formulate legislation or regulations governing the protection of data gathered by social scientists for legitimate research purposes.

THE RIGHT TO PRIVACY
FOR FAMILIES IN THE EXPERIMENT

From the inception of the experiment, the research staff was concerned with protecting the rights of privacy of the experimental subjects, for several rather obvious reasons. The first was ethical. The planners felt that the families would be making a substantial contribution to the development of public policy, and to place them individually under public scrutiny because of their participation in the experiment would clearly deny them their right to privacy. Second, from the standpoint of obtaining good data from the experiment, it was important that the experimental families not be subjected to publicity and pressures that would not be similarly focused on control families. Finally, the interviews asked for very personal information, not only details about income and assets but a whole range of attitudinal and behavioral information that many families were understandably reluctant to give. It was felt necessary to ensure participants complete anonymity in order to obtain such information. Even a suggestion that names, or information associated with names, might become public property would have threatened the collecting of critical items of information from the families.

Measures to Ensure Confidentiality

Given these concerns, it was assumed that all information collected in the experiment would remain privileged, to be published only in aggregate form. The assumption that all data were privileged was further reinforced by the original contract approved by OEO, Article XIII:

> Individual personal and financial information pertaining to all individuals and families who participate as respondents in this study shall remain strictly confidential. If case histories are used, precautions will be taken to prevent the identification of the persons or families described.[1]

Furthermore, the rules of operation,[2] the administrative regulations developed by Mathematica and the University of Wisconsin, stated:

> All information obtained from families participating in the Basic Income Program [the name given to the experiment in order to avoid more complex terms, such as Negative Income Tax, Income Maintenance, or Graduated Work Incentives] will be kept in strictest confidence. . . .

In addition to the formal confidentiality provisions, several additional steps were taken to protect the families and to ensure that staff members understood the importance of protecting the identities of families and the information collected from them. The first was the brochure describing the experiment that was given to every family. This brochure, entitled "A Basic Income for American Families," stated, in part:

---

[1] OEO Grant No. CG-8486 between the Regents of the University of Wisconsin and Mathematica, July 1967, Data Center Archives, Institute for Research on Poverty, University of Wisconsin-Madison.

[2] See Appendix B.

Besides informing [the staff of the experiment] of its size and income, the family is asked to reply to a questionnaire four times each year for the duration of the study. The purpose of these questionnaires is to evaluate the success of the program; all information about the family will be kept strictly confidential.[3]

Second, each family also received a short version of the rules of operation ("Basic Income Program—Summary of Rules of Operations"), which stated, in part:

The Basic Income Program is conducted by ... Mathematica of Princeton, New Jersey, and the University of Wisconsin. Funds are provided by the United States Office of Economic Opportunity. Information gathered during the program is kept in the strictest confidence and is used only by these organizations to evaluate the program.[4]

Third, an administrative decision was made as soon as the enrollment process began to use family numbers instead of names wherever possible.

All office managers and field personnel were instructed about procedures for maintaining confidentiality and for working with the press. The office-procedures manual stated:

It is of great importance that all information about the families in the experiment, particularly their names, be kept strictly confidential. A family may choose to discuss its participation in the experiment with others, but under no circumstances should the family's name, or any information about a specific family, be released by a member of the office staff. Insofar as feasible, all files, tabulations, and other information kept in the field office should be kept by family number.

All requests for information from members of the press should be referred to the Princeton office. It is very important that a consistent policy be pursued with respect to publicity; therefore, all such requests must be processed through the main office.[5]

Finally, all staff members, including members of the research staff at the University of Wisconsin and the entire interviewing staff, were required to sign the following "confidentiality agreement":

I understand that all information pertaining to families interviewed in connection with the survey conducted by Mathematica is strictly confidential. I further understand that under no circumstances may I mention, discuss, or name any such family to any person or persons other than full-time employees of Mathematica who show good reason for having to know such name or information. Finally, I understand that this pledge of confidentiality will remain in effect after the experiment is completed and/or after my association with the experiment is ended.

[3] See Scranton Enrollment Kit, September 1969, Data Center Archives.
[4] Ibid.
[5] "Office Procedures Manual," Data Center Archives.

Given the contract with the Office of Economic Opportunity (OEO), the rules of operation of the experiment, and the internal safeguards afforded the families, little additional thought was given to the possibility that these measures might be insufficient protection. As subsequent events were to show, however, none of these provisions afforded the protection regarding the names of families or information about them that the experimental staff assumed they would.

INCIDENTS IN THE EXPERIMENT
TREATENING CONFIDENTIALITY

Infringements on the confidentiality guaranteed to the participants in the experiment, and those most likely to be faced by other experiments in the future, were of three types: (1) relationships with representatives of the mass media; (2) problems with local public officials—in this case, welfare officials instigating the investigation of the experiment by the Mercer County Grand Jury and instituting civil suits against participating families and Mathematica in Passaic County—and (3) requests for data on individuals by the United States Senate.

The Mass Media and the Experiment

Substantial interest in the experiment in its early stages was shown by representatives of the press. Early and favorable articles appeared in the *New York Times, Business Week,* and the *Wall Street Journal,*[6] in addition to substantial coverage in various local newspapers—particularly in Trenton, where the pilot sample was being selected. No thought was given to hiring a public relations firm or to the development of a systematic public relations policy, except for the decision that all media requests be directed to the central project office in Princeton. OEO received public relations advice from its own Office of Public Affairs.

The beginning of the experiment's problems with the press came as a result of a request by CBS-TV to do a program on the experiment for their "60 Minutes" show. Daniel Schorr requested permission to interview families for the program. The request put OEO in a difficult position; they greatly respected the opinion of the research staff that the experiment was too new for any detailed publicity and that public attitudes should not be formed about the negative-income-tax

[6] Ronald Sullivan, "Jersey Sets Test for Negative Tax," *New York Times,* 19 May 1968; "A Think Tank That Thinks for the Poor," *Business Week,* 22 June 1968; Jonathan Spivak, "Test of 'Negative Tax' to Help Poor Families Starts in New Jersey," *Wall Street Journal,* 11 October 1968.

concept and the experiment itself on the basis of incomplete and highly preliminary information or on the basis of interviews with one or two families. On the other hand, they argued that some publicity was inevitable and that a good presentation, sensitive to the subtleties and complexities of social experimentation, would be a useful public service. Given Schorr's reputation, it seemed evident that he was qualified to give the experiment such treatment. The research staff finally agreed to the program after several meetings with CBS.

Further meetings were held with Schorr and CBS officials at which details of the broadcast were discussed. To avoid endangering the sample selection process (still incomplete at that time), CBS agreed not to air the program until after all the enrollment interviews had been completed. While Mathematica had no control over the form or content of the broadcast, CBS agreed to work closely with the experimental staff. Both CBS and OEO suggested that twelve families be selected as candidates for the final program, on which two would be interviewed, provided that releases could be obtained from the families. In order to be fair to all the networks, OEO suggested obtaining releases from six families in all, holding two each for ABC and NBC. While CBS wanted exclusive rights, Mathematica refused, and legal counsel confirmed that they could not grant such a right. Two families were finally selected and readily agreed to take part in the television broadcast, which was filmed over a two-day period in November of 1968. The results of the CBS effort were reasonably impressive, the final product being comprehensive and accurate. The initial OEO judgment that media treatment by sensitive and knowledgeable people would be helpful to the experiment seemed to be borne out. However, the release of the program triggered a series of events that created substantial difficulties for some of the families and for the experiment.

The head of one of the families interviewed worked at a local welding shop in Trenton and was filmed at his home and at his place of work. He subsequently reported to the Trenton office manager that as a result of the filming at the shop he was "being ridden" by his boss and fellow employees for "being somebody special" and for being called poor (he made $99 per week and his foreman disagreed that he was underpaid). In March, he was laid off from his job and reported that "due to a misunderstanding at the plant I am now unemployed." In July of 1968, his wife left him, partially because he could no longer support the family. A court order followed instructing him to make support payments of $15 per child per week (two children), which he was unable to do. He reported to the office manager in September that he was in danger of being jailed for nonsupport. It is, of course, unclear whether or not the television program was actually the direct cause of his trouble, but the incident had enough impact when added to the initial concerns to cause Mathematica to decide never again to release names of participants, even with the written permission of the families. While considering action in support of the man, Mathematica learned that he finally had found another job.

On a more general level, the policy of identifying six families, two for each network, was clearly unworkable. To consider that only the network groups were interested in interviewing families was an error. Following the release of the CBS program, requests from fifteen different sources were received for names of families to interview. It was realized that the integrity of the experiment would be threatened if any additional families were interviewed and that a change in policy was required. In a memorandum dated 5 December 1968, prior to the showing of the CBS film, Mathematica proposed to OEO that a change in policy take place:

> We feel a very strong sense of responsibility for the rights of privacy of the families we enrolled. They were assured that all information, including their identities, would be kept confidential. They will not fully understand [the future implication] even if they sign a release, and we can expect families whose names we release to be trampled on: reporters will follow them to the market, escort their children to school, and invade their homes.[7]

OEO agreed to this request in the spring of 1969, and a new policy was instituted of giving no information to the media.

This new policy was obviously difficult to maintain, given the fact that names had already been released to CBS. NBC, in particular, was doggedly persistent in seeking out families to interview. In August of 1969, NBC correspondent Ron Nessen and his producer came to the office to seek family names. They were informed of the new policy, and a series of discussions took place between NBC, Mathematica, and OEO. The OEO Public Affairs Office at first suggested that Mathematica provide NBC with the names of the original two families since they were already "in the public domain" and then asked that the name of another family already found and interviewed by a *Newsweek* reporter (without Mathematica's permission) be given; Mathematica refused both requests. Mathematica did agree to an interview with staff people, but only if the policy of no family interviews was respected. NBC finally agreed, and the research staff cooperated. When the program was aired in August, however, it was evident that NBC had, after all, found and interviewed a family. They allegedly both told the family head that they had Mathematica's permission to interview him and prodded him into answering questions that had no bearing on his own situation, but which apparently fit into the producer's steroetype of welfare recipients. He subsequently told the research staff that the news crew asked him the same questions over and over until he gave the answer they wanted. Aside from registering

---

[7] Baumol et al. to OEO, Internal Memorandum, December 1968, Data Center Archives.

complaints with NBC, there was nothing that could be done about the situation.[8]

During the course of the experiment, materials were prepared for reporters, including a random selection of quotations from anonymous families. In addition, members of the staff were available for interviews, and a set of composite family profiles was developed. While this satisfied few reporters, several did respect the rights of privacy of the families and used composites very effectively. The two best examples appeared in the *Washington Post*[9] and the *New York Times Magazine*. A quotation from Fred Cook's *New York Times Magazine* article of 3 May 1970 illustrates how human interest can be achieved without using family interviews:

> They were living "a life of quiet desperation." The husband, 26, tall, very thin, dark-haired, was mired in a poor job; his wife, a 22-year old brunette, was small, smiling and gracious. The couple and their children, aged 1 and 2, lived in what the wife accurately described as a "dump". . . . Behind it was a grim alleyway; the steps to the tiny back porch were broken. . . . The family was trapped in the kind of dead-end situation that afflicts some 25 million Americans.[10]

Mr. Cook never spoke with a family, relying solely on interviews with staff members and composite profiles.

The lesson here is that a firm, consistent policy toward the media is critical for an experiment. Although the legitimate needs and rights of the press must be recognized, they should be placed in the context of the need to protect both the families involved and the reliability of the data gathered.

Local Welfare Officials and the Experiment

In January 1969, the state of New Jersey introduced a public-assistance program—Aid to Families with Dependent Children, Unemployed Parents (AFDC-UP)—that expanded public-assistance eligibility to families with an unemployed or underemployed male present in the household. Underemployment was defined simply on the basis of insufficient earnings, making most families previously selected for the experiment eligible for the more generous AFDC-UP

---

[8] The fact that it is easy to obtain family names is illustrated by a more recent experience from the rural experiment, where a *Wall Street Journal* reporter, Neil Maxwell, found eight families by asking a local grocer for the names of families cashing checks there. See, "In a Novel Experiment, Some Rural Poor Get a Guaranteed Income," *Wall Street Journal,* 19 September 1972.

[9] Eve Edstrom, "It's an Honor to Work," *Washington Post,* 30 March 1970.

[10] Fred Cook, "When You Just Give Money to the Poor," *New York Times Magazine,* 3 May 1970, p. 23.

program. The new program and the subsequent payment overlaps of experiment and welfare payments caused a major problem.

The first indication that there were problems with the welfare people in Trenton came in October 1969, when it was learned that the Mercer County prosecutor's office was investigating overlapping welfare and experimental payments in the case of one family. The experiment staff attempted to convince both the prosecutor's office and the welfare officials that the coexistence of two similar transfer programs was confusing to the families, and that in the interest of experimentation on an important public issue the problem should be settled out of court. A major concern was that a public investigation of a family would cause other families to drop out of the experiment.

The prosecutor, however, subpoenaed the records of the family. Mathematica complied by providing information on payments made to the family by the experiment, and again suggested that a settlement was in the public interest. The Mercer County Welfare Board then requested the names of other sample families who were also on welfare. The experiment staff cooperated by supplying the board with a list of thirteen additional families reporting welfare income, and indicated a willingness to meet to determine the existence of unreported overlap.[11] The prosecutor's response was to issue thirteen more subpoenas, one for each newly obtained family record.

In view of the small size of the Trenton sample and the potential attrition problem, it was felt that the experiment would be seriously endangered if the records of these families were released. Moreover, the contract with OEO contained tight confidentiality clauses, and the staff felt bound not to release information without a court order. Accordingly, Mathematica's lawyers moved to have the subpoenas quashed.[12] The prosecutor's office countered with a court order to show cause why the director of the experiment should not be held in contempt of court.[13]

Mathematica's motion to quash the subpoenas claimed (1) that the information sought was confidential; (2) that the experiment was in the national interest (its contribution to planning for the President's Family Assistance Plan); (3) that, as the pilot, Trenton was the key city, and that losing families there would damage the experiment; and (4) that the action would be detrimental to the experiment as a whole. Prior to an actual hearing, we explained the background

---

[11] A sharing of names with selected government agencies on a confidential basis was determined by OEO and counsel to be allowable and advisable under the terms of the grant. Other information was restricted, of course, and families were informed of the possible necessity for sharing names. See, for example, Letter to Families, October 1969, Data Center Archives.

[12] Notice of Motion to Quash, November 1969, Data Center Archives.

[13] Show Cause Order, December 1969, Data Center Archives.

and objectives of the experiment to the prosecutor and requested an amicable settlement to avoid the damaging effect of publicity.

After several weeks of negotiating with the prosecutor's office, it was agreed that the best solution would be for the families to repay the amount of the overlap to the welfare department. All the families in question had had some overlap during the eighteen-month period since the beginning of the experiment (involving approximately $20,000 in welfare overpayments). In order to provide as little disruption to the experiment as possible it was decided that the experiment would make the repayment to the welfare department on behalf of the families. In addition, Mathematica filed a stipulation with the court that noted that families may have been confused by the change in procedures on the part of both the welfare board and the experiment.[14]

After the repayments on behalf of the families were made, the rules of operation were changed: Trenton families could no longer receive experimental and welfare payments simultaneously. In addition, a system of checking records quarterly was proposed to the Mercer County Welfare Department and instituted with its approval.

In spite of this apparent settlement, however, a headline article, "Mercer Jury Begins Probe of U.S. Welfare Experiment," appeared on the front page of the *Trenton Times* in March 1971. The article included the following statement:

> A special Mercer County Grand Jury today began investigating welfare fraud charges against an affiliate of Mathematica, Inc., the Princeton research firm conducting a federal experiment in guaranteed annual income here. The Prosecutor's office is understood to contend that Mathematica officials instructed low income families taking part in the experiment not to report income subsidies to city and county welfare authorities. . . . An informed source said criminal indictments on conspiracy charges have been prepared against Mathematica and at least two of the firm's officials.[15]

Nobody at Mathematica had been informed of the investigation or of the indictments, but it was later pieced together that the same detective who had done the original investigation had reopened the old case, dealing only with the period prior to January 1970. While the stipulation had provided for full reimbursement to the welfare department of all overpayments, it did not include any punitive or criminal sanctions. Why the prosecutor's office would want to raise the old issue again was puzzling, and the reasons for the new investigation were never made clear.

Despite a four-month grand jury investigation, which included testimony from

[14] Stipulation, January 1970, Data Center Archives.
[15] Thomas H. Green, "Mercer Jury Begins Probe of U.S. Welfare Experiment," *Trenton Times*, 10 March 1971.

several experimental families, welfare officials, the detective, and representatives of the experiment, no indictments were returned. The grand jury eventually produced a draft presentment. At Mathematica's insistence, it was modified, and with the consent of the presiding judge, a rather mild document was finally issued.[16]

Unfortunately, the Mercer County situation was not the last of the problems with local welfare officials. As soon as the original problem in Trenton arose, the director of the Passaic County Welfare Board asserted that there had been overlapping payments in his county (which included both Paterson and Passaic) and demanded restitution of funds from the experiment. The different circumstances of the two counties were repeatedly explained to him, and cooperative efforts for cross-checking records were instituted. Despite conversations between the welfare director and representatives of the experiment at Mathematica, Passaic County still refused to give up the notion of recovery of funds. The situation was made more difficult by the fact that there were at the same time outcries from the public and the Passaic County Board of Freeholders regarding alleged welfare fraud and welfare-board inefficiency, in general. The welfare officials were frantic to do something to please the public, and suing experimental families could serve to divert attention from other problems.

The situation became acute when, late in December 1970, a newspaper article in the *Paterson News* gave details of a meeting of the welfare board at which overlapping payments were discussed. The names of eighteen families in the experiment, some of whom had never received more than the experiment's biweekly filing fee, were placed in the newspaper as "welfare frauds," in flagrant violation of even the welfare board's own confidentiality regulations. The staff of the experiment vigorously protested this breach of confidentiality and suggested more frequent audits, a suggestion that was rejected. No further action was taken for a full year, at which time another newspaper article appeared reporting that Mathematica and twenty-four families were being taken to court in a civil suit to recover $24,000 in overlapping payments. Mathematica was indeed served with the complaint, as were the families. In response, Mathematica reiterated that the Passaic County Welfare Board had had in its possession from the beginning of the experiment a complete list of the Paterson families participating in the experiment, but requests to the welfare board to sit down and discuss the situation were refused.

Because the issue continued after payments had ended in the Passaic cities and publicity would no longer damage the experiment, the staff did not feel the same constraints against a vigorous counterattack as they had in Trenton. Mathematica therefore informed Passaic County officials of their intention to file a suit of their own, and the Passaic suit was dropped.

---

[16] Presentment, April 1971, Data Center Archives.

THE POLITICAL PROCESS AND THE EXPERIMENT

The preceding section described three incidents in the experiment that illustrate the potential vulnerability of any social experiment to the antagonism of local officials. This section describes the situation that occurs when an experiment becomes politically relevant on the national level and is thrust into the spotlight of political debate.

When the experiment was planned, the negative-income-tax concept was very controversial. OEO used great caution in presenting the experiment to the public, and it was felt that it would be years, even a decade, before experimental results would be directly applicable to public-policy decisions.

When President Nixon made his statement to the nation in August 1969 announcing the new Family Assistance Plan (FAP), the relationship of the experiment to the political process suddenly changed. It became clear to many that, while the experiment was by no means a replication of the proposed Family Assistance Plan, it could provide the only empirical evidence bearing on the new legislation. The researchers had planned to wait until the end of the experiment before publishing findings, but the increasing demand for *any* data from the experiment intensified the pressure to produce results. The research staff, obviously interested in making a contribution to the formulation of new policies, were frustrated by their inability to come up with experimental data, particularly on the central work-response issue. A letter written by David Kershaw to James M. Lyday, of the Office of Planning, Research, and Evaluation at OEO, following Kershaw's testimony with Harold Watts (principal investigator of this experiment) and D. Lee Bawden (principal investigator of the Rural Negative Income Tax Experiment) before the House Committee on Ways and Means, indicates this feeling of frustration:

> It became clear at the hearings that there are five or ten questions which are central to the decision on FAP, most of which I mentioned above [work response, expenditures, family stability, etc.]. In the next week or ten days I can have some findings (primarily frequency distributions, before and after in a couple of cities) which will supply answers to these questions. We stressed the fact that families have a strong work ethic, that administrative costs will be relatively low . . . but I think these points would be more effectively reinforced if I wrote a letter to [Congressman] Byrnes with some additional concrete findings.[17]

The letter was circulated at OEO with no response for some time. Fred Cook, in the *New York Times* article cited previously, quotes John Wilson (Director of Planning, Research, and Evaluation at OEO):

---

[17] Kershaw to Lyday, Letter, 28 January 1970, Data Center Archives.

> Pat [Moynihan] jumped all over me. He stomped around the room, waving his
> arms . . . "Wilson," he said, "you mean to tell me that you've had a $5 million
> experiment running in New Jersey for almost two years now and you don't know
> what you've got?" I tried to explain that you had to let the experiment run its
> course before you could evaluate your data. . . . [18]

Nevertheless, Wilson called Wisconsin and Mathematica and asked if some preliminary data could be run. After a frantic two weeks of hand tabulations, a preliminary report was put together at OEO and was issued as "Preliminary Findings of the New Jersey Work Incentives Experiment" on 18 February 1970.[19]

Soon after the release of the report, the General Accounting Office (GAO) arrived at Mathematica's Princeton office and stayed thirteen weeks to "verify and/or trace to the source" the data contained in the report. This particular purpose was regarded by the research staff as legitimate, but the GAO attempted to extend its investigation into areas not covered in the report. The research staff argued that, while a "research audit" was appropriate, "parallel and extended research" was not justified and that more sophisticated analysis should be done by the researchers before the experiment could be evaluated or independent research undertaken by the GAO.[20]

During this period, some members of the Senate Finance Committee decided that even an extensive GAO audit was insufficient; they wanted to look at individual family files. After extensive negotiations conducted through OEO, the research staff agreed to supply the Senate Finance Committee with a listing of family numbers, and with income before and after participation in the experiment, occupation and industry code before and after, and total payments made to date. This did not suffice. The first list made it impossible to identify individual families, and the committee wanted case histories. Wilson at OEO received a call from the committee indicating that the members wanted six family files to determine if they would be useful to the committee. They had expressed skepticism over the preliminary figures and wanted to "add them up themselves." The research staff pointed out that not only were all names and data on individuals confidential, but that six files would tell nothing about an experiment with 1357 participating families. What concerned the research staff most was the chance that families would be subpoenaed to appear before the Senate committee, a development that would end their usefulness as experimental subjects and perhaps submit them to the pressures experienced by families interview by the press. (Mathematica knew by then that it probably

[18] Cook, "When You Just Give Money," p. 110.

[19] OEO, "Preliminary Findings in the New Jersey Work Incentive Experiment," 18 February 1970, Data Center Archives.

[20] Kershaw to Wilson (OEO), Letter, 29 June 1970, Data Center Archives.

could not resist such a subpoena.) As an alternative, the staff offered to act as a resource for the committee and to answer any legitimate questions over a one-month period. This offer was refused.

On 18 August 1970, members of the experiment staff, OEO officials, and the GAO were called to testify before the Senate Finance Committee. Members of the committee hoped to support their contention that the experiment was not cooperating with the Senate and the GAO, in order to legitimize their demand that individual records be turned over. While the GAO had been critical of the earlier preliminary report,[21] primarily on the basis that it had been issued too quickly and too early and with too small a sample (all of which were mentioned in a University of Wisconsin paper amplifying the original OEO document), the support that the experiment received from the GAO at the hearing appeared to save the experiment from having to fight a congressional subpoena for individual records, a battle it would probably have lost. Only the GAO's affirmation that OEO and its contractors had cooperated with its investigation prevented additional pressure to turn over family files.

SUMMARY

Certain lessons learned from the New Jersey experience can be generalized for those involved in social experimentation. Remedies have already been successfully transferred to other social experiments similar to New Jersey in size, public interest, and relevance to national policy.

First, detailed arrangements at a high level should be made in advance with local agencies, such as public assistance and public housing. Such precautionary action has not prevented the income-maintenance experiments in Seattle, Denver, and Gary from experiencing some problems with overlapping payments, but agreements on the procedures to follow have been reached easily and the scope of the problems consequently reduced.

Second, special preparations should be made in advance for adequate media coverage of the experiment without involving the release of names or permitting families to be interviewed. It is a simple matter to prepare background information, composites on families that provide human interest, and conversations with field workers who have interesting stories to tell.

With regard to other public threats to experiments, be they from an ambitious district attorney or a frightened welfare official, the only answer is solid administrative guidelines (or, better yet, legislation) to protect, at the very least,

---

[21] GAO Report, "Preliminary Comments on the New Jersey Graduated Work Incentives Experiment," June 1970, Data Center Archives.

certain data under specified circumstances.[22] It seems clear that good data cannot be gathered unless respondents are assured of protection; it is also clear that responsible, capable people will not conduct social experiments in the future unless they can promise their respondents such protection.

Congressional interest and concern pose a more sensitive issue. It is helpful to establish a relationship with the GAO when the experiment is launched, so that the agency knows what the experiment is, how it was designed, the kinds of research being done, and when results can reasonably be expected. When results are obtained, they should be published with suitable qualifications, and the GAO should see them before they are released. Problems need not arise except in cases where political events pressure the research staff to publish preliminary data. If experiments are designed as policy-making tools, then policymakers have the right to have timely results made available to them. However, the Congress should also be educated to understand the time horizon involved in gathering good information from an experiment and to accept tentative statements and early impressions of experimental results for what they are.

When an experiment becomes as relevant to the policy-making process as the New Jersey experiment did, it requires a difficult but essential balance between the interests of research and policy to ensure that high quality data will continue to be generated, that encroachment on the data in preliminary form will be minimized, and that the rights to privacy of the families will be protected. In such a situation, research staffs composed of personnel who are committed to policy issues face a real dilemma. To release data too soon (as was the case with the 1970 OEO report) is to place the experiment in jeopardy from its enemies. On the other hand, to refuse to yield any information denies policymakers experimental data when they need it most.

The approach subsequently taken with H.R. 1 ("Social Security Amendments of 1971") is probably the best course. The research staff disclaimed for the experiment any central relevance to the legislation but indicated to both the House Ways and Means Committee and the Senate Finance Committee that members of the experiment's research staff were very willing to act as a resource for equestions that fell within the scope of the experimental experience. The Ways and Means Committee took advantage of this offer by sending a detailed, five-page letter of questions to which the staff was able to respond. Neither OEO nor the experiment staff supported or criticized the legislation, only supplying answers to specific questions raised.

---

[22] For a more detailed discussion of legal remedies and protections, see Paul Nejelski and Lindsey Lerman, "Research-Subject Testimonial Privilege: What to Do before the Subpoena Arrives," *Wisconsin Law Review* (1971): 1085–1148; David Kershaw and Joseph Small, "Confidentiality and Privacy, Lessons from the New Jersey Experiment," *Public Policy* **20** (Spring 1972): 257–280.

13 Stopping payments at the end of the experiment

In a limited-duration negative-income-tax experiment, the payments must, by definition, come to an end. The basic hypothesis of the experiment was that meaningful changes in the lives of the families would occur as a result of the introduction of the treatment. This carried with it another hypothesis, namely, that equally meaningful—and possibly harmful—effects might take place when the treatment was withdrawn. Given this concern, a plan for terminating the experiment was developed.

The termination plan had to meet the following objectives:

· It had to end the participation of treatment families in as humane a way as possible, ensuring insofar as feasible that no family was worse off after the experiment than it had been before.
· Its consequences had to be such as would reassure policymakers not only that it was possible to obtain valuable data from large-scale, limited-duration social-science experiments but that such endeavors could be conducted (and ended) within a reasonable time and at reasonable cost.

The data in this chapter come from analysis performed by Arnold Shore, first Trenton field-office manager and later staff sociologist for the experiment.

- It had to meet ethical objections that the disruption of the lives of the experimental families overrode the scientific value of the undertaking.
- It had to ensure that the data gathered near the ned of the experiment were as valid as those obtained during the preceding experimental period.

The research staff and OEO together designed a pilot program for termination in Trenton. At first, some thought was given to a long grace period, slowly letting the families down from high to low payments and then terminating them after a relatively long period of time. The opposite view, voiced by psychologist Tom Tomlinson of OEO, was that the least disrupting procedure for the families was to end the experiment abruptly, making it clear to them that the end of the payments had come. This would avoid any added uncertainty about the end of the experiment. The Wisconsin staff commented:

> We strongly disagree with the proposition that there be any "grace period" of *regularly calculated* payments. Tomlinson made the point about disappointing the expectations of families. Our psychologist [Vernon Allen] emphatically agrees with him on this—i.e., if you extend [the experiment] unexpectedly you *will* let them down harder the second time you announce termination. . . . Our view is that what we do in Trenton should be regarded as a pilot, not only for the rest of our families, but also for Iowa, North Carolina, Seattle, Denver, and Gary. We must do it in an experimentally justified way (i.e., with no extra warning before the final interview) so that we really get some information on family and public reactions.

> Only 15 families in Trenton are receiving sizable payments. If the worst happens we shall administratively be able to pick up the pieces. Then will be the time to consider further early warning devices.[1]

The procedure finally decided upon was the following:

- Payments to families would be stopped at the scheduled date.
- No special payments would be made.
- The last quarterly interview would be administered before the last payment, to maximize the validity of the interview.
- Families would be reminded of the date of their last payment immediately following the administration of the final quarterly interview.
- The field office would remain open as a referral agency, to assist families in locating other agencies that could help them with financial and other problems.
- A special interview (the thirteenth quarterly) would be administered three months after the last payment, to assess what changes, if any, took place in the families' lives immediately after the termination of the experiment; to

[1] Wisconsin to Mathematica, Internal Memorandum, December 1970, Data Center Archives, Institute for Research on Poverty, University of Wisconsin-Madison.

determine how well the families understood the experiment; to measure the families' attitudes toward the interviews; and to obtain data on postexperiment income and labor-force participation.
- Families would receive a "certificate of participation" as a gesture of appreciation for their participation in the experiment.

The phase-out plan was deliberately severe, designed to highlight any potential problems, so that the plan could be revised, if necessary, for the other sites. As the results discussed in the next section indicate, this plan did not turn out to have any observable adverse effects on the families and was used unchanged in all sites.

Although the field offices were kept open as referral agencies, no families made use of this service. Several families called the field offices to find out what had happened to their payment. Letters were received from several families, most expressing appreciation for being chosen to participate in the program. The following are some examples:

I will miss our little get-togethers once a month by mail. I trust our reports will help somehow in the future of our government. We seem to be on the "mend" now. My husband has started a new occupation and it is quite a change—working days for the first time since we are married. I expect to have a larger knitting class next month and the Tupperware will pick up in the fall. So for now and always, every blessing to you and yours.

The members of our family would like to thank you for the assistance that you rendered during the past three years. We were able to improve our lives a great deal with your added help and once again say thank you with our love and respect that we will always have for the members of your program.

I am writing to let you know how much we really appreciated being a member of the [experiment]. It was just three wonderful years. It was something we had never expected to happen from the beginning and it is now something we regret very much to know that [it] is coming to an end. We sure wish it could have lasted forever. With the great help of these checks we bought a mobile home. And without the checks we never would have been able to think of buying one. This is the reason we feel we put the money to very good use. Now with the checks ending we will miss them tremendously and we also will have quite a struggle until we pay it off, but we can always look back on the three wonderful years we had with the great help of the [experiment]. Without you wonderful people we wouldn't have what we have today. I know I can't thank you people enough, but I do want to say *Thank you, Very, Very Much.*

Dear Sir or Madam:
I got the report this week. And, I did not get the check. Is this the last report I will have to fill out? I enjoyed every cent I got. Thank you very kindly.

Since there was very little overt reaction by the families to the end of the experiment, the only data available to measure the effects of the phase-out was the thirteenth quarterly interview, administered in each site three months after the termination of payments.

The interview was designed to measure responses to the termination, needs during the three months after the experiment, and outlook on the future. Because data on these topics were available only for experimental families, the analysis compared family responses within the experimental group on two variables: the generosity of the plan and the proportion of total family income represented by the actual payments. These two variables represent, respectively, the amount families would expect to get during the course of the experiment given the level and fluctuation of their incomes, and the amount they actually received.

Three interview questions asked about overall reaction to the end of the experiment—whether or not the family ever thought much about the end of the experiment, whether or not they worried how they would manage when payments stopped coming, and whether or not they did anything differently during the last six months of the program because the program was coming to an end. As Tables 13.1 and 13.2 show, there were a number of differences in response that were related to generosity of plan and actual payment received. Not surprisingly, the more generous the plan, the more likely the family was to have given considerable thought to the end of the experiment; more families on generous plans worried how they would manage when payments stopped; and a larger proportion of them did some things differently during the last six months of the program in anticipation of its end.

As Tables 13.3 and 13.4 show, there are noticeable differences in every area of activity listed, with the exception of "called experiment office more." According to field-office records, families did not utilize the experiment staff's offer to act as a referral agent, and this is confirmed here. A fairly substantial number of families said they worried more, although many of them seem actively to have changed spending and saving practices to cope better with the end of the program.

Table 13.1 **Percentages of "Yes" Answers to Questions Related to Phase-Out, by Generosity of Plan**

	Low (N=116)	Medium (N=196)	High (N=271)
Never thought much about end of program	55	39	32
Worried how would manage when payments stopped	23	27	50
Did things differently during last six months because program was ending	8	10	25

Table 13.2 **Percentages of "Yes" Answers to Questions Related to Phase-Out, by Percentage of Total Income Represented by Negative Tax Payments**

	0–10 (N=328)	11–40 (N=194)	41–100 (N=62)
Never thought much about end of program	50	25	23
Worried how would manage when payments stopped	20	57	63
Did things differently during last six months because program was ending	6	30	32

It is interesting to note that there are no distinct differences by plan or by proportion of total income represented by payments, in terms of special needs—budgeting, emergency needs, medical care—that families said they had during the experiment (Tables 13.5 and 13.6).

To determine the financial impact of termination, four questions were analyzed: How many families said they needed help from some public agency three months after the completion of the experiment? Of these, how many needed help but did not apply to an agency? How many needed help, applied for, and did not receive help? How many needed, applied for, and received help? Of these four question categories, the third—those who did not receive help although they applied for it—can be said to represent the number of families having needs that were not met after the completion of the program.

There were 179 families who said they needed help at the end of the program. Of these, 94 did not apply for help, and 77 applied for and were granted public assistance. Only 8 families, therefore, applied for and were denied assistance.

Table 13.3 **Percentages of "Yes" Answers to Questions Related to Things Done Differently Because Program Was Ending, by Generosity of Plan**

	Low (N=117)[a]	Medium (N=198)[a]	High (N=271)
Altered weekly spending	18	20	34
Saved money	6	10	16
Bought things not able to afford after program ended	3	7	11
Did something about job	3	8	12
Worried more	17	15	35
Called experiment office more	2	1	3

[a]Numbers differ slightly from those in Table 13.1 because of response and coding problems.

Table 13.4 Percentage of "Yes" Answers to Questions Related to Things Done Differently Because Program Was Ending, by Percentage of Total Income Represented by Negative Tax Payments

	0–10 (N=328)	11–40 (N=194)	41–100 (N=62)
Altered weekly spending	13	43	39
Saved money	7	15	19
Bought things not able to afford after program ended	3	13	11
Did something about job	4	14	16
Worried more	12	37	52
Called experiment office more	1	3	6

Insofar as families considered receiving aid from a public agency as a viable option, then, very few families were left in difficult situations because the experiment terminated; but it should be noted that to the extent that less stigma was attached to participation in the experiment than to applying for public assistance, this estimate of hardship is biased downwards.

Finally, families were asked to compare their circumstances before and after the experiment. As Table 13.7 indicates, a very high percentage of families thought that they were either the same or better off after the experiment than before it. Although it may be that the simple passage of time improved the experimental families' absolute level of well-being, these figures provide one more general indication that short-term experiments can be conducted without serious adverse effects on participants.

Table 13.5 Percentages of Families Saying Additional Aid Needed during Program, by Generosity of Plan

Type of Aid Needed	Low (N=115)[a]	Medium (N=193)[a]	High (N=268)[a]
Budgeting	17	17	21
Emergency needs	37	53	52
Medical care	50	53	58
Job placement	30	37	35
Job training	28	39	37
Family counseling	17	23	16
Housing	34	41	39
Child care	16	24	14
Referral to other programs (food stamps, legal aid)	37	45	38

[a] Numbers differ slightly from those in Table 13.1 because of response and coding problems.

Table 13.6 Percentages of Families Saying Additional Aid Needed during Program, by Percentage of Total Income Represented by Negative Tax Payments

Type of Aid Needed	0–10 $(N=322)$[a]	11–40 $(N=193)$[a]	41–100 $(N=62)$
Budgeting	16	21	27
Emergency needs	52	56	56
Medical care	48	64	68
Job placement	31	42	37
Job training	34	40	34
Family counseling	17	22	19
Housing	35	45	40
Child care	19	17	21
Referral to other programs (food stamps, legal aid)	35	44	48

[a]Numbers differ slightly from those in Table 13.2 because of response and coding problems.

The purpose of this volume has been to describe the operational underpinnings of the New Jersey Income-Maintenance Experiment. As we have seen, these details are important because they may have far-reaching consequences for the data collected, and thus for the research analysis and conclusions.

The basic objective of the experiment, however, was to measure the behavioral responses of the experimental families to their negative-income-tax payments. The operations, surveys, and administration described in the chapters above were planned and carried out to this end. Volumes 2 and 3 of the series contain the research analyses of the New Jersey data and represent the research staff's efforts to come to grips with the basic objective.

Table 13.7 Percentages of Families Saying Their Situation Was the Same or Better after the Experiment than before

By Plan[a]		By Percentage of Total Income Represented by Negative Tax Payments[b]	
Low $(N=115)$	90	0–10 $(N = 321)$	88
Medium $(N = 190)$	86	11–40 $(N = 181)$	87
High $(N = 255)$	89	41–100 $(N = 57)$	88

[a]Numbers differ slightly from those in Table 13.1 because of response and coding problems.

[b]Numbers differ slightly from those in Table 13.2 because of response and coding problems.

Appendices

Chronology of events

1965
Summer   The Office of Research, Plans, Programs, and Evaluation (RPP&E), Office of Economic Opportunity (OEO), assigns James M. Lyday and Walter Williams to study the feasibility of a national income-maintenance program.

Independently, White House Task Force on Income Maintenance, chaired by Gardner Ackley, chairman of the Council of Economic Advisers, is established.

August   Robert Lampman provides OEO with a paper entitled, "Negative Rates Income Taxation," which discusses design, administration, and cost of various negative-income-tax plans.

September   White House Task Force sends its report on income-maintenance programs to the White House.

October   OEO presents a national antipoverty plan, including the negative income tax, to the Bureau of the Budget.

1966
June   OEO plans experiment to measure socioeconomic effects of a negative income tax.

OEO sends more detailed plan for a negative-income-tax program, developed by Lyday and Harold W. Watts, to the Bureau of the Budget.

December   Heather Ross prepares paper, "A Proposal for a Demonstration of New Techniques in Income Maintenance," suggesting an experiment be conducted in

Washington, D.C., under the auspices of the United Planning Organization, a local Community Action Program.

1967

March   Guy Orcutt, of the University of Wisconsin, responds to Ross's paper with "Experimental Studies of Negative Income Taxation."

June   Mathematica, drawing upon the Ross and Orcutt papers, submits a proposal to RPP&E at OEO to administer and study the experiment on negative income taxation in New Jersey.

Sargent Shriver, director of OEO, recommends that the experiment be administered through the OEO-funded Institute for Research on Poverty at the University of Wisconsin (directed by Harold W. Watts).

July   Mathematica and the University of Wisconsin sign a contract with OEO to administer and analyze an experiment on the negative income tax.

1968

January   President's independent Commission on Income Maintenance is set up.

Mathematica seeks bids from survey-research organizations to select, enroll, and administer quarterly interviews to participant families.

February **John Kervick, state treasurer, state of New Jersey, confirms that the state of New Jersey will contribute data-processing services to the experiment.**

March   Tax rates and guarantee levels are set by Wisconsin and Mathematica for the experiment.

Trenton, Jersey City, and Paterson–Clifton–Passaic SMSAs are tentatively chosen as target sites by Mathematica.

A "Request for Ruling" that experimental transfer payments will not constitute taxable gross income is submitted to the Internal Revenue Service on behalf of the experiment.

April   Screening questionnaire is developed by Mathematica and Institute staffs.

Mathematica grants contract on field work to Opinion Research Corporation.

May   Mathematica makes contact with selected officials and community leaders in Trenton to inform them of the experiment and request their cooperation.

June   Mathematica begins to hire personnel to administer the experiment.

Final version of the Trenton screening interview is completed by Mathematica **and approved by the Bureau of the Budget (later to become the Office of Management and Budget, OMB).**

Screening interview is administered in Trenton.

A Certificate of Firm Name is filed in the Mercer County Clerk's Office setting up the Council for Grants to Families as a separate corporate entity.

Tax-free status of negative-income-tax payments is granted by Internal Revenue Service.

Trenton Housing Authority is contacted to request waiver of maximum income-level requirements for experimental families, so that payments pushing them over the maximum will not lead to loss of housing.

Pre-enrollment interview is pretested.

July   The New Jersey state legislature proposes an amendment to the state welfare laws to include needy parents and relatives living together with needy children (AFDC-UP).

August   Field office is set up in Trenton. Preenrollment interview is administered there.

First family is enrolled in the experiment and first transfer payment made in Trenton.

September Mathematica decides to administer screening and pre-enrollment interviews in the remaining sites and to let the survey-research organization administer only quarterly questionnaires.

October   Experiment staff meets with community leaders in Paterson–Passaic.

Decision is made to drop survey-research organization altogether and to have Mathematica administer all interviews. To implement this decision the Urban Opinion Surveys (UOS) division of Mathematica is established.

A disagreement arises between Mathematica and Wisconsin over assignment of experimental families to negative-income-tax plans.

Daniel Schorr, of CBS, interviews two families for "60 Minutes." CBS agrees not to show it until all families are enrolled.

November First quarterly interview in Trenton and screening interview in Paterson–Passaic are administered by Mathematica.

Jersey City is selected as the third experimental site, and community leaders are contacted.

December Schorr, of CBS, discusses CBS's interview with the two families on the radio before all families have been erolled in the experiment.

Mathematica decides that no names of the experimental families can be released to the press. Appeal is made to Robert Levine, OEO, to support this decision, and he agrees.

1969
January Pre-enrollment interview is administered in Paterson–Passaic.

Paterson–Passaic families are enrolled.

The state of New Jersey institutes a welfare program for two-parent families (AFDC-UP).

Design controversy between Mathematica and the University of Wisconsin intensifies.

First transfer payment is made to Paterson–Passaic families.

Passaic County Housing Authority is contacted about waiver of eligibility criteria for experimental families.

February   The Trenton second quarterly interview and the Jersey City screening interview are administered.

The Family Security System (later called the Family Assistance Plan) is presented to the Cabinet by Secretary Finch, of the Department of Health, Education, and Welfare (HEW).

March   Scranton, Pennsylvania, is chosen as the fourth experimental site.

April   First quarterly interview is administered in Paterson–Passaic.

Schorr's interview with the two families is shown on "60 Minutes."

Mathematica and the Wisconsin staff decide to submit design-model problem to James Tobin, Yale University, for arbitration.

May   Trenton third quarterly interview and Jersey City pre-enrollment interview are administered.

Scranton community leaders are contacted.

June   Scranton screening interview is administered.

Jersey City families are enrolled.

$10.00 filing fee replaces $2.50 minimum payment.

Yearly accounting period is decided upon for sixty-five of the sample families in Jersey City and Scranton.

Tobin submits compromise recommendation on the design model, which is agreed to by Mathematica and the University of Wisconsin staffs.

First transfer payment is made to Jersey City families.

Carry-over system of accounting is proposed.

July   Paterson–Passaic second quarterly interview is administered.

August   Paterson–Passaic special screening interview for additional control families and Scranton pre-enrollment interview are administered.

Mercer County Welfare Board calls Princeton office about a family receiving overlapping payments.

A family appears on the Huntley–Brinkley News Report (NBC), and David N. Kershaw, project director, is interviewed.

President Nixon announces his welfare-reform proposal, the Family Assistance Plan (FAP).

September   Trenton fourth quarterly interview, screening interview for new Trenton controls, and Jersey City first quarterly interview are administered.

Scranton families are enrolled.

First cost-of-living increase in experimental guarantee levels is put into effect (July 1968–July 1969, up 5.5 percent).

The Nixon proposal, to be known as the Family Assistance Plan (1969), is sent to the House Ways and Means Committee.

Carry-over system of accounting is introduced.

First payments are made to Scranton families.

Decision is made to allow deductions for child care.

First monthly $8 address-card fee is made to Jersey City control families.

October   Special pre-enrollment interview is administered to new controls in Trenton and Paterson–Passaic.

Additional control families are enrolled in Trenton and Paterson–Passaic.

Subpoena is delivered to Kershaw requesting records on a Trenton family.

Scranton Housing Authority waives eligibility criteria for experimental families.

Kershaw and Arnold Shore deliver records to the Mercer County Court.

House Ways and Means Committee begins hearings on Nixon's first Welfare Reform Proposal.

November   President's Commission on Income Maintenance Programs releases final report.

Trenton fifth quarterly interview, the second special interview for Trenton new controls, the Paterson–Passaic third quarterly interview, and the Scranton first quarterly interview are administered.

Control families in Trenton, Paterson–Passaic, and Scranton receive first $8 payment for monthly filing of address card.

Subpoenas are issued for the records and canceled checks of thirteen additional Trenton families. Mathematica decides not to hand over records.

December   In-depth "perception of experiment" interview is administered to sixty-eight families.

First payments are made in rural income-maintenance experiment in Iowa and North Carolina, funded by OEO and run by the Institute for Research on Poverty.

Watts, D. Lee Bawden (director of the rural experiment), and Kershaw testify on FAP before the House Ways and Means Committee.

1970

January   Kershaw tells Lyday that the experiment can provide results of a preliminary nature to OEO, for use by the Ways and Means Committee.

Stipulation is signed with Mercer County officials whereby Trenton families are no longer eligible to receive both welfare and experimental payments. OEO refunds amount of overlap to county on behalf of fourteen Trenton families.

February   OEO agrees that data on experiment can be released for congressional hearings on the Family Assistance Plan.

Data are collected for OEO report.

Trenton sixth quarterly interview, Paterson–Passaic fourth quarterly interview, and Jersey City and Scranton second quarterly interview are administered.

OEO releases first preliminary report on findings of the experiment.

March   General Accounting Office (GAO), responsible to the U.S. Congress, makes its first visit to Mathematica office.

Passaic County Welfare Board threatens to prosecute if any overlap is discovered and suggests that "restitution would be appropriate," as in Trenton.

Senator John Williams (D. Del.) makes initial request to HEW, which forwards it to OEO, for data on the experiment.

House Ways and Means Committee report on the welfare reform proposal, now HR16311, and referred to as the Family Assistance Act of 1970.

April   House passes H.R. 16311.

Jersey City third quarterly interview is administered.

Senate Finance Committee begins public hearings on H.R. 16311.

Senator Williams makes additional requests for information.

The GAO sets up an office in the Mathematica Princeton office and makes requests for more data.

May   Fifth quarterly interview and second special interview for new controls are administered in Paterson–Passaic.

Senator Williams makes additional requests for information and is sent aggregate data.

Senate Finance Committee defers hearings on H.R. 16311 pending submission of new material on the effect of cumulative tax rates.

The GAO writes a critique of the preliminary results prepared for the Senate Finance Committee and sends it to John Wilson, OEO. The Office of Planning, Research, and Evaluation is asked to comment.

A rebuttal is prepared by Mathematica and Wisconsin staffs.

June   The seventh quarterly interview is administered in Trenton.

Administration comes back with a modified bill, and the Senate Finance Committee resumes hearings on H.R. 16311.

Wisconsin issues discussion paper by Watts, "Revised and Extended Preliminary Results from the Urban Graduated Work Incentive Experiment."

July   Jersey City fourth quarterly interview and Scranton third quarterly interview are administered.

The GAO writes Donald Rumsfeld, OEO, questioning the advisability of using New Jersey further as a sample site.

Rees, Watts, and Kershaw prepare memo to Wilson rebutting the GAO letter.

Secretary Richardson, of HEW, in testimony before the Senate Finance Committee, indicates that he will do what he can to see that more information gets to Senator Williams.

Senator Williams calls OEO and requests individual files on six families and access to payments files on all experimental families.

August   Paterson–Passaic sixth quarterly interview is administered.

Watts testifies on experiment before the Senate Finance Committee.

Rees, Watts, and Kershaw meet with OEO officials to discuss future relationship with GAO and Senator Williams. Issue on whether to let Senator Williams have files is not resolved, but it is agreed the Senate Finance Committee will be supplied with answers to any questions for which there are data.

OEO persuades the GAO to do a "data audit" rather than attempt an analysis of their own.

Senator Williams does not press his request for individual files. Instead, it is agreed by all sides that the GAO can continue to visit the Princeton site on a regular basis and that unlimited aggregate data will be provided to the Senate Finance Committee.

Data on industry and occupation, earnings, sample size, and attrition are sent to Wilson at OEO to be given to Senator Williams.

Wilson and Kershaw appear before the Senate Finance Committee with the GAO.

September Trenton eighth quarterly interview and Scranton fourth quarterly interview are administered.

October   Second cost-of-living increase in guarantee levels is put into effect (July 1968–July 1970, up 11.7 percent from original guarantee levels).

Jersey City fifth quarterly interview is administered.

November Paterson–Passaic seventh quarterly interview is administered.

December Jersey City sixth quarterly interview, Trenton ninth quarterly interview, and Scranton fifth quarterly interview are administered.

Names of eighteen families appear in the *Paterson News* as having defrauded welfare. Mathematica registers strong objections to the breach of confidentiality agreement.

H.R. 16311 killed by the Senate.

1971

January   A new welfare-reform bill (H.R. 1) goes to the House Ways and Means Committee.

First payments are made in the income-maintenance experiment in Gary, Indiana, funded by HEW, run by an independent group, and with a special interest in the interaction of day-care provision and income-maintenance schemes.

February Paterson–Passaic eighth quarterly interview is administered.

March   Jersey City seventh quarterly interview and Scranton sixth quarterly interview are administered.

House Ways and Means Committee requests additional information.

Three Trenton families call the Trenton field office to say they have been summoned by the Mercer County prosecutor's office for alleged fraud. The prosecutor begins another investigation.

Fraud charges appear in local Trenton newspapers.

The Hudson County Welfare Board threatens to sue. Kershaw and Jersey City office manager, meet with the Hudson County Welfare Board. The parties come to an amicable understanding.

April   Trenton tenth quarterly interview is administered.

Kershaw appears before the Mercer County Grand Jury.

Kershaw, Arnold Shore, and Marsha Shore meet with Mercer County Prosecutor's office to review records of all experiment families receiving welfare.

May   Paterson–Passaic ninth quarterly interview is administered.

H.R. 1 reported out of Ways and Means Committee.

Wisconsin issues discussion paper by Watts, "Mid-Experiment Report on the Basic Labor Supply Response."

June   **Trenton eleventh quarterly interview, Jersey City eighth quarterly interview and Scranton seventh quarterly interview are administered.**

H.R. 1 passed by the House and referred to Senate Finance Committee.

August   **Paterson–Passaic tenth quarterly interview, Scranton eighth quarterly interview, and Trenton twelfth quarterly interview are administered.**

September   Third cost-of-living increase in guarantee levels is put into effect (July 1968–**July 1971, up 16.6 percent from original guarantee levels).**

Jersey City ninth quarterly interview is administered.

Final transfer payment is made to Trenton families.

October   Paterson–Passaic eleventh quarterly interview is administered.

November   Scranton ninth quarterly interview is administered.

First payments are made in the income-maintenance experiment in Seattle, **Washington, and Denver, Colorado, funded by HEW, run by the Stanford** Research Institute and Mathematica, and with a special interest in the interaction of manpower-training and labor-market services with income maintenance.

December   Trenton thirteenth quarterly interview, Paterson–Passaic twelfth quarterly in**terview, and Jersey City tenth quarterly interview are administered.**

Passaic County Welfare Board files a civil complaint against Mathematica and several families.

Decision is made to try to locate and interview attrited families.

1972
February   Final transfer payments are made to Paterson–Passaic families.

Scranton tenth quarterly interview is administered.

	Two validation interviews are made in Trenton.
March	Trenton office closes down.
	Jersey City eleventh quarterly interview is administered.
April	Paterson–Passaic thirteenth quarterly interview is administered.
May	Jersey City twelfth quarterly interview and Scranton eleventh quarterly interview are administered.
	First efforts are made to locate attrited Trenton families to administer the attrition interview.
June	Paterson and Passaic field offices close down. Final transfer payments are made to Jersey City families.
August	Scranton twelfth quarterly interview is administered.
September	Attrition interview is completed on 50 percent of the attrited Trenton sample. Decision is made to try to locate attrited families in other sites.
	Jersey City thirteenth quarterly interview is administered.
	Final transfer payments are made to Scranton families.
	H.R. 1 killed in Senate Finance Committee.
October	Jersey City field office closes down.
	Attrition interview in Paterson–Passaic, Jersey City, and Scranton is begun.
November	Scranton thirteenth quarterly interview is administered.
December	Scranton field office closes down.

1973
| December | Final report submitted to HEW and released. |

B   Rules of operation for the basic income program[1]

I. *Auspices of the Program*

The Basic Income Program is being conducted by the Council for Grants to Families, an organization established jointly by Mathematica, Princeton, New Jersey, and by the Institute for Research on Poverty of the University of Wisconsin, Madison, Wisconsin. Funds and overall guidance to the program are provided by the United States Office of Economic Opportunity.

II. *Confidentiality*

All information obtained from families participating in the Basic Income Program will be used only to operate and to evaluate the program, and will be kept in strictest confidence by the Council.

III. *Family Participation*

  A. *Initial Eligibility*

The eligibility of a family to enter the Basic Income Program is established by the Council after two separate interviews with the family. Families are selected to be interviewed at random from among all families living in certain neighborhoods of the following cities:

Trenton, New Jersey
Paterson, New Jersey

---

[1] The "Rules of Operation" went through several versions; this is the final text. They were not printed. Typewritten copies were on file in each field office. (A short version was printed as a booklet and given to families.)

Passaic, New Jersey
Jersey City, New Jersey
Scranton, Pennsylvania

Once preliminary interviews are completed in these cities, and families found to be eligible are enrolled, no new families may be added to the program.

B. *Continued Participation*

Eligible families may continue to participate in the program, which will last three years, as long as they maintain their residence within the United States and provide the Council with the correct information it needs to operate the program. (See Section IV, *Obligations of Participants* and Section VII, *Penalties*.)

IV. *Obligations of Participants*

In order to continue in the program, families must report their income and the size of their family unit once every four weeks on Family Income Report Forms provided by the Council. All information requested on these forms must be filled in fully and accurately and filed promptly.

The Council utilizes a comprehensive definition of income which is described in detail in *Appendix B1, Definition of Income.*

The family unit is defined as the head of the family and his or her dependents. A person is considered a dependent if he or she resides with and is supported by the head of the family.

A more detailed definition of dependency and provision for adding persons to the family unit after the start of the program, institutionalization of family members, and separation of family members into two or more households is given in *Appendix B2, Definition of Family Unit.*

V. *Payments to Participants*

A. *Calculation of Payments*

1. The amount of each family's Basic Income Payment will depend on the number of people in the family unit, the family income, and the Basic Income Plan assigned to the family.

2. Two methods of income averaging will be used to determine Basic Income Payments.

a. For some families, income reported to the Council during each four-week reporting period will be averaged with income reported in the previous two reporting periods. This three-period (twelve-week) moving average, plus or minus any imputation or deduction as described in *Appendix B1, Definition of Income*, will become the income base for calculating Basic Income Payments in the next four-week period. If that income base in any four-week period is greater than the income level at which a family's Basic Income Payment for that period would drop to zero (the breakeven point) then the excess income over that level will be carried over and added to the income base in the next four-week period. Such excess income will be used to raise the subsequent income base or bases up to but not over the breakeven point, and will be carried over from period to period until exhausted or for thirteen periods (one year), whichever is sooner.

If, in computing the carry-over sume for any period, there is excess income available from more than one of the preceding twelve periods, or if there is actual income in a period plus excess income from one or more of the preceding twelve periods, then the source of the carry-over sum and the amount of any new excess income arising from the current period will be determined as follows: A carry-over sum is first taken from the unused excess income of the earliest period of the preceding twelve periods. If this amount is insufficient to reach the breakeven level than an additional carryover sum is taken from the next earliest period of the preceding twelve periods. If carry-over sums plus actual income exceed the breakeven level, then the excess constitutes excess income for the purpose of computing carry-over sums in subsequent periods.

b. For other families, income reported to the Council during each four-week reporting period will be averaged with income reported in the previous twelve reporting periods. This thirteen-period (fifty-two-week) moving average plus or minus any deduction or imputation as described in *Appendix B1, Definition of Income,* will be come base for calculating Basic Income Payments in the next four-week period.

3. A family that files its four-week Family Income Report Form correctly will receive a flat biweekly filing fee from the Council. This fee will be in addition to any Basic Income Payment for which the family may be eligible.

B. *Filing Requirements*

In order to receive regular biweekly payments from the Council, a family must submit its regular four-weekly Family Income Report Form correctly and on time to the Council. A more detailed definition of the filing requirements is given in *Appendix B3, Filing Periods and Procedures.*

C. *Interview Fees*

Families will be interviewed once every three months for the full period of their participation in the program. These interviews are designed to evaluate the operation of the program, and have no bearing on the amount or timing of Basic Income Payments. Families will be paid a special fee for their participation in each of these interviews.

All members of the household over eighteen years of age who move from the original household residence will be interviewed. They will receive the same payment for the interview as is received by the original household unit.

Minor discrepancies between information reported on the Family Income Reports and the interviews will not be checked by the Council. Information from the interviews will only be used if (1) there is a major discrepancy between information reported on the Family Income Reports and the interviews or (2) there are signs that there is widespread misreporting by the families. In the latter two cases, the interview information will be used as grounds for investigation by the field-office managers. Interview information, however, may not be used as fact on which to base decisions or treatment.

D. *Reporting Payments to the Internal Revenue Service*

1. The interview fees and the flat biweekly fees for filing Income Report Forms are taxable income and must, under Federal law, be included in any income tax declaration submitted to the Federal Government.

2. The Internal Revenue Service has ruled that the biweekly Basic Income Payments are not taxable income. No Federal income taxes should be paid on these payments.

3. In addition, all families enrolled in the Basic Income Program and receiving more than the filing fee will be reimbursed, in whole or in part, for Federal income taxes paid during the time they are enrolled in the program. The amount due the family will be calculated at the end of each year, provided that the family has given the Council adequate evidence of its final Federal income tax liability for that year.

E. *Receiving Payments*

All payments will be received by families through the mails. In special cases checks may be sent to the field office to be picked up there. In no case can a check be given to a family member at the Princeton office.

VI. *Rights of Recipients*

A. *Disputing a Council Decision*

1. A recipient may, at any time, dispute a decision by the Council with respect to

his family's biweekly payment. The status of payments to families contesting a Council decision is given in *Appendix B3, Filing Periods and Procedures.*

2. A recipient disputing the disposition of a matter by the Council must contact the local office, either orally or in writing, to initiate reconciliation procedures.

B. *Administrative Remedies*

The office manager will make arrangements to discuss the matter with the recipient and to achieve a mutually satisfactory disposition. The recipient may be accompanied by any representative he chooses to assist him in such discussion, and the office manager may be accompanied or assisted by other staff members of the Council.

In the event that the discussion does not result in a mutually satisfactory disposition of the matter, the office manager shall inform the recipient of his right to appeal. To exercise this right, the recipient shall make oral or written application for review to the office manager within five days. The office manager will then file a request for a hearing with the Review Board, and will make all other documents relating to the case available to the Board.

1. *Overpayment*

In the event of overpayment, the procedure to be followed will depend on whether the Council was responsible for the overpayment or the family was responsible. In cases in which reasonable doubt exists as to who was responsible for the overpayment, the Council will assume full responsibility.

If the Council was responsible for overpayment, or if the responsibility cannot be determined, the amount of overpayment will be applied to the family's income at the time the overpayment was made. If the amount of overpayment is $300 or less, the overpayment will be ignored. If the amount of overpayment is more than $300, the Council will meet to decide upon further action.

If the responsibility for the overpayment lies with the family, the amount of the overpayment is divided by the tax rate of the family plan and that amount is added to the family's income in the period in which the error is discovered by the Council.

2. *Underpayment*

If an underpayment is $300 or less, the underpayment will be paid immediately. If the underpayment is more than $300, a $300 sum will be repaid immediately and the rest will be paid in six-month installments.

C. *The Right of Appeal*

The council shall maintain a Review Board of three hearing officers whose sole function shall be to review the proposed decision of the Council. A more detailed description of the Review Board and its functions is given in *Appendix B4, Review Board.*

VII. *Penalties*

Families who are otherwise eligible for full participation in the Basic Income Program may be penalized by the Council for any of the following activities:

1. Failure to provide the Council in a timely fashion with the information on family size, income, and address which it needs to operate the program.
2. Knowingly supplying false information to the Council on family size, income, or residence.
3. Deliberately false statement of nonreceipt of any Council payment.

Penalties for these actions will range from delay or forfeiture of particular payments (see *Appendix B3, Filing Periods*) to recapture or unwarranted payments by direct assessment or deduction from later payments to permanent exclusion from the program.

VIII. *Policy Decisions*

Policy decisions will be appended to and take precedence over this document.

APPENDIX B1:
DEFINITION OF INCOME

For the purposes of the Basic Income Program, the term "income" is defined as it is for the Federal income tax, with the following exceptions and modifications.

A. *Additional Items Included in Income*

1. The entire amount of any payment received as an annuity or pension.

2. The amount or value of all prizes or awards.

3. The aggregate life insurance proceeds, in excess of $1000, which a family unit receives on the death of any one individual.

4. Gifts, support payments, inheritances, and trust distributions of capital, from sources outside the family unit, in excess of a total of $100 per year. But amounts received from a person who is living with a family unit but is not a member of the family unit, to the extent that such amounts represent reimbursements or contributions for the actual cost of maintaining such nonmember person, are not income.

5. Interest on all governmental obligations.

6. Any amount received in the form of damages, insurance payments, workmen's compensation, or in any other form if it is paid as compensation for physical, mental, or any other personal injuries or sickness or for wage or income continuation.

7. The full amount of all dividends, including periodic payments that are in whole or in part a return to capital.

8. The amount of any scholarship or fellowship, including the value of room and board supplied without charge, to the extent that such scholarship or fellowship exceeds the costs of tuition, fees, and books.

9. The amount of current or accumulated income that could, within the discretion of any person, be paid to a family member from a trust or estate, except that any such amount that is in fact paid to some other person shall not be so included.

10. Alimony and court-ordered support payments whether periodic, lump sum, or installment.

11. The rental value of public housing, to the extent that such value exceeds the amount paid as rent, and the rental value of owner-occupied housing. Such value will be allocated across household members on a per capita basis and will be attributed as income to the head of the family if the house belongs to him or to one of his dependents. Housing value allocated to members of the household who are not also part of the family unit will not be included in family income.

12. Any direct or indirect cash payments (other than payments that are required by the terms of payment to be used for purposes other than meeting general living expenses), and the value of lodging received in kind, from any job or public or private agency, including, but not limited to payments or transfers made pursuant to the following programs or plans, regardless whether received as a lump sum or as periodic payments:

    a. Unemployment compensation

    b. Strike benefits or unemployment benefits paid to any person by any union or any other organization or agency.

    c. Social Security (Old Age, Survivors, Disability, and Health Insurance) benefits.

    d. Veterans Disability benefits

    e. Training stipends.

13. Income received from nonfamily members, such as roomers, who live with the family. For a roomer receiving meals, $12 per week will be subtracted from the income

received from the roomer and the net will be counted as income to the family unit. For a roomer without meals, the gross rent paid will be counted as income to the unit.

B. *Deductions and Exclusions*

No deductions or exclusions shall be allowed except for the following:

1. Businessmen and independent contractors may deduct the direct costs incurred in earning income.

2. Mortgage interest and real property taxes plus a fixed amount for property maintenance may be deducted in computing the income from owner-occupied housing.

3. Alimony and court-ordered support payments to persons outside the family unit, whether periodic, lump sum, or installment, shall be fully deductible for each person whom the family supports outside the home, providing such person was being supported outside the home or was a member of the family unit at the beginning of the program. A family will be considered to be supporting a person outside the home if they make cash payments of $30 per month or more toward the upkeep of that person.

In cases in which support payments are made to more than one person, the following rule shall apply. The total amount of support payments divided by $30 equals the number of allowable deductions, providing that the number of deductions is less than or equal to the number of persons to whom support payments are made. Thus, if a total of $180 is paid by a family for the support of two children, two $30 deductions are allowed. If the $180 were paid for the support of six or more children, six $30 deductions would be allowed.

4. The cost of caring for any child or incapacitated member of the household if such cost is incurred for the purpose of enabling a member of the unit to be gainfully employed, shall be deductible from the income of the released earner up to $80 per four-week accounting period for one such member receiving care, or $120 per four-week accounting period for two or more such members. In no report period can the deduction exceed the income of the released earner; and there can be only one released earner per family who can claim the deduction. The deduction may be made only if releasing the earner results in immediate earnings. If releasing a member of the household results in delayed earnings, as in the case of a member going to school or taking job training, no deduction will be allowed.

5. A disregard of $1200 per year, or $92 per four-week period, will be made for ineligible members of the unit who are 65 years of age and older. This $1200 disregard is retroactive to April 1971.

C. *Capital Gains and Losses*

Capital gains shall be taken into income at 100 percent and capital losses shall be deductible to the extent of capital gains realized at any time during the course of the program.

D. *Public Assistance*

1. No family in the program may receive any payments from a government agency for which the size of the payment or benefit is based on demonstrated need, at the same time the family is receiving more than a biweekly filing fee from the Council. Such excluding payments include the following:

    a. Aid to the Permanently and Totally Disabled

    b. Old Age Assistance

    c. Aid to the Blind

    d. Aid to Families with Dependent Children including Unemployed and Under-employed Parent.

    e. General Assistance.

2. Families receiving other payments or benefits at the time of enrollment may enroll in the Basic Income Program and will receive a biweekly filing fee from the

Council as long as they continue to get these other payments or benefits and continue to report their income and family size to the Council.

3. A family may choose to receive Council payments instead of other payments at any time during the experiment. Following the family's declaration of intent to receive Council payments and a suitable demonstration that it is not receiving other payments, regular Council payments will begin.

4. Similarly, a family may choose to receive other payments instead of the Basic Income Program payments at any time during the experiment. Following the family's notification to the Council that it wishes to receive other payments, Basic Income Payments will cease and the family will receive only the biweekly filing fee.

5. There is no limit set by the Council to the number of times a family may choose to change from one to the other form of payment.

6. Public Assistance payments received by ineligible members of the unit shall not disqualify the unit from regular Council payments provided that the Welfare Department is notified of the Council payments to the unit.

7. Public Assistance payments received by an eligible member of the unit for an ineligible member shall not disqualify the unit from regular payments provided that the assistance payments are not means-tested for the entire family. The person for whom public assistance payments are made shall not be included in the family unit for the purpose of calculating Council payments. The Welfare Department will be notified of the Council payments to the unit. This rule is retroactive to March 1971.

8. Token grants of less than $10 per month awarded by the Welfare Board for the sole purpose of making a family eligible for Medicaid and/or other noncash benefits will not disqualify the family from full payment from the Council. The Council must have written notification from the Welfare Board of the amount and purpose of the grant. The Council must notify the Welfare Board in writing that the family is receiving full payments and that they will become eligible for only the filing fee if welfare payments are increased.

9. For purposes of calculating the moving average, assistance payments will not be counted as income. Welfare income which is included in the carry-over, if any exists, as of June 1971 (effective date of this policy) will be disregarded. Assistance payments, however, must be reported by the family on the Income Report Form.

APPENDIX B2:
DEFINITION OF FAMILY UNIT

A. *Family Members*

1. A person will be considered to be a member of the family unit if he or she is the head of the family or one of the dependents of the head.

2. A person is considered a dependent of the head of the family if he or she meets one of the following two considerations:

a. If the person is the wife, child, or stepchild of the head or any descendant of any child or stepchild and lives with the head of the family.

b. If the person is not so related to the head, but lives with and receives no more than thirty (30) dollars income per month from sources other than the head of the family or his dependents described in *a*.

B. *Adding Members to the Original Family Unit*

A person who joins an eligible household after the start of the program will *not* be eligible for payments by the Council for Grants to Families unless one of the following conditions applies:

1. The new person is a child born to a female member of the initial family unit.

2. The new person is under eighteen years of age and has been living in the household for more than six months.

C. *Institutionalization of Family Members*

A member of the original family unit will not be an eligible recipient of Council payments during any period in which he or she is serving in the U.S. Armed Forces or institutionalized, unless such institutionalization is voluntary and the family unit makes payments for his or her care.

D. *Separation of Family Members*

An original family unit whose members separate into two or more units, i.e., whose members form or become part of two or more households maintaining separate and independent residences, will divide its original Basic Income Payments between or among those new units. This division will be achieved by splitting the total payment of the original unit into its component parts attributable to various adult and dependent members of the unit as follows.

A new economic unit is established when a member of the originally enrolled household moves to a separate residence. Separate residency will define separate households regardless of any desire by the family members to share income payments.

1. A family head or spouse who leaves the original unit will take with him or her one of the two adult payments initially assigned to that unit. Such head or spouse will carry over the basic tax rate (the rate at which Basic Income Payments are reduced as other family income rises) assigned to the original unit, which rate will be applied to the pooled income of his or her new unit in determining payment. If this new unit is already enrolled in the Basic Income Program, its basic tax rate will take precedence. The remainder of the original family unit will lose the payment attributable to the head or spouse who has left.

2. A dependent eighteen years of age or older who leaves the original unit will take with him or her the maximum dependent's payment, that is, the payment attributed to the third member of the original unit. Such person will carry over the tax rate of the original unit, which will be applied to the pooled income of his or her new unit, unless that new unit is already enrolled in the Basic Income Program, in which case its tax rate will take precedence. The original unit from which the dependent has departed will lose the marginal payment, that is, the payment attributed to the last member of the family unit at the time the dependent left. There is no provision for independent filing by persons under eighteen years of age.

3. A family which separates so that head and spouse live apart, each with at least one of the original unit dependents, will be treated as two families with only one adult member. These new families will carry one tax rate and pool income as described above.

E. *Procedure for Establishing Additional Filing Units*

As part of the procedure for establishing a new economic unit the following shall be completed:

1. *Agreement Form*

An agreement form, similar to the Enrollment Agreement, but including these additions, must be signed: "I certify that I have moved from my former place of residence and no longer live with all members of the family who lived at that address. I understand that I will receive Council payments at my new address. I also understand that any payments received by me from my former household or any income shared with that household must be reported on my Family Income Report."

2. *Establishing Age*

For Council purposes, eighteen is the age of majority. It shall be the responsibility of the local office manager to determine if the potential filer is eighteen years of age. If the office manager deems identifying proof unnecessary, he will note this as part of office correspondence on the matter. If identifying proof is deemed necessary, identification such as driver's license or voting card is acceptable. The manager will note having asked for and seen proof of age.

3. *Establishing Payments to the New Filing Unit*

A new filer will take with him the marginal amount for a dependent according to the payment plan of the original unit. No additional payments or members will be added for this unit except for the following:

a. Children born to a female member of the initial family unit.

b. Children under eighteen years of age who have been living in the new household for six months or more and who are dependent upon the head of the household. If a child is dependent upon a nonmember, he will not be added to the family unit.

Grants will be allotted to these dependents in the following way:

a. A dependent will take with him the marginal guarantee.

b. If two or more dependents leave a unit simultaneously (that is, within the same IRF period) and subsequently file from the same residence, on the same form, the payment to the new unit shall equal the sum of the marginal payments of the unit from which they left.

If two or more dependents leave a unit simultaneously (within the same IRF period) and file from separate residences, their payments shall be the same and equal to the highest marginal payment which would have been paid had they left at different times. The remaining unit shall lose payments as if the dependents had left at different times.

c. If, after the new unit has been established, an additional dependent from the original unit joins the new unit, he takes the marginal guarantee of the original unit at the time the new unit was established and all other members of the new unit move up one guarantee level.

d. If a person who was not a member of the original unit joins the new unit and he becomes eligible for benefits, he takes the marginal payment of the original unit at the time the new unit was established, but the guarantee levels of the other members of the new unit are not changed.

e. Dependents of the original units of more than eight persons may not be eligible for payments since the marginal payment is zero dollars.

f. The original family loses the marginal guarantee or guarantees when one or more dependents leaves the unit.

g. If a person is added to the original unit the family plan is increased by one.

h. If the original family has no carry-over, each new unit will be attributed a proportion of the moving average of the original unit equal to the new unit's contribution to the original unit's moving average.

i. If the original family unit has carry-over in its account, a proportion of the moving average up to the monthly breakeven point, equal to the proportion of contribution to the family's income, will be attributed to both units. The amount above the monthly breakeven point (that is, the total accumulated carry-over) will be attributed to the new units according to the proportion of original family members in each new unit.

j. The new unit will receive a $5 filing fee.

k. If possible, full payment will be sent by the date established for receiving a check if normal filing procedures were followed. If this is not possible, the filing fee will be sent no later than two weeks after the new unit enrolls, and the full payment will be sent as soon as complete information is provided.

l. Income earned by noneligible members of a new unit shall be included in the new unit's income.

4. *Establishing Payments to New Filing Units under Lagged Accounting Treatment*

The procedure for establishing payments to new filing units received the lagged accounting treatment is similar to that for regular accounting period families, with the following exception. Each new unit will be attributed a portion of the moving average of the original unit proportional to the number of members in each new unit.

F. *Death*

Survivors of a dead earner will be said to have "usable" income that will be carried over in their moving average, although their plan will be reduced by one. Whether the surviving unit remains intact or whether some survivors leave the family unit, those constituting a family unit will be attributed usable income according to their percentage of the total number of survivors in the original unit.

Example: If three children leave a surviving unit of family size five, the remaining spouse and child would be attributed 2/5 of the usable income (the moving average last figured when the deceased earner was alive). Likewise, the three persons leaving, if eligible to be a new unit, will be attributed 3/5 of the moving average.

G. *Notification of Change in Family Composition*

A family should notify the Council of a change in household composition by their income report, by letter, or by contact with the local field office. In the cases of institutionalization or leaving the country the family will be instructed to continue to notify us of institutionalization or absence of the family member. We will assume until otherwise notified, that the newly born child remains in the family unit.

1. *Effective Date of Administrative Plan Change*

a. *Institutionalization*

A change will go into effect in the payment period after notification that a family member has been institutionalized is received.

b. *Leaving the Country*

No change in family plan will be made until one full report period has passed after a member has left the United States, i.e., until one report form has been submitted following initial notification.

c. *Returning to the Original Plan: Institutionalization and Leaving*

As soon as the family member returns to the unit, the family should notify the Council. The plan will then be readjusted and take effect in the next payment period.

d. *Birth*

A change will be made in the next payment period.

2. *Division of Payment Based on Jointly Filed Income Report Form*

If the two check payees of a family unit split after filing a joint Income Report Form but before payment for that period is received, they may request that the payments and filing fees for that period be divided in proportion to the number of members in each unit. If the family unit is eligible only for the filing fee, each of the payees will receive a separate fee of $10. The total payment for the period will not be recalculated. If the payees do not request that the payment and filing fee be divided, the entire payment will be sent to the household from which the Income Report Form was filed.

APPENDIX B3:
FILING PERIODS AND PROCEDURES

It is necessary that a family submit a four-weekly Family Income Report Form to the Council correctly and on time in order to receive regular biweekly payments. Failure to submit a complete and correct form to the Council on time will result in late payments or, in the case of excessively late filing or unclear Income Report Forms, forfeiture of particular payments. Families have the right, however, to dispute the Council's decision with regard to the timing of any particular payment.

A. *Filing Periods*

1. Family Income Report Form will be considered on time if it is received in the Princeton office within two weeks of the date on which it was mailed to the family. These two weeks will be known as the *Regular Filing Period*.

2. A Family Income Report Form which is not received in Princeton during the Regular Filing Period will be considered late. A family whose Income Report Form is late will be notified of this fact by a letter mailed from Princeton on the final Friday of the Regular Filing Period.

3. Payment will be made on a late report if it is received within fourteen days of the end of the Regular Filing Period. These fourteen days will be known as the *Late Filing Period*. Such payment will be made to the family one week after the regular biweekly payment date. The second check for that period will be mailed at its usual time.

4. A Family Income Report Form which is not received in Princeton by the end of the Late Filing Period will be considered void and neither of the payments based on that report will be made. The examiner in the Princeton office, in consultation with local Council representatives, may in special circumstances determine that payment will be made on a report which would otherwise be declared void. In order for families who have had an Income Report declared void to resume receiving Council payments in a later period, they must provide satisfactory evidence of their previously unreported income to a local Council representative. An Income Report Form will not be considered late even though it is not received in Princeton during the regular filing period if a family claims to have mailed the report. The Council field office or the Princeton Office must receive, however, another Income Report Form for the period before payment will be made. If this situation occurs repeatedly, however, and does not appear to be a postal problem for the city in question, the Income Report Form will be considered late.

5. If a Family Income Report Form is received on time but requires clarification before it can be used as a basis for payment the family will be notified of this fact by a letter mailed from Princeton on the final Friday of the Regular Filing Period. In order to receive payment at the regular time, the family must call or come to the nearest Council office and clear up the problem within five days of the end of the Regular Filing Period. These five days will be known as the *Adjustment Period*.

6. A Family Income Report Form with problems which remain unclarified at the end of the Adjustment Period will be considered late. If clarification is subsequently made within fourteen days of the end of the Regular Filing Period, the family will receive a late payment as described in Item 3 above.

7. An insufficient report which is not clarified within fourteen days of the Regular Filing Period will be said to have lapsed, and both of the payments based on that report will be set equal to the flat filing fee. In special circumstances, the examiner in Princeton, in consultation with local Council representatives, may decide to make regular payment on a report which has lapsed. Families must provide the necessary clarification of a lapsed report before they can resume regular biweekly payments in any amount greater than the filing fee.

8. Families who fail to file or clarify an Income Report Form in any period in order to conceal unusually large income receipts in that period will immediately, upon discovery, have that income included in their current moving average.

9. The length of time necessary to be considered an absence from the United States is twenty-eight days or more. No payment will be made for the period of absence, that is, from twenty-eight days after a family has left the United States until it returns.

10. In figuring income report periods which have been skipped due to absence from the program, the following shall be observed: Any absence such as a leaving of twenty-eight days or more from the United States or a failure to report income in one or more income report period(s) (including dropping and returning to the program) necessitates a review and disclosure by the family to the local office manager of all monies earned or received during this time (but not over one year). Income reports, although late, must be filed providing this information, which will be used to calculate the family's first payment upon reentering the program. Information for the program's current three-month period and possible carry-over from prior months must be provided before payments can be resumed.

11. If vacation pay is received in advance and covers weeks in a future report period, the income so reported will be held over to that future period.

12. Payments to a family which has decided to discontinue participation in the program will end immediately upon receipt of such notice in the Princeton Office.

B. *Payments Status of Families Contesting a Council Decision*

1. At any time, a family may contest a Council decision with respect to the amount or timing of a Basic Income Payment.

2. A family shall be considered to be contesting a Council decision at the time of receipt, in the local office, of written or oral notice by the family stating its wish to challenge a decision and describing the disputed item(s).

3. Immediately upon receipt of such notice from the local office, the Princeton office shall accept the family's statement on the item(s) in dispute, and shall calculate payments accordingly. The family shall continue to receive payments calculated according to the statement initially sent to the Princeton office, until the matter is resolved.

4. A family in the process of discussing a disputed item with the Council will retain its regular obligation to report all sources of income and changes in family size. Aside from the disputed items, all other procedures will be followed as set forth in these rules.

5. Any additional dispute(s), either related or unrelated to the first, will be considered separately.

6. If the matter is settled in favor of the family, payments will continue without adjustment. If settled in favor of the Council, an adjustment in the family payments will be made over a reasonable amount of time to correct any over- or underpayment which may have occurred before or during the discussion of the matter.

C. *Filing and Payment Status of Families Leaving the United States*

1. The Council will process only those Income Report Forms which are filed inside the United States. Payment based on reports not filed from the United States will not be made.

2. A family must assume the responsibility of having checks forwarded by the Post Office or friends should the family move outside the United States or assume a temporary U.S. address. Checks will be mailed only to families' or family members' legal address within the United States. No checks will be mailed outside of the United States or to temporary addresses.

APPENDIX B4:
THE REVIEW BOARD

1. The Review Board shall consist of three hearing officers, whose function will be to review disputed issues brought before it by the office manager on request of a recipient.

2. The Review Board shall maintain a docket of all proceedings. Upon receipt of the request for hearing, the proceeding shall be assigned a docket number in chronological order. Each proceeding shall be considered in the order in which docketed.

3. Hearings shall be conducted as soon as possible after receipt of the hearing request, in the Council office located in the community in which the recipient resides.

4. Upon receipt of the hearing request, the Review Board shall set the time and the date on which the hearing will be held; the date shall be no later than two weeks after receipt of the hearing request.

5. The Review Board shall assign one of its members to conduct the proceedings as hearing officer.

6. Immediately after the Review Board has set the date and the time of the hearing, the hearing officer shall mail to the recipient a notice of the time, the date, and the place of the hearing. This notice shall also include:

a. A full description of the procedure and rights of the recipient as outlined in these rules.

b. A statement of the recipient's right to be assisted by a representative of his own choice.

c. A statement of the availability of copies of the substantive and procedural regulations and of past decisions of the Review Board, the place where such copies are kept, and the hours during which the recipient and his representative may examine them.

d. A statement of the recipient's or his representative's right prior to hearing to examine the documents to be presented at the hearing upon two days' notice to the hearing officer.

e. A statement of the recipient's right to object to the time and the date of the hearing, within three days' receipt of the notice, by mailing to the hearing officer a written statement of the reasons for the recipient's objections and his choice of dates and times for the hearing.

7. The hearing officer may for good cause shown by the recipient set a new date and time for the hearing.

8. Immediately after receipt of the recipient's objection to the time and the date of the hearing, the hearing officer shall notify the recipient of his decision to accept or reject the recipient's objection, and of the new date and time of the hearing if one is set.

9. The hearing shall be conducted by the hearing officer and shall be attended by the recipient, his representative, and any witnesses the recipient decides have information relevant to the issues.

10. If, prior to or during the hearing, the recipient or his representative decides that cross-examination of the local office manager or the other Council personnel is necessary for full exploration of the recipient's case, he shall ask the hearing officer to ensure the presence of the local office manager and such other personnel during the hearing; he may grant a continuance of the hearing if necessary.

11. The procedure at the hearing will be informal. Legal rules of evidence shall not apply, but the hearing officer shall have discretion to refuse to hear obviously irrelevant evidence. The hearing officer shall determine the order in which issues are to be explored and evidence presented. He shall ensure that the recipient and his representative have a full opportunity to present the recipient's case. He shall inquire fully into the matter at issue and shall receive in evidence the testimony of witnesses and any documents which are relevant to such matters, including affidavits of witnesses unable or unwilling to attend. The hearing officer may examine the witnesses. He shall give the recipient or his representative full opportunity to cross-examine all witnesses. He shall allow the recipient or his representative to present an oral or written statement of the recipient's reasons for disputing the local office manager's decisions on the contested issues, including arguments against the agency's interpretation of substantive regulations.

12. As soon as possible after the close of a hearing, the hearing officer shall make his decision on each of the contested issues. The decision shall be based on the evidence and arguments presented at the hearing and on the files of the case.

13. The hearing officer's decision shall be in writing and shall contain the following:

    a.   His statement of the issues and his resolution of each.

    b.   His explanations and interpretations of the substantive rules and past Review Board decisions deemed controlling.

    c.   Findings of fact together with a statement of the reasons for each finding, the evidence relied upon and a summary of the evidence rejected or considered insufficient and the reasons for such judgment.

    d.   Where appropriate, an outline of the action necessary to implement the decision.

14. The hearing officer shall submit his written decision, together with the file of the case and the documentary evidence, to his colleagues on the Review Board for confirmation. On approval of one other Board member, the decision shall be final. If both of the hearing officer's colleagues disapprove the decision in any part, the entire Board shall review the files and the documentary evidence and shall resolve the issues involved. The Review Board's final decision shall conform to the standards set out in *12* above.

15. Immediately after deciding, the Review Board shall return the completed file, together with any record of the hearing, and a copy of the Board's decision to the local office manager for action appropriate to implement the decision.

16. Immediately after deciding, the Review Board shall mail a copy of its opinion to the recipient at his home address, together with an explanation of the effect of this decision on future payments to the recipient. If a representative appeared with or on behalf of the recipient, a copy shall be mailed to such representative.

17. The Review Board shall have its decision rephrased to eliminate any references to the identity of the recipient. It shall transmit copies of the rephrased decision to the agency's central office for indexing and inclusion in the information made available to the public.

18. The Review Board's decision shall be final and shall not be subject to any administrative or judicial review or attack.

19 a.   Until the Review Board's decision, payments to the recipient as to the issues contested shall be based on the recipient's statement.

b.   After the Review Board's decision, payments to the recipient as to the issues contested shall be based on the Review Board's disposition thereof.

20. At its central office, the agency shall maintain copies of all of the agency's substantive and procedural regulations and copies of all decisions of the Review Board. Each decision of the Review Board shall be indexed according to subject matter and according to substantive or procedural regulations interpreted therein. The files shall be open to the public. The agency shall allow a recipient or his representative to obtain copies of any rules or decision.

Subject index